RAVEN

a JOURNAL OF VEXILLOLOGY

AMERICAN CITY FLAGS

Part 1: United States

150 Flags From Akron to Yonkers

John M. Purcell

with James A. Croft & Rich Monahan

David B. Martucci, Art Editor

Edward B. Kaye, Managing Editor

North American Vexillological Association

Volume 9/10 — 2002/2003

Subscriptions & Submission of Articles

Raven: A Journal of Vexillology is published by the North American Vexillological Association (NAVA), PMB 225, 1977 North Olden Avenue Extension, Trenton, New Jersey 08618-2193, USA. Address manuscripts and correspondence concerning them to the attention of the *Raven* editor or to raven@nava.org.

Subscriptions: Free to NAVA members; US$20.00/CAN$25.00 per year for non-NAVA members—add US$3.00/CAN$4.00 for postage outside of North America. Back issues are post-paid US$20.00/CAN$25.00 for single issues, US$35.00/CAN$45.00 for double issues. Wholesale pricing available for 24 or more copies. Membership information is available by contacting the NAVA membership committee.

Submission of Articles: For guidelines and schedule, contact the *Raven* editor, c/o NAVA. Send a paper copy of the article to the *Raven* editor, along with copies of any photographs or figures plus the text on computer disk in WordPerfect or MS Word with a minimum of formatting. (To have the material returned, include a self-addressed envelope with sufficient postage.) Articles are subject to an annual juried review and accepted based on criteria set by the Editorial Board. Authors of accepted articles must sign a publication agreement assigning copyright to NAVA and affirming that the material is original and not previously published elsewhere. Articles will be edited for style, consistency, and length.

Material appearing in *Raven* does not necessarily reflect the policy or opinion of NAVA, the NAVA executive board, or the *Raven* editor.

Information concerning permission to reprint articles is available from the *Raven* editor. Articles appearing in *Raven* are abstracted and indexed in *HISTORICAL ABSTRACTS* and *AMERICA: HISTORY AND LIFE.*

Cover: The flags of (top row) Fresno, St. Louis, Minneapolis, Cleveland, Baltimore, Jackson, Phoenix, Chicago, Irving; (middle row) Augusta [Maine], Fort Smith, Los Angeles, Montgomery, Fremont, Madison, San Francisco, Portland [Oregon], Charlotte; (bottom row) Akron, Denver, Corpus Christi, Des Moines, Anchorage, Cincinnati, Louisville, and Wichita.

Raven: A Journal of Vexillology
© 2003 North American Vexillological Association
ISSN 1071-0043
Printed in USA

RAVEN

Volume 9/10 — 2002/2003

CONTENTS

American City Flags

Editor's Notes viii

Introduction x

Acknowledgments xv

Definitions, Conventions, & Authors xvii

Akron, Ohio 1

Albany, New York 4

Albuquerque, New Mexico 7

Anaheim, California 9

Anchorage, Alaska 12

Annapolis, Maryland 14

Arlington, Texas 16

Atlanta, Georgia 18

Augusta, Georgia 20

Augusta, Maine 22

Aurora, Colorado 24

Austin, Texas 26

Bakersfield, California 28

Baltimore, Maryland 30

Baton Rouge, Louisiana 33

Billings, Montana 36

Birmingham, Alabama 38

Bismarck, North Dakota 41

Boise, Idaho 43

Boston, Massachusetts 46

Bridgeport, Connecticut 49

Buffalo, New York 51

Burlington, Vermont 54

Carson City, Nevada 57

Casper, Wyoming 60

Cedar Rapids, Iowa 62

Charleston, South Carolina 64

Charleston, West Virginia 66

American City Flags

Charlotte, North Carolina 68

Chesapeake, Virginia 70

Cheyenne, Wyoming 72

Chicago, Illinois 74

Cincinnati, Ohio 77

Cleveland, Ohio 79

Colorado Springs, Colorado... 82

Columbia, South Carolina 84

Columbus, Ohio 86

Concord, New Hampshire 89

Corpus Christi, Texas 92

Dallas, Texas 94

Denver, Colorado 97

Des Moines, Iowa 99

Detroit, Michigan 101

Dover, Delaware 104

El Paso, Texas 106

Fargo, North Dakota .... No Flag

Fort Smith, Arkansas............ 109

Fort Wayne, Indiana 112

Fort Worth, Texas 114

Frankfort, Kentucky............. 117

Fremont, California 120

Fresno, California 122

Garland, Texas 124

Glendale, Arizona 126

Glendale, California............. 129

Grand Forks, North Dakota .. 132

Grand Rapids, Michigan 134

Greensboro, North Carolina . 136

Gulfport, Mississippi 138

Harrisburg, Pennsylvania 140

Hartford, Connecticut 142

Helena, Montana 145

Hialeah, Florida 147

Hilo, Hawaii .... No Flag

Honolulu, Hawaii 149

Houston, Texas 152

Huntington, West Virginia .. 155

Indianapolis, Indiana 157

Irving, Texas......................... 160

Jackson, Mississippi 162

Jacksonville, Florida 164

Jefferson City, Missouri 167

Jersey City, New Jersey 169

Juneau, Alaska 172

Kansas City, Missouri 174

Lansing, Michigan 180

Las Vegas, Nevada 182

Lexington, Kentucky............ 185

Lincoln, Nebraska 187

Little Rock, Arkansas 189

Long Beach, California 191

Los Angeles, California 194

Louisville, Kentucky 196

Lubbock, Texas 198

American City Flags

Madison, Wisconsin 201

Manchester, New Hampshire .. 203

Maui, Hawaii (county) 206

Memphis, Tennessee 209

Mesa, Arizona 212

Miami, Florida 214

Milwaukee, Wisconsin 216

Minneapolis, Minnesota 219

Mobile, Alabama 221

Montgomery, Alabama 224

Montpelier, Vermont 226

Nashville, Tennessee 229

New Orleans, Louisiana 233

New York, New York 235

Newark, New Jersey 244

Norfolk, Virginia 246

Oakland, California 248

Oklahoma City, Oklahoma .. 250

Olympia, Washington 253

Omaha, Nebraska 255

Philadelphia, Pennsylvania ... 257

Phoenix, Arizona 260

Pierre, South Dakota 262

Pittsburgh, Pennsylvania 265

Plano, Texas 268

Pocatello, Idaho 270

Portland, Maine 272

Portland, Oregon 274

Providence, Rhode Island 280

Provo, Utah 283

Raleigh, North Carolina 285

Rapid City, South Dakota 287

Richmond, Virginia 289

Riverside, California 292

Rochester, New York 294

Sacramento, California 297

St. Louis, Missouri 300

St. Paul, Minnesota 303

St. Petersburg, Florida 305

Salem, Oregon 308

Salt Lake City, Utah 310

San Antonio, Texas 312

San Diego, California 315

San Francisco, California 317

San Jose, California 320

Santa Ana, California 322

Santa Fe, New Mexico 324

Scottsdale, Arizona 327

Seattle, Washington 329

Shreveport, Louisiana 333

Sioux Falls, South Dakota .. No Flag

Spokane, Washington 335

Springfield, Illinois 338

Stockton, California 340

Tacoma, Washington 342

Tallahassee, Florida 345

American City Flags

Tampa, Florida 347

Toledo, Ohio 351

Topeka, Kansas 354

Trenton, New Jersey 356

Tucson, Arizona 358

Tulsa, Oklahoma 360

Virginia Beach, Virginia 363

Warwick, Rhode Island 365

Washington, District of Columbia ... 367

Wichita, Kansas 371

Wilmington, Delaware 374

Worcester, Massachusetts 376

Yonkers, New York 378

Contributors to this Issue 380

www.NAVA.org

NAVA

The North American Vexillological Association (NAVA) is a nonprofit organization dedicated to the promotion of vexillology, the scientific and scholarly study of flag history and symbolism. Its members come from all fields of vexillology, including flag collectors and historians, government officials, museum directors, flag manufacturers, and encyclopedia editors, as well as those interested in flags as a hobby. NAVA publishes *Raven: A Journal of Vexillology* and a newsletter, *NAVA News*, hosts the website www.nava.org, holds annual meetings, undertakes special projects, and participates in international vexillological events.

For membership information, contact the Membership Committee, North American Vexillological Association, PMB 225, 1977 North Olden Avenue Extension, Trenton, New Jersey 08618-2193, USA, or visit http://www.nava.org.

2002-2003 Executive Board

Editorial Board

Editor's Notes

It has been an honor and a pleasure to bring to print the most significant body of information about United States city flags ever compiled. Not since 1915, when the Chicago Municipal Flag Commission polled all U.S. cities with populations over 30,000, has such a research project been successfully attempted. Hats off to John Purcell for his 40-year effort to complete this work, and a big thank-you to those who helped. Of course, the work is never done; cities will continue to adopt and change their flags. However, we hope this documentation of the current state of the civic flag world will spur continued interest in such flags, and perhaps even lead to improvements in their designs (see NAVA's guide to flag design *Good Flag, Bad Flag*).

As the Dutch consul-general remarked, when presenting the New York City flag to the city in 1915, "There are people who decry the idea of a city flag: I am sorry for a man so unimaginative that he cannot see in a flag a festive and decorative emblem in and through which the historical truths and noble traditions are preserved and transmitted from generation to generation."

As usual, *Raven* generally follows the *Chicago Manual of Style;* however, it adopts the more logical British style of presenting quoted material inside the commas and periods that belong to the surrounding sentence. See the Descriptive Conventions below for some stylistic attributes unique to this text. A note on color: the term "gold" can have two meanings when describing a flag color, either a golden yellow hue or an actual metallic gold fabric. The first is a deep yellow and is quite common, while the second is known to flag manufacturers as a "foil" and is very rare. In this text, therefore, "gold" should be read as a color synonymous with "golden yellow" unless specifically noted otherwise.

Raven hopes to publish a companion volume on Canadian City Flags. NAVA members and other readers may help by contacting NAVA with relevant information.

This book ultimately reflects the support of the many hundred members of NAVA and the dozens of generous donors who contributed toward its publication. The world of vexillology thanks you!

To Dorothy Hite Claybourne

and the memory of

Kenneth Robert Huff (1923-1989)

*for their staunch dedication to
the advancement of knowledge in
U.S. civic vexillology*

Introduction

This work documents, as far as possible, the past and current civic flags of the major cities of the United States, including the capitals and largest cities of each state. Included is every city in these groups: the largest 100 U.S. cities (based on the 2000 census), all 50 state capitals, and at least two cities in each state, for a total of 150 different cities.[1] Of course, hundreds more cities have flags, but the study was limited because of that very abundance; such a project is enormously time-consuming and expensive.

For the most part, not until the last few years of the 19th century did cities in the United States begin to adopt official flags, for a number of reasons. Until that time, the nation had been preoccupied with simply establishing itself, recovering from the wars of independence and a devastating civil war, and rushing westward to settle new lands. The idea of civic flags just did not occur to people. Further, until that time—and indeed, for several decades beyond—many citizens felt that the only flag needed was the national flag, and to show allegiance to any other was unpatriotic. Even many states had not adopted flags. By the late 1800s, however, cities began to take an interest in their civic image, not only among their own citizens but to attract business and industry, to further commerce, and to promote tourism. A civic flag represented a colorful means to distinguish the city among many others.

As might be expected, the older established cities in the East led the way. New York appears to have used a civic flag at least as early as 1825. Among the first cities to adopt flags officially were Philadelphia in 1895, Cleveland and Knoxville in 1896, and Pittsburgh and Raleigh in 1899. (Cincinnati's flag, designed in 1895, was not adopted until 1940.) By 1915, when a Chicago alderman initiated a survey of cities with flags as part of an effort to create a Chicago flag, 31 cities had adopted flags, two more used flags unofficially, and four cities were in the process of adopting flags. Only three of these cities—Kansas City (Missouri), Colorado Springs, and San Francisco—were west of the Mississippi River.[2] As the century progressed, of course, more and more

1. In states with smaller cities, we chose the capital and the largest or second-largest city depending on the capital's size. Where a city doesn't have a flag, we chose the next city in size that has a flag.

2. *Municipal Flags*, prepared under the direction of Alderman James A. Kearns (Chicago: Chicago Public Library, November, 1915; reprinted by the North American Vexillological Association): 7.

cities adopted flags—some, indeed, adopting one flag only to replace it once or more in later years.

Today nearly all major cities in the United States have adopted flags, either officially or unofficially. However, for the most part the flags are largely unknown—even by the cities' own citizens. In the larger cities, such as New York and Chicago, the city flag is frequently seen and generally recognized, but in many American cities the flag is relegated to the mayor's office or city council chambers, and few people have the opportunity to see it. Largely for this reason, civic flags seldom inspire a sense of civic patriotism, and are mostly ignored—unless they become embroiled in controversy, as in those cities that have recently been targeted by lawsuits for having flags that display some sort of religious symbol that some citizens find objectionable.[3] Civic flags are also the victims of politics, as one administration of a different political party seeks to disassociate itself from the flag adopted during a previous administration by changing the flag, or when civic leaders feel it is time for a "new image" and change the flag accordingly.[4] Yet another reason that flags are unknown is due to poor record keeping. As administrations in city halls change over the years, flags adopted years before are lost and current staff know nothing about them. Flags may be adopted by a city council unaware that a previous council had done the same thing years before; city officials will sometimes maintain stoutly that there is no city flag, even though official documents or actual usage prove otherwise.

The history of this project may prove informative. In 1962, I chaired the Athenaeum of Cincinnati, a society devoted to academic and literary pursuits. One of its projects that year was to undertake a survey of

---

3. A number of court cases, usually vehemently defended by the cities, have resulted in court orders to remove symbols such as crosses, churches, and temples as contravening the separation of church and state mandated in the U.S. Constitution. See John M. Purcell, "U.S. Civic Flags in Conflict with the Courts", *Flags from Sea to Sea: The Proceedings of the XVIII International Congress of Vexillology*, Victoria, B.C., Canada (July 1999): A45-A51.

4. At the time these materials were being prepared for publication, at least four cities were considering changing their city flags: Anaheim, California; Fort Worth, Texas; Tallahassee, Florida; and Washington, D.C.

the civic flags of the cities with a population of over 100,000 based on the 1960 census, as well as the state capitals not included in that group, with the idea of publishing a volume of the findings. The cities were surveyed by letter, and work began. Three years later, working independently and unknown to us in the Athenaeum, Kenneth R. Huff, an editor for a major encyclopedia working in Chicago, began virtually the same project, surveying the same cities. As the decade wore on, publisher after publisher told both the Athenaeum and Huff that the project was too expensive for a potentially limited readership. Ultimately, both parties abandoned the project, but the materials gathered were carefully preserved. With the founding of the North American Vexillological Association in 1967, Huff and I met and talked of one day working together to bring our abandoned project to fruition.

Then, in the early 1970s, Dorothy Hite Claybourne set out to do just what Huff and I had attempted a decade earlier. She did her own survey of the cities—the same criteria, but based on the 1970 census. In an attempt to avoid the pitfall of rejection by publishers, she first secured what she believed to be a contract for her book, and produced a manuscript with a black-and-white version of each flag, along with its history. She thought that such illustrations would keep the publishing costs down and make the book more feasible. However, after the praiseworthy manuscript was completed following many months of careful research and writing, the publisher withdrew, to the great disappointment of all of us with a special interest in civic flags.

There the situation remained for the remainder of the century. At various times over the years, the topic was raised, and some interest was voiced in reviving the project, but no one seemed to have the time available, and the prospects for publication had not seemed to improve greatly. Meanwhile, Kenneth Huff met an untimely death in 1989 after a long illness. He bequeathed to me his city flag archives.

Things changed in 2001. Many of my fellow vexillologists in NAVA (led by its president, Dave Martucci) felt that it was time to revisit the project, because by then, computer-generated images could significantly reduce the publication costs. However, the materials on file were mostly out of date, since, with the exception of a flag here and there, I had not attempted to keep them current. This meant, of course, doing a complete new survey of cities, based on the census of 2000.

The survey began in April of 2001. I sent letters to the city clerks of all the cities on the list, derived from the census with the help of James Croft. After a reasonable time, if the city clerk did not respond, I sent another letter to the library in the city, asking for the same information. When there was no response from the library either, I followed up with a letter to the mayor or city manager. I examined each city's website for any information about the city flag. Only about a dozen cities did not respond at all. I then called each city hall individually asking for the needed information, and made a long trip by car to six cities in five southern states to visit some of them. David Martucci also visited three New England cities to obtain information, and James Croft followed up with another visit to two of them. As a result, we compiled some information about all the cities surveyed within 18 months.

We found that only three of the cities surveyed have no flag: Fargo, North Dakota (the largest city in that state); Hilo, Hawaii (the state's second largest city); and Sioux Falls, South Dakota (the state's largest city). We replaced these with Grand Forks, North Dakota; the county of Maui, Hawaii; and Rapid City, South Dakota.

The quality of the information received varies considerably from excellently detailed to sketchy. In some cases, desired information has been lost or is vague at best, and on occasion inaccurate information has been inadvertently provided by well-meaning informants. In each case, we have tried to ascertain what we believe to be the most authentic data, and have followed up in many cases trying to resolve apparent inconsistencies. Consequently, the information that follows is as accurate as we have been able to establish from the records available.

Flag ordinances are usually very general and are often terse regarding the flag's description and specifications. Interpretation of these ordinances then often varies greatly from manufacturer to manufacturer, especially with respect to proportions. In those cases where the proportions are officially prescribed, we have always indicated them as such, but if not, then the proportions that seem to be most in use with the flag are indicated. In the cases where information about past flags is known (and the earlier files from the 1960s were very helpful here), it has been added, but it is very likely that not all the past flags have been included, simply because they have been forgotten or records have been lost.

The reader will note two major characteristics of the civic flags discussed here. The first is the widespread use of the city seal (or in some cases, civic arms); the second is the preponderance of flags with lettering on them. The reasons for this have been discussed fully elsewhere, but may be summed up with a few brief observations.[5] Americans have long considered the seal the single most important sign of authority of a governing body, probably because of its frequent use on documents in the country's early history. The seal represented legitimacy. Consequently, when the cities wished to demonstrate their dominion, the symbol that first came to mind was always the city seal, and as civic flags were developed, it was displayed on those flags as a symbol of the city's jurisdiction.

Similarly, from colonial times, Americans have had great regard for the printed word; literacy was a badge commanding respect. Important documents, often with the seal, were a way to promulgate ideas and preserve them for history. Hence, it seemed important to civic flag designers to be sure that the city's name would be prominent on the flag for all to see and read. They seem to have ignored how the seal and the lettering would make the flag unattractive or more costly to manufacture. The seal and lettering appear in the earliest examples of U.S. civic flags and their use continues to the present day. In a new trend, a logo replaces the seal, but lettering still frequently accompanies the logo.

Countless U.S. civic flags remain to be catalogued. It is my hope that this project will be just the first step toward a compilation of the many flags still known only to the mayor or city council members, or that remain only as historical information filed away in libraries or old newspaper files. Civic flags come and go; the work for the vexillologist to record them is never finished.

John Purcell

---

5. See Whitney Smith, "American Perspectives in Heraldry and Vexillology", *Raven: A Journal of Vexillology* 6 (1999): 41-53.

ACKNOWLEDGMENTS

Two authors, James Croft and Richard Monahan, joined me in writing these articles. Peter Orenski led a spectacularly successful effort to photograph city flags from the collections of NAVA members, especially Rich Kenny, who generously shared his extensive knowledge and personal collection—by far the largest number of municipal flags of the United States ever assembled. Mason Kaye also provided an article and Ted Kaye contributed two.

Other NAVA members furnished valuable information to the project. Special thanks go to David Breitenbach, Carita Culmer, Jim Ferrigan, Scot Guenter, Kevin Harrington, Patrick Ka'ano'i, Ted Kaye, Clay Moss, David Ott, Whitney Smith, Annie Platoff, Charles "Kin" Spain, and a helpful friend, Ralph Carter. Doug Lynch designed most of the cover. And Dave Martucci, as president of NAVA, deserves recognition for enthusiastically making this project a priority for the organization, then volunteering his time and exceptional talent to produce all the images in the book.

It is impossible to list all the other special people, beginning in 1962, to whom we owe so much for their generous contributions of information, specifically the city personnel, reference librarians, flag manufacturers, museum personnel, and newspaper staffs. The vast majority of these people have willingly taken time from their busy schedules to respond to questions that frequently required them to dig into old records, or find a missing flag image, or contact others for the answer to a puzzle. Their help was invaluable, and we thank them yet again for their assistance. The vexillologist, like Blanche DuBois of Tennessee Williams' *Streetcar Named Desire*, must often "rely on the kindness of strangers". To all of these kind strangers, a sincere salute.   JP

DONORS

NAVA thanks the generous members whose financial contributions made this volume of *Raven* possible.

Phil Allen
Elmer Bauer, Jr.
J. E. Beard
Andrew Biles
Gloria Krug Bortell
Daniel Broh-Kahn
Lois Campbell
Carita Culmer
Flag Tech
Scot Guenter
It's About the Flag, Inc.
Ted Kaye
Albert S. Kirsch
Rev. Richardson Libby
David A Maggi
David B. Martucci
John D. McGlynn
Truman G. Pope
John Purcell
Jon T. Radel
Kenneth R. Ray
Loyal Rohrbaugh
Henry T. Sampson
Rev. Michael B. Smith
Whitney Smith
TME Co., Inc.
Gustavo Tracchia
Steven Wheatley
Cindy Williams

DEFINITIONS, CONVENTIONS, & AUTHORS

KEY DEFINITIONS

Canton
A distinct section of a flag, usually rectangular or square and located in the upper hoist corner.

Dexter
A heraldic term for "the left as seen by the viewer" or "the right as seen from the object".

Field
The background of a flag or seal, often of a solid color, on which symbols or images are placed.

Fimbriation
A narrow line or edging separating two areas of a flag, often to enhance their contrast.

Fly
The far edge of a flag, opposite the flagpole—the part that "flies".

Hoist
The near edge of a flag, next to the flagpole—the part that is "hoisted".

Quarter
One of four sections of a flag, coat of arms, or seal.

Saltire
A diagonally-oriented cross, similar to an "X", usually extending to the edge of the field.

Sinister
A heraldic term for "the right as seen by the viewer" or "the left as seen from the object".

Supporter
A heraldic image of a person or animal flanking ("supporting") a shield.

Tribar
A flag of three horizontal or vertical stripes; the colors are given top-first or hoist-first.

Vexillology
The study of flags.

DESCRIPTIVE CONVENTIONS

Proportions of flags are presented as width(height):length, for example 2:3.

Bold type denotes an inscription on a flag, for example **Rose City**.

Italics indicate a title, quotation, or foreign words, for example *History of Jacksonville, The Flag shall be of the Lord Baltimore colors,* and *de jure* or *Urbs in Horto.*

"Official" and "Unofficial" denote legal status, indicating whether or not the flag has been adopted by ordinance or other legal process.

Locations on circular seals are often described by the comparable position on a clock, for example "Dots at 8 o'clock and 4 o'clock separate the two legends".

Population ranks are listed for each city's place among U.S. cities and among cities within its state, for example POCATELLO, IDAHO: *Population Rank:* U.S. .... # 586; Idaho .... # 2.

Capital cities are marked with a star, for example BISMARCK, NORTH DAKOTA ✪.

AUTHORS

Authors are noted at the end of each article:

> **JC**   James Croft
>
> **JP**   John Purcell
>
> **RM**   Rich Monahan

Akron, Ohio

Population Rank: U.S. ..... # 81
              Ohio ...... # 5

Proportions: 3:5 (usage)

Adopted: March 1996 (official)

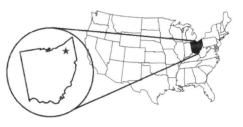

DESIGN: Akron's flag has a white field with the city seal in the center. The seal features an American shield, which recalls the design of the All-America City program's shield, awarded to cities meeting the program criteria. Akron's shield is divided roughly into thirds horizontally. At the top of the shield are two rows of five white five-pointed stars on a dark blue field. In the center section is **AKRON** in black on white. The lower third displays six red and five white vertical stripes. Around the shield and the white field on which it rests is a dark blue ring on which **1981-ALL-AMERICA CITY-1995** curves clockwise above, and **CITY OF INVENTION** curves counterclockwise below, all in white.

SYMBOLISM: Akron, having twice won the distinction of "All-America City" (in 1981 and 1995), has chosen to pattern its seal to commemorate that award. The ten stars represent the ten wards of the city. **CITY OF INVENTION** refers to Akron as home to the National Inventor's Hall of Fame at Inventure Place, a museum of inventors and inventions.

HOW SELECTED: Prepared by the mayor and his chief of staff.

DESIGNER: Mayor Don Plusquellic and his chief of staff, Joel Bailey.

FORMER FLAG: Akron's former flag also places the city seal in the center of a white field. That former logo-type seal is oval, oriented horizontally. On a blue background is a rhomboid (a diamond shape). A horizontal blue line that narrows at both ends at the two horizontal points of the diamond divides it horizontally, producing two isosceles triangles. At the inner ends of the line are two short vertical lines the same width as the greater part of the horizontal lines, in a "T" turned sideways. Between the two inner ends, a white tree trunk expands above into five straight white branches tipped with arrowheads: two horizontal, one vertical, and two halfway between the others. The branches are on a field of red, with a white border that forms an "A" with very short feet. The trunk extends below the centerline to form five white roots, similarly placed below as the branches are above, but on a blue background, again with the white "A" border, this time inverted. Curved clockwise over the top of the oval is **THE CITY OF**, curved counterclockwise below the oval is **AKRON •** **OHIO**, all in blue. Between the two groups of letters on either side are five small red isosceles triangles resembling sun's rays emanating from the oval. The overall effect is that the bottom half is a virtual mirror image of the upper half, with the differences noted. The flag's proportions are 5:7 (usage).

This flag, designed by Sam Scherr, an industrial designer, was officially adopted in August 1965. Mr. Scherr, explaining the symbolism of his design, said that it was *based on historic concepts as well as future image desires. The small triangles represent the 10 wards—also expansion—growth. The triangle shapes represent Summit, and Akron means Summit in Greek. The letter 'A' is for Akron. The abstract tree represents life—growth—expansion. The top part represents direction—progress; and the bottom part represents planning—traffic—street layout. Two triangles represent the original two Akrons and are enclosed in quartic shape to form present-day Akron. The passage between the 'A's represents Akron, the City of Bridges.* Summit is also the name of the county of which Akron is the seat.

JP

ALBANY, NEW YORK ✪

Population Rank: U.S... # 249
New York .... # 6

Proportions: 3:4 (usage)

Adopted: 1916 (official)

DESIGN: Albany's flag centers the city's coat of arms on a field of three equal horizontal stripes of orange, white, and blue. The city describes its arms in heraldic terminology:

The shield: Gules, two wheat sheaves Or, on a chief Azure a beaver felling a tree proper; For a crest: a Dutch sloop proper; For supporters: dexter, a farmer holding a sickle on his right arm and sinister is an Indian resting his left hand on a bow. For a motto: ASSIDUITY.

The coat of arms consists of a shield divided horizontally. The top third section is blue with a beaver felling a tree in natural colors. The lower two-thirds section is red with two yellow wheat sheaves. Above the shield is a Dutch sloop under sail in natural colors on a heraldic wreath. On the hoist side is a farmer holding a sickle on his right arm; on the fly side is an Indian resting his left hand on a bow, both in natural colors. The motto on the scroll at the bottom of the arms is **ASSIDUITY**.

SYMBOLISM: The orange, white, and blue stripes allude to the city's early Dutch heritage. In 1609, explorer Henry Hudson sailed his ship the *Half Moon* to present-day Albany. He flew the flag of his sponsor, the Dutch East India Company. That flag, the first flown in the area, had three horizontal stripes of orange, white, and blue, with **V.O.C.A.** on the center stripe. In 1614, Fort Nassau was founded there as a trading post, later leading to the establishment of the Dutch settlement of Fort Orange. Twelve years later the Dutch West India Company succeeded the Dutch East India Company, and used a flag of three horizontal stripes of red, white, and blue, with **G.W.C.** on the center stripe. In 1664, the British took control of the city and the Union Jack replaced that flag.

The coat of arms signifies the early occupations of the city. The wheat sheaves and the colonial farmer holding a sickle are for farming and agriculture. The beaver reflects the fur trade between the Native American people, symbolized by the Indian supporter, and the Dutch, and later English, settlers. The Indian also represents the people who first lived in this area. The Dutch sloop represents the commerce of the area and Albany as a major port on the Hudson River.

HOW SELECTED: By the Hudson Fulton Celebration Committee.

DESIGNER: Unknown.

MORE ABOUT THE FLAG: In 1909 the Hudson Fulton Celebration Committee first used the current city flag for the commemoration of the 300th anniversary of the founding of Albany. Seven years later, in 1916, the common council officially adopted this design.

SEALS: There have been at least three seals used in Albany's history. The first dates from 1686, when several towns were incorporated into the municipality of Albany. The seal was octagonal with the letters **ALB** in monogram, with a crown above.

In 1752 the seal was altered—although similar in shape, it consisted only of a beaver cutting down a tree and the date, 1752.

The current seal was designed in 1789 and the common council legalized it through an ordinance in 1888. It is a seal with the coat of arms described above, except below **ASSIDUITY** appears **Charter 1686**. At the top of the disk is **The Seal of the City of Albany**.

FORMER FLAGS: As early as 1884, Albany flew a white flag, apparently unofficially, with the coat of arms on it in blue and white.

JC

ALBUQUERQUE, NEW MEXICO

Population Rank: U.S. ..... # 35
New Mexico ...... # 1

Proportions: 10:17 (unofficial)

Adopted: February 1969 (official status uncertain)

DESIGN: Albuquerque uses the Zia sun symbol from the New Mexico state flag, but with the colors reversed: the sun is yellow on a crimson field. The symbol is also proportionately larger on the Albuquerque flag, and located slightly above center rather than in the exact center of the field. On a field of 10 by 17 units, the two interior rays of the sun's four arms measure about 2.4 units long. As on the state flag, the two exterior rays measure slightly less. On the center of the sun, in yellow, is **1706**. Centered below the sun symbol, in italics, is *Albuquerque*, about 9 units in length. In the upper hoist is a stylized Native American thunderbird in flight, descending toward the center, measuring about 2.7 units from beak to tail.

SYMBOLISM: The sun symbol of the Native American Zia Pueblo has four arms signifying the importance of the number four in their spiritual beliefs: four figures in the four cardinal directions, the four seasons, the four aspects of the day (sunrise, noon, sunset, and night), and the four stages of life (childhood, youth, adulthood, and old age). Additionally, the Zia believe that a person has four sacred obligations: to develop a strong body, a clear mind, a pure spirit, and a devotion to the welfare of the people. Aside from the obvious link to the state's flag with the Zia sun symbol, the thunderbird on the flag of Albuquerque may represent the city's great progress in recent years.

HOW SELECTED: The Zonta Club (an international women's organization) of Albuquerque apparently solicited a design.

DESIGNER: Said to be Dr. Richard T. Vann, a local optometrist, but the microfilm records are now barely legible.

MORE ABOUT THE FLAG: On 13 January 1969, representatives of the Albuquerque Council of Camp Fire Girls presented a city flag it had made to the city aviation director, Clyde Scharrer. This flag measured 5 by 8 feet. The ceremony was repeated for the city commission on 26 February 1969. Nearly a year later, on 26 January 1970, the Zonta Club presented four city flags to the city commission.   JP

ANAHEIM, CALIFORNIA

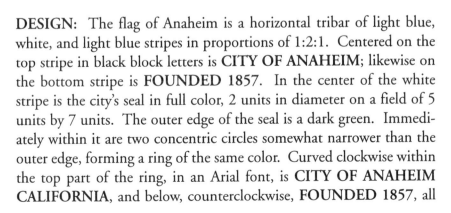

Population Rank: *U.S. ..... # 55*
California ...... # 9

Proportions: 5:7 (usage)

Adopted: 11 April 1967 (unofficial)

DESIGN: The flag of Anaheim is a horizontal tribar of light blue, white, and light blue stripes in proportions of 1:2:1. Centered on the top stripe in black block letters is **CITY OF ANAHEIM**; likewise on the bottom stripe is **FOUNDED 1857**. In the center of the white stripe is the city's seal in full color, 2 units in diameter on a field of 5 units by 7 units. The outer edge of the seal is a dark green. Immediately within it are two concentric circles somewhat narrower than the outer edge, forming a ring of the same color. Curved clockwise within the top part of the ring, in an Arial font, is **CITY OF ANAHEIM CALIFORNIA**, and below, counterclockwise, **FOUNDED 1857**, all in dark green. Dots at 8 o'clock and 4 o'clock separate the two legends. Within the inner edge of the ring is another green circle that matches the outer edge of the seal in width and surrounds the body of the seal, which depicts a colorful view of a typical agricultural farm. In the foreground on the hoist side are nestled a half-dozen yellow lemons; on the fly side are five oranges, some with leaves attached. A wreath of dark green citrus leaves extends from the lemons and oranges to the top of the circular scene, diminishing in width as it rises. Five sun-dappled brown walnuts rest atop the pile of lemons and oranges. As a background to the fruit, a vineyard of 11 green rows appears in the distance. A white house with a red roof stands to the left of the vineyard. Behind it is another taller building, also white with a red roof. Beyond the vineyard, the land is divided into two strata, green over yellow, above which rises a snow-covered mountain range in blue and white, topped by low-lying white clouds and a bright blue sky. Spaced across the strata are five oil derricks, appearing to be at varying distances, in dark blue.

SYMBOLISM: The seal depicts the agricultural origins of Anaheim and Orange County that centered on Valencia oranges, walnuts, grapes, and lemons. The oil derricks represent industry; the San Gabriel Mountains are visible from many parts of the city. The city's seal was adopted on 24 May 1960. The artwork is very reminiscent of a fruit box label.

HOW SELECTED: By the mayor, Fred Krein.

DESIGNER: Howard C. "Bud" Nagel, Public Information Officer.

MORE ABOUT THE FLAG: The first flag was presented by Mayor Krein in a pre-game ceremony when the Los Angeles Angels and the Detroit Tigers opened the 1967 American League season at Anaheim. Governor (later President) Ronald Reagan and Gene Autry, star of western-themed movies, took part in the ceremony.

FORMER FLAG: The city does not consider that there was a former flag, as such. However, the flag presented in the 1967 ceremony differs from the current version in that the first flag was swallow-tailed, with proportions of 3:5. The city seal, without the outer ring and lettering, was set near to the hoist, instead of occupying the center of the white stripe. Otherwise, the details are the same. It is not known when the shape changed to a rectangle.   JP 🏴

ANCHORAGE, ALASKA

Population Rank: U.S. ..... # 65
Alaska ...... # 1

Proportions: 2:3 (usage)

Adopted: Unknown (unofficial)

DESIGN: The flag of Anchorage has a gold field of 6 units by 9, with the municipal seal in the center, 3.5 units in diameter. The field of the seal is white. In its center, and extending nearly to its inner circumference, is a blue anchor with its tangs curving upwards halfway along each side of the seal, ending in barbed inward-facing points. The anchor overlays an 18th-century sailing ship in yellow under full sail toward the hoist. A wavy yellow line below the ship suggests the ocean. In the upper left above the ship's prow is a small rayless yellow sun. Above the ship's stern, in blue, is a modern airplane, flying toward the hoist. Two narrow blue concentric circles set closely together enclose the seal. Curved and centered above the outer edge of the seal is

ANCHORAGE, curved and centered below is **ALASKA,** all in small blue letters.

SYMBOLISM: The ship on the seal symbolizes the voyages of British Captain James Cook (1728-1779) who explored the site of Anchorage in today's Cook Inlet. The airplane represents Anchorage's pivotal role as a transportation hub, and the sun symbolizes the city's northern latitude and wide variation of daylight hours from summer to winter. The anchor represents the city's name and origin as an anchorage.

HOW SELECTED: The flag was developed sometime after the municipality's seal was adopted.

DESIGNER: Unknown.   JP

ANNAPOLIS, MARYLAND

Population Rank: U.S. ... # 983
Maryland ...... # 7

Proportions: 2:3 (usage);
originally 3:4

Adopted: 11 January 1965 (official)

DESIGN: The flag of Annapolis is white with the royal badge of Queen Anne (1665-1714) occupying most of the center of the field. The badge consists of a purple thistle and red Tudor rose with a white center appearing to issue from the same stem, the thistle on the hoist side with two of its distinctive dark green serrated leaves, and the rose on the fly side, with two dark green rose leaves. Centered above the flowers is a royal crown in gold with a red bonnet, lined at the bottom in ermine. The official description of the crown in the ordinance of adoption describes the jewels on the crown: *...a large green stone at the peak, one large purple stone, two small green stones, two small red stones and twenty-four small white stones....* The placement of these gems is not specified, except for the first, but it appears that the colored stones grace the lower part of the crown, while the white stones (perhaps pearls), encrust the cross-arch over the bonnet. Below the entire badge is a heraldic scroll in yellow, with red lining and the Latin motto in black **VIXI LIBER ET MORIAR** ("I Have Lived Free and Will Die So").

SYMBOLISM: The city is named for Queen Anne of Great Britain, who granted the original charter to Annapolis in 1708. The thistle represents Scotland, and the rose, a united England (after the fifteenth century "War of the Roses" between the House of Lancaster—the red rose, and the House of York—the white rose). The motto was chosen by the flag's designer as "one that might be acceptable".

HOW SELECTED: The city council asked the Peggy Steward Tea Party Chapter of the Daughters of the American Revolution to design a flag.

DESIGNER: Anna Dorsey Linder.

MORE ABOUT THE FLAG: The original flag hung under glass in council chambers. When the production costs of additional flags were found to be prohibitively expensive because of the many colors on the flag, the colors of the gemstones on the crown were changed to black in practice.   JP

ARLINGTON, TEXAS

Population Rank: U.S..... # 53
Texas...... # 7

Proportions: 3:5 (official)

Adopted: 27 May 1980 (official)

DESIGN: The ordinance of adoption describes the flag of Arlington: *The City of Arlington Flag is ... rectangular having its width equal to 60% of its length. The Flag shall consist of a white background with the City of Arlington logo imprinted or embossed thereon and the words* **City of Arlington Texas** *printed or embossed beneath such logo. Such lettering shall be in black or navy blue. The distance from the top of the Arlington logo to the top of the Flag shall be one-sixth (1/6) of the width of the Flag, and the distance from the bottom of the lettering to the bottom of the Flag shall be one-sixth (1/6) of the width of the Flag. The entire width of the lettering and logo shall be two-thirds (2/3) of the length of the Flag. The height of the lettering shall be one-tenth (1/10) of the width of the Flag. Plus or minus 5% of all the foregoing measurements and proportions is permitted.*

The city's logo is a large stylized letter **A**, composed of two broad strokes on either side that extend outwards, resembling two hockey sticks back to back. The hoist stroke is dark blue, the fly stroke is red. In place of a crossbar for the "A" is a five-pointed star divided vertically in half: the hoist side red, the fly side dark blue. The lettering is an unusual sans-serif font; the letter "i" is not dotted in **City** or **Arlington**, and the "C" and "i" in "City" are joined.

SYMBOLISM: The "A" stands for "Arlington". The colors are those of the state and national flags. The single star suggests the state's nickname, "The Lone Star State".

HOW SELECTED: The flag was developed seven years after the logo was adopted in 1973, presumably by city hall personnel simply placing it on a white background.

DESIGNER: Unknown. The name of the logo's designer is also not available, but was likely a graphic arts firm.

MORE ABOUT THE FLAG: The chapter devoted to Arlington's flag ordinance is seven pages long and has 34 regulations governing its use and display. JP

ATLANTA, GEORGIA ✪

Population Rank: U.S. ..... # 39
Georgia ...... # 1

Proportions: 2:3 (usage)

Adopted: Unknown

DESIGN: Atlanta's flag centers the city seal in gold outline on a blue field. On a field of 2 by 3 units, the seal's diameter is roughly 1.5 units. The city seal features a phoenix, with eight rays ringing its head, rising from flames. Above the phoenix is **RESURGENS**. Around the lower edge is **1847 ATLANTA, GA. 1865**. The two dates, although appearing below the wings of the phoenix, are oriented clockwise to read in the direction of "**RESURGENS**"; the city's name and state abbreviation run counterclockwise. The seal is edged with a solid line, within which is a double beaded line; the phoenix's wings extend slightly beyond the outermost line. All letters are in an outline font.

SYMBOLISM: The phoenix refers to the rising of the city from the ashes of its destruction in the Civil War. An official pamphlet explains: *Just as the phoenix, fabled bird of myth and story, rose from its ashes to begin a new life, the people of Atlanta returned to the ashes of their city without bitterness or self-pity, and began the gigantic task which lay before them. Their seal is an enduring symbol of the courage, vision and selfless-ness they brought to that task ... reminders of a gallant past, of the civic spirit which will make tomorrow the full realization of today's hopes and plans.* (In Latin, *Resurgens* means "Rising again".)

HOW SELECTED: Officially adopted by ordinance of the city council (date unknown).

DESIGNER: Information unavailable.

MORE ABOUT THE FLAG: Atlanta adopted its charter and seal in 1847. In 1865, rebuilding of the city began after the devastation of the Civil War. The ordinance of adoption also mentions a city pennant and a city ensign, but it is uncertain if these have ever been used.

RM

AUGUSTA, GEORGIA

Population Rank: U.S...... # 97
Georgia...... # 2

Proportions: 2:3 (usage)

Adopted: 5 December 2000

DESIGN: Augusta's flag bears the city's official service mark logo, in black figures and outline on a gold oval disk, centered on a field of dark forest green. On a field of 2 by 3 units, the oval is 1.5 units high and 2.1 units wide. The logo was designed for the consolidated government of Augusta and Richmond County created in May of 1996. It features the old Government House, a stately two-story structure with four windows on the top floor and a door to a balcony. The four windows on the first floor are partially obscured by bushes. The balcony is supported by what appear to be wrought iron pillars, forming archways about the first floor windows and door. Shutters flank all the windows. A chimney caps off each side of the house. Below the image is **OLD**

GOVERNMENT HOUSE c.1800. Centered below this legend appears 1736 in larger numerals. In a ring around this inner oval field are AUGUSTA at the top and GEORGIA at the base.

SYMBOLISM: The selection of the Old Government House seems to show the appreciation and continuity of history in the municipality of Augusta. The stately, dignified structure is undoubtedly a source of pride in Augusta. The year 1736 marks the founding of the city.

HOW SELECTED: Approved at a meeting of the Augusta Commission.

DESIGNER: Information unavailable.

MORE ABOUT THE FLAG: The dark forest green of the flag seems nearly blue in practice.   RM 🛡

AUGUSTA, MAINE

Population Rank: U.S. # 2,070
                 Maine ...... # 9

Proportions: 2:3 (usage)

Adopted: 20 February 1961

DESIGN: The field of Augusta's flag is divided diagonally, from the lower hoist to the upper fly, blue over green. In the center of the flag is the central portion of the city's seal in white, outlined in red. Above the seal is **CITY · OF · AUGUSTA**, and below it **1754**, all in white. The order of the city council establishing the flag states: *ORDERED, that the official flag of the city of Augusta be a rectangular blue and green flag with the name of the city, the date 1754, and the city seal in the center thereof.* The lower center of the seal depicts an Abenaki warrior in a canoe on the eastern side of the Kennebec River, viewing Fort Western along with its storehouses and the southwest blockhouse. A guard in colonial-era dress stands with his musket at the open gate door. Further behind is the 1829 statehouse. Clouds and trees embellish the design.

Note: The design does not follow the ordinance, as the complete seal should be shown on the flag, including the outer ring with **CITY OF AUGUSTA** at the top of the seal, and **ESTABLISHED** 1754 below, separated by two Abenaki arrowheads pointing downward.

SYMBOLISM: Augusta was founded in 1754 with the building of Fort Western during the French and Indian Wars; the building still stands and serves as the city's museum. The image of the 1829 statehouse, which opened in 1832, honors Augusta's status as Maine's state capital.

HOW SELECTED: A contest in the elementary school system.

DESIGNER: Unknown.

MORE ABOUT THE FLAG: The symbolism of the colors, if any, is not given. When displayed indoors the flag is bordered with gold fringe. The city seal was designed by an Augusta policeman, Officer Caroll W. Black, who took artistic license with the placement of the buildings, since Fort Western and the 1829 statehouse actually stand on opposite sides of the river.   JC

AURORA, COLORADO

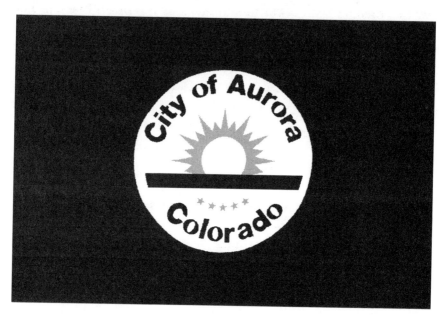

Population Rank: U.S. ..... # 67
Colorado ...... # 3

Proportions: 2:3 (usage)

Adopted: 1969 (official status uncertain)

DESIGN: Aurora's flag has a dark blue field with a large city seal in the center. On a flag of 2 by 3 units, the seal has a diameter of about 1.5 units. The seal has a narrow ring in bright yellow around its edge enclosing a white field. A dark blue bar, nearly as long as the circle's diameter, runs horizontally below the midpoint of the seal. A white sun surrounded by 15 yellow rays, alternating short and long, rises from the blue horizon bar. Immediately below the blue bar, in a semi-circle completing the circle of the sun's rays, are 5 small yellow five-pointed stars, evenly spaced. Arched over the sun is **City of Aurora**; curved below the stars counterclockwise is **Colorado**, all in a blue sans-serif font.

SYMBOLISM: Aurora means "Dawn" in Latin, hence the rising sun, which also represents a rising community letting its light shine and making its voice heard throughout the Rocky Mountain Empire. The five stars stand for Home, Church, School, Business, and Industry, which the city considers essential to a healthy, progressive community. The city's colors are blue and gold. The blue symbolizes the azure sky; the gold represents the minerals that made Colorado famous and resulted in its settling in the early days of the West. The seal was adopted in 1907 when the town of Fletcher changed its name to Aurora.

HOW SELECTED: No information given.

DESIGNER: Albert Christen, an artist who painted many murals of the early Aurora, designed the seal (date not given).   JP

AUSTIN, TEXAS ⭐

Population Rank: U.S. ..... # 16
Texas ...... # 5

Proportions: 2:3 (usage)

Adopted: 12 April 1919 (official)

DESIGN: Austin's flag has a white field with a heraldic shield in the center. On a field of 2 by 3 units, the shield, which has a triangular shape at its bottom, is about 1 unit high overall and about 2/3 of a unit wide. The shield is divided vertically in three equal stripes of red, white, and red. The top of the shield, or chief, is an inverted blue isosceles triangle bearing an ancient oil lamp, in gold, its spout toward the hoist. The shield is fimbriated with a narrow gold border. The crest of the shield rests on a white wreath, from which two large white wings outlined in blue rise vertically on either side of a gold cross bottonny. Silhouetted behind the crest in red is the dome and upper part of the state capitol. Centered in a curve counterclockwise below the shield is **CITY OF AUSTIN** in blue, across the center third of the flag.

SYMBOLISM: The crest comes from the coat of arms of Stephen F. Austin, for whom the city is named. (Austin was an early settler in Texas and the first Secretary of State of the Republic of Texas, and is often called the "Father of Texas" for his efforts in helping it win independence from Mexico.) The colors of the shield match the Texas state flag and the United States flag. The ancient lamp symbolizes knowledge, citing the educational advantages of living in Austin, where the University of Texas is located. The image of the state capitol and its distinctive dome marks Austin's status as the state's capital.

HOW SELECTED: In mid-1915, Mrs. William R. Wyse, editor of *Gossip*, suggested to Mayor A. P. Wooldridge that the city ought to have its own flag. The mayor appointed a committee of some 38 citizens to study the issue. That committee led to another committee of 10 to develop a process for selecting a flag. The city, through this committee, set up a contest and offered two prizes, one of $50 for first place, and another of $25 for second place, for an appropriate design. A third committee judged the more than 100 entries, a process which took several months.

DESIGNER: Ray F. Coyle, of San Francisco, took first place. Second place went to G. A. Geist, a faculty member at Texas A&M College.

MORE ABOUT THE FLAG: Coyle's original design had a white star and crown on the chief, representing "The City of the Violet Crown", but the committee suggested substituting the gold lamp in their place as more appropriate to Austin's role as a center of education. The committee also added the blue to the wings of the crest to make them more visible.

In 1991, a citizen identified as "Murray" sued the city, protesting the use of the Christian cross on the crest as violating the separation of church and state mandated by the U.S. Constitution. The court ruled that the use of the cross was a historically valid part of Austin's arms, and could therefore be retained on the flag.   JP 🛡

BAKERSFIELD, CALIFORNIA

Population Rank: U.S. ..... # 69
California .... # 11

Proportions: 5:8 (usage)

Adopted: 9 March 1983 (official)

DESIGN: The field of Bakersfield's flag is white with a narrow gold beveled border. In the center is the city's seal with a diameter of 3 units on a field of 5 by 8 units. The seal has a gold beveled outer edge matching the field's border. Immediately within the edge is a dark blue ring on which **CITY OF BAKERSFIELD** arches clockwise over the top and **CALIFORNIA** curves counterclockwise below, separated by a star on each side, all in gold. The field of the seal is white. On it, immediately below the blue ring, **INCORPORATED** arches clockwise over the top and **JANUARY 11, 1898** curves counterclockwise below, all in smaller gold letters. The center of the seal bears a large dark yellow cornucopia, its mouth toward the hoist. It appears to be filled to overflowing with various fruits, mainly melons and grapes, and several stalks of grain extend from the opening.

SYMBOLISM: Blue and gold are the city's official colors. The cornucopia's abundance of fruits represents the area's agricultural wealth.

HOW SELECTED: The Bakersfield Beautification Committee, on 2 February 1983, petitioned the city council to consider the adoption of a city flag, city colors, a city flower, and a city bird. The committee had commissioned the flag design and presented it to council.

DESIGNER: Rick Alton, a local artist.

MORE ABOUT THE FLAG: At the same time that it adopted the city flag and city colors, the city council adopted the Miss Bakersfield Camellia as the city flower and the western robin as its city bird.

JP

BALTIMORE, MARYLAND

Population Rank: U.S..... # 17
Maryland...... # 1

Proportions: 2:3 (official)

Adopted: 11 February 1915 (official)

DESIGN: Baltimore's flag is heraldic in design. The ordinance of adoption describes it:

The Flag shall be of the Lord Baltimore colors, to wit: black and gold, heraldically arranged as in his armorial bearings, that is to say, paly of six pieces, Or and Sable, a bend counterchanged; and superimposed thereon, as an augmentation of honor, a shield, Sable, bordered, or, charged with the Battle Monument argent, in memory of the Defenders of Baltimore during the War of 1812-14.

In non-heraldic language, the field of the flag is divided into six equal vertical stripes, alternating from the hoist gold and black. From the top of the hoist to the bottom of the fly is a diagonal stripe (the same width as the vertical stripes) that reverses the colors, beginning with black. Overlaying the center is a heraldic shield with a black field bordered in gold. The center of the shield depicts Baltimore's Battle Monument in white.

The ordinance specifies that on a flag of 6 by 9 feet, the shield is two feet six inches wide by three feet and three-eighths of an inch high.

SYMBOLISM: The city was named for Lord Baltimore (George Calvert, the first English Baron of Baltimore, seated in County Longford, Ireland). His arms also appear on the first and fourth quarters of Maryland's flag, and were the colors first brought ashore by the early settlers of the state in the 17th century. The Battle Monument, the central figure on the city's seal, was designed by Maximilian Godefroy in 1815 to commemorate the successful defense of the city against the British in the War of 1812, the same attack that gave rise to the national anthem, *The Star-Spangled Banner*.

HOW SELECTED: Mayor James H. Preston appointed a flag commission on 10 July 1914 to develop a city flag design in cooperation with the municipal art commission, in time for the September 1914 centennial of the writing of *The Star-Spangled Banner*. The centennial committee offered a prize of $50, and 40 designs were submitted to the flag commission. However, finding none of them "entirely acceptable", the commission itself "evolved and accepted" a suitable design.

DESIGNER: The flag commission, consisting of Judge Henry Stockbridge, Mr. Carroll Lucas, Mr. Wilbur F. Coyle, and Mrs. Hester Dorsey Richardson.

MORE ABOUT THE FLAG: The original design submitted by the flag commission also showed a green laurel wreath around the shield, perhaps because of concern whether it would be heraldically correct to place a black shield on a black field. Later someone wrote to the heraldic experts at the College of Arms in London to inquire about this matter. Keith W. Murray, Portcullis Pursuivant, replied that the flag was correct without the wreath because the field was "paly or and sable" (vertically divided yellow and black), so the "rule of tincture" was not violated. He did suggest changing the "inescutcheon" (shield) to "azure" (blue), but the all-black-and-gold design with the white monument won out, and the wreath was dropped.

FORMER FLAG: From about the turn of the 20th century, Baltimore used a blue banner with the Battle Monument in white. One early version also included a wreath of green around the Battle Monument, perhaps the inspiration for the wreath suggested by the flag commission.   JP 🏴

BATON ROUGE, LOUISIANA ✪

Population Rank: U.S. .. # 74
                  Louisiana ...... # 2

Proportions: 2:3 (usage)

Adopted: 13 December 1995 (official)

DESIGN: The flag of Baton Rouge has a field of crimson. In about the center of the top half of the field, beginning at the hoist, *Baton* runs horizontally in white in a large italic script that extends five-eighths of the flag's length. *Rouge,* in the same white script, appears below, beginning five-eighths of the flag's length from the fly, in the upper quarter of the lower half of the field. Centered in the space below *Baton* and before *Rouge* at the fly is a heraldic shield, its top extending to slightly above the mid-point of the flag's width, and its base extending nearly to the flag's bottom edge. The shield is divided horizontally into two parts. Above, on a blue field, is a white *fleur-de-lis* on the hoist side and a white castle tower on the fly side. Below, occupying the rest of the shield, is an adaptation of the British Union Flag of 1606-1801, combining the white Cross of St. Andrew on blue with the red Cross of St. George on white.

SYMBOLISM: The crimson field recalls the "*Rouge*" (French for red) of the city's name. The red, white, and blue colors of the shield are also those of the United States. The emblems on the shield represent the three foreign powers whose flags have flown over Baton Rouge: the fleur-de-lis for France; the *castillo* (castle) for Spain, and a variant of the then-current Union Jack for the United Kingdom.

HOW SELECTED: By the metro council on recommendation of a special committee established for the purpose.

DESIGNER: A committee appointed by the city-parish administration.

MORE ABOUT THE FLAG: The flag was adopted despite opposition by several prominent citizens who wanted to retain the earlier flag. In an effort to appease the opponents, the earlier flag was enclosed in a glass case for permanent display in council chambers.

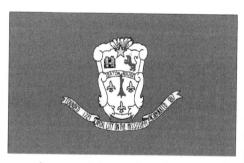

FORMER FLAG: The first flag of Baton Rouge has a green field, described as a "lime" green, although the mayor at the time of the flag's adoption said it was intended to be "emerald" green. In any case, the green color sufficiently annoyed some citizens that they complained to the city-parish administration, which gave rise to the movement to change the flag.

The green flag is elaborate. In the center of the field is an elongated rococo shield, bordered with white plumes. The field of the shield is also white. The upper portion of the shield depicts, dexter, a *castillo*, for Spain, and sinister, an upright red lion with a halo crown facing the hoist, for England. Centered above and between these figures in the crest position is a five-pointed yellow star above which are seven white feathers of a Native American headdress. The star recalls Baton Rouge's role as capital of the Republic of West Florida for 74 days in 1810. Below these figures an arched white ribbon runs across the shield, separating the two portions, with **BATON ROUGE** in blue. Below this ribbon are three yellow *fleurs-de-lis*, one each on the hoist and fly sides and one below in the center for France. Between the upper pair of fleurs-de-lis is a truncated red cypress tree, symbolizing the *baton rouge* (red stick) of the city's name. Below the shield, in an extended heraldic ribbon curved upward in three folds appear **FOUNDED 1721** on the first part, **CAPITAL CITY ON THE MISSISSIPPI** on the second (center) part, and **INCORPORATED 1817** on the third part, all in blue.

This flag was designed by a committee established by the mayor, W. W. Dumas, and was adopted officially on 11 December 1968.   JP ▨

BILLINGS, MONTANA

Population Rank: U.S... # 250
　　　　　　Montana...... # 1

Proportions: 3:5 (usage)

Adopted: 3 February 1986 (official)

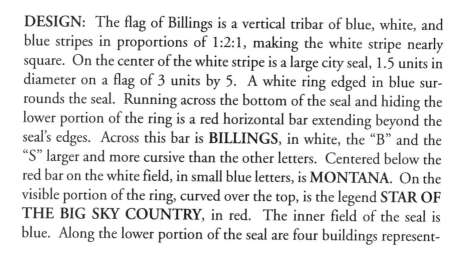

DESIGN: The flag of Billings is a vertical tribar of blue, white, and blue stripes in proportions of 1:2:1, making the white stripe nearly square. On the center of the white stripe is a large city seal, 1.5 units in diameter on a flag of 3 units by 5. A white ring edged in blue surrounds the seal. Running across the bottom of the seal and hiding the lower portion of the ring is a red horizontal bar extending beyond the seal's edges. Across this bar is **BILLINGS**, in white, the "B" and the "S" larger and more cursive than the other letters. Centered below the red bar on the white field, in small blue letters, is **MONTANA**. On the visible portion of the ring, curved over the top, is the legend **STAR OF THE BIG SKY COUNTRY**, in red. The inner field of the seal is blue. Along the lower portion of the seal are four buildings representing the skyline of the city, in blue shaded in white. Behind the buildings on the hoist side are the Rimrocks, a city landmark, jutting from the hoist side and slanting downward in the center, in blue with a white line running down it. The blue sky above has a red sun hovering over the buildings, slightly to the fly side of center.

SYMBOLISM: The seal depicts what the city calls "a progressive image of Billings", showing the city's three tallest buildings. Montana's nickname is "Big Sky Country".

HOW SELECTED: On 23 January 1986, the Flag Committee of Billings met to discuss the need for a city flag and a new city seal to replace the former seal adopted in 1885. Two contests were held, one for the seal and one for the flag, with a top prize of $500 in each. The committee received 66 entries.

DESIGNER: Fernando Méndez received a plaque and his prize of $1,000 at the council meeting of 9 June 1986 for designing both the flag and the new seal.   JP 🏴

BIRMINGHAM, ALABAMA

Population Rank: U.S. ..... # 71
                     Alabama ...... # 1

Proportions: 10:19 (usage)

Adopted: 15 December 1925 (official)

DESIGN: Birmingham's flag is a vertical tribar of red, white, and red stripes in proportions of 4:7:4. In the center of the white stripe is a large red five-pointed star inscribed in a circle of stars 5.5 units in diameter, on a flag with overall dimensions of 10 by 19 units. In the center of the star is the city seal in gold with black figures and lettering. The outer edge of the seal, which has seven notches somewhat like a gear (which the designer called a "hub"), extends nearly to the five inner points of the star. Along the inner notches of the gear are two concentric circles forming the traditional ring around the seal proper. Curved clockwise over the top part of the ring is ★ **Official Seal** ★. Curved counterclockwise in the lower part of the ring is **Birmingham, Alabama**, beginning at 9 o'clock and ending at 3 o'clock. In the center of the seal, its baseline bisecting it horizontally, is the skyline of the city. Radiating from the midpoint of that baseline in the lower half of the seal are eight ray-like lines, equidistant from each other. Slightly to the fly side of the seal's center, and appearing to be in the seal's foreground, is a statue of the Roman god Vulcan on a pedestal, facing the city skyline, his right arm upraised.

Encircling the red star are 67 tiny gold stars, pointing outwards and forming a circle. Radiating out from these stars are eighty-five gold rays, forming another circle of 6.5 units in diameter. The rays start with a longer one (one-eighth of a unit in length) at the red star's top point and alternate long and short around the star. The shorter rays are about three-fourths the length of the longer ones.

SYMBOLISM: The seal suggests that Vulcan, Roman god of smiths and metalworkers, and hence, of industry, is bestowing his blessing upon the city. In the late 19th and early 20th centuries, Birmingham was the center of the iron and steel industry in the Southern states. The designer carefully explained the remainder of the flag's symbolism:

The WHITE is symbolic of the purity of our women; the RED typifies the valor of our men; the GOLD hints not only of the fabulous mineral wealth of this district, but also represents the high standard of purpose and character of our citizens.

The larger RED star represents our marvelous young city; in its center is the golden official seal (with the year of our City's birth, 1871, added to it), and surrounded by a golden "hub", which signifies that Birmingham is considered the industrial, financial, and aerial "hub" of the South.

The SIXTY-SEVEN GOLD stars surrounding the large RED star, represent the sixty-seven counties of Alabama enjoying correlative glory of our 'Magic City.'

The GOLDEN RAYS or sunbeams depict our city's fame and prosperity, and also suggest that 'all roads lead to Birmingham'—à la Imperial Rome.

HOW SELECTED: The designer, assisted by the junior chamber of commerce, presented a flag to the city council, which adopted it.

DESIGNER: Mrs. Idly King Sorsby.

MORE ABOUT THE FLAG: In spite of the mention of the 1871 date on the seal in Mrs. Sorsby's explanation of the symbolism, the date is sometimes omitted on depictions of the flag today.   10:19 are the same proportions as the United States flag.   JP 🏴

BISMARCK, NORTH DAKOTA

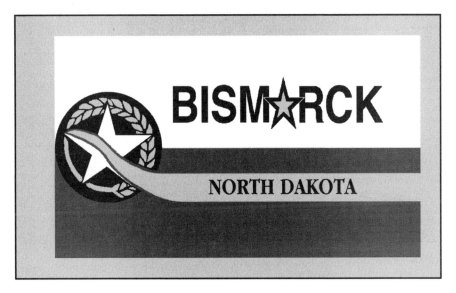

Population Rank: U.S... # 628
North Dakota ...... # 2

Proportions: 3:5 (usage)

Adopted: September 1986 (official)

DESIGN: Bismarck's flag is a horizontal bicolor, 3 units by 5 units. The stripes are white over red, each of 1.25 units, and are surrounded by a yellow border .25 units wide, except at the hoist, where the border is .5 units wide. Centered on the white stripe is the legend BISM☆RCK, in dark blue letters .4 units high. The five-pointed star that replaces the "A" in the name is distorted slightly so that the top point is slightly longer than the others; it has a gold interior, with the outline of the star in dark blue. Set at the hoist is a large dark blue disk 1.25 units in diameter, half of which is on the white stripe, and half on the red stripe. Within the disk, and almost to its inner edge, is a circle formed of a gold wheat stalk, the stem of which starts at 9 o'clock; the grains of wheat begin at 6 o'clock and complete the circle. Within the circle thus formed by the wheat is a large five-pointed white star, two points of which extend toward the edge of the wheat stem at 9 and 7 o'clock. The points at 12 and 3 o'clock extend to where the wheat grains join the stem. The remaining point, which would be at 5 o'clock, is hidden by a red-edged yellow ribbon that issues narrowly from the upper part of the star's point at 9 o'clock and swirls down across the star and on out horizontally across the red stripe, gradually widening to three-quarters of a unit, to join the yellow frame's edge at the fly. The ribbon, which at its horizontal position is nearly .25 units from the top of the red stripe, bears the legend **NORTH DAKOTA** in dark blue letters that are about half the size of the letters on the white stripe.

SYMBOLISM: The large white star encircled by wheat represents Bismarck as the capital city of an agricultural state, while the horizontal ribbon represents the freeway (Interstate 94) through North Dakota, on which Bismarck is located.

HOW SELECTED: Mayor Marlan Haakenson and the city commission held a contest to design a new city flag. The city commissioners appointed a "Betsy Ross Committee" to judge the entries. Its members were Fran Gronberg, Mary College; Dorothy Jackman, Bismarck Public Schools; Karen Syvertson, Bismarck Arts and Galleries Association; Nancy Hart, homemaker; and Susan Anderson, a Bismarck free-lance photographer.

DESIGNER: The winner of the contest and the $100 prize was Mark Kenneweg, a commercial production manager at KXMB-TV, with a degree from Columbus College of Art and Design in Columbus, Ohio.

JP

BOISE, IDAHO ✪

Population Rank: U.S... # 105
Idaho ...... # 1

Proportions: 2:3 (usage)

Adopted: March 2001 (official status uncertain)

DESIGN: The flag of Boise has a blue field with the city's logo slightly below its center. A narrow horizontal white stripe extends from the lower half of the logo to the flag's edges. The logo shows the dome of the state capitol in blue and white with trees on either side in the foreground. The capitol forms the upper half of the logo; behind it is a narrow gold ring forming a semi-circle around the logo's top half. The spire of the capitol juts above the ring, which crosses behind it on the dome's roof. The lower half of the logo intersects the horizontal white stripe, which is 8 units of the 48 units of the flag's width. The white stripe has **BOISE** in gold letters about 5 units high above a thin blue line. Below the line is **CITY OF TREES** in blue letters about 3 units high. Below the white stripe, the gold ring continues on the blue stripe, completing a circle. The words on the white stripe extend on either side slightly beyond the circle formed by the gold and blue ring, 24 units in diameter. (Only an image of the logo was available in determining the flag's design. The flag has been reconstructed based on an oral description from the city's administration.)

SYMBOLISM: The capitol dome denotes Boise's role as capital city of Idaho. The trees reflect its motto, "City of Trees". The motto suggests the origin of the name of the city, corrupted from the French *Les Bois*, "The Woods".

HOW SELECTED: By the city council.

DESIGNER: Unavailable.

FORMER FLAG: An earlier flag designed by Mrs. Delton (Marguerite) Irish, was adopted by city council on 3 January 1972 and used until March 2001. This flag placed the city's seal of 19 units in diameter in the center of a blue field 34 units by 60 units.

The seal, which was adopted in the 19th century, is very elaborate. Its gold beveled edge has 60 small triangular gold points emanating from around it. The seal itself has a white field, and is heraldic in appearance. In the center is an ornate shield with gold edges. Four thin gold lines emanate from a tiny gold-edged blue rhomboid in the center of the shield, thus quartering it. The first quarter shows a golden yellow sunrise over the area's Shaw Mountain, with a cultivated field and cottonwood trees, in natural colors, to suggest the origin of the city's name, *Les Bois*. The second quarter has a white-winged caduceus with two brown snakes entwined around it on a green field, to represent the first doctors and medical missionaries in the area. The third quarter has a gold sheaf of wheat on a green background, to symbolize the area's agriculture. The fourth quarter shows a burnished gold cornucopia spilling out golden coins toward the dexter side of the shield, to represent the mining wealth of the region.

At the base of the shield is a small golden yellow ribbon with 1865 in gold numerals outlined in black. The dexter supporter is a white-bearded miner, symbolizing the gold rush and early mining development of the area; his left arm leans on the shield, his right arm holds the handle of a pickaxe to his side. A long-handled shovel lies at his feet, pointed toward the base of the shield. He wears a brown broad-brimmed hat, a light blue shirt with a scarf around his neck, and dark blue trousers. The sinister supporter is a soldier in full 19th-century uniform, commemorating Fort Boise as a military post; his right arm supports the shield, his left hand rests on his sword. His jacket and broad-brimmed hat are dark blue, his trousers a lighter blue, and his boots, brown. The shield and the supporters stand on a brown platform of hewn logs.

Immediately below the platform is a blue heraldic ribbon with **BOISE CITY** in gold, curved to follow the inner edge of the seal. At the top of the seal, curved along its inner edge, is a similar ribbon reading **SEAL OF**. Below this ribbon, in the crest position, is a brown beaver on a log, facing the hoist, commemorating an early name for the Idaho Territory, "Beaver Territory". Between the beaver and the shield is yet another blue heraldic ribbon with the motto in gold: **PERIL, ENERGY, SUCCESS**, summarizing Boise's settlement history.

The seal was first colored by Mayor Eugene W. Shellworth in 1963; it was previously embossed or depicted only in black and white.   JP 🛡

BOSTON, MASSACHUSETTS ✪

Population Rank: U.S..... # 20
    Massachusetts...... # 1

Proportions: 7:10 (official)

Adopted: 30 January 1917

DESIGN: Boston's flag centers the city's seal on a blue field. The seal consists of a white disk with its features outlined in blue. It shows a city scene in the early 1800s with the state house, built in 1790, featured prominently in the center, along with several sailing ships in Boston Bay. In the lower part of the seal appears, in three lines, **BOSTONIA/ CONDITA A.D. / 1630.** ("Boston Founded AD. 1630"). On a ring of "continental buff" surrounding the seal is **SICUT PATRIBUS SIT DEUS NOBIS** ("God be with us as He was with our fathers") at the top, and **CIVITATIS REGIMINE DONATA AD. 1822.** ("Presented with the government of a body politic in the year of Our Lord 1822"), at the bottom, all in blue. A thin white line fimbriates the outer edge of the ring.

SYMBOLISM: Governor John Winthrop founded Boston in 1630 and made it the capital of the Massachusetts Bay Colony in 1632. The ships signify the importance of maritime commerce to the city's development. The motto "God be with us as He was with our fathers" comes from 1 Kings, 8:57.

HOW SELECTED: In 1913 the Columbus Day Committee designed a civic flag for its parade and later proposed to the mayor that it be adopted. An ordinance was introduced into the city council on 16 January 1914, after the municipal art commission had been consulted, but it was not adopted until 30 January 1917.

DESIGNER: Unknown.

Seal of the Boston Society, showing an image of the Trimountain.

MORE ABOUT THE FLAG: The city seal was created in 1823 and has no colors. Since the ordinance does not specifically define the flag, except to specify that *the colors herein specified shall be the official colors of the city of Boston, namely: Continental blue and Continental buff* (the colors derive from the uniforms of Boston soldiers during the Revolutionary War), the flag has been manufactured differently. One version has the seal is in blue and white with the buff circle on a light blue field. Another has a colored seal that appears on a dark blue field. The city ordinance creating the civic flag described "a City Flag and a Municipal Standard". The flag was to be flown from public buildings such as city hall, and made of bunting with the seal showing through to the reverse side. The standard was to be used in parades and other functions when the mayor could attend, and made of silk with the reverse showing the Trimountain (three hills of Boston). Apparently the standard was never manufactured, as no reports, examples, illustrations, or photographs of it exist.

FORMER FLAGS: In the 19th-century booklet (n.d.) *City Flags*, published by Allan and Ginter, the civic flag of Boston is illustrated as a colored city seal on a white field with wreath below it. Whether this flag was actually used remains unknown, as no other evidence has appeared to either verify or refute its use.   JC 🛡

BRIDGEPORT, CONNECTICUT

Population Rank: U.S... # 160
           Connecticut...... # 1

Proportions: 3:5 (usage)

Adopted: 17 February 1936

DESIGN: The city resolution states: *The field of the official flag shall be dark blue and the figures on said field shall consist of the following: The Official Seal and the words* **City of Bridgeport, Connecticut** *in gold under the seal and a suitable fringe shall be provided.*

The *de facto* design does not follow exactly the official description in the above resolution. The current flag places **City of Bridgeport** above the seal and **Connecticut** below. The lettering is gold in an Old English font. The seal is rendered in natural colors rather than in gold. The seal portrays a view of the city's economic and civic life.

In the center of the lower third of the seal are an anvil and a cogwheel; below the anvil is a cornucopia. Above the anvil is a shield bearing a right arm holding a hammer, with a rising sun behind three hills. Above the shield is an American eagle with wings spread, facing the hoist, upon a globe, with a scroll in its beak reading **INDUSTRIA CRESCIMUS** ("By Industry We Thrive"). On the observer's right of the seal is a section of a bridge, with mills above and a train below. To the observer's left are a sailing ship and a harbor scene. Above this are a grain elevator, railroad roundhouse, and church spire. Below the ship is an old-fashioned fire engine. A sewing machine is below the train and next to the anvil. In the blue ring surrounding the seal appear **SEAL OF THE CITY OF BRIDGEPORT, CONNECTICUT** clockwise above, and **INCORPORATED 1835** counterclockwise below, all in gold.

SYMBOLISM: Bridgeport is an industrial city whose manufacturing development accelerated after the Civil War. The anvil, cogwheel, and hammer symbolize industry; the cornucopia is for wealth. The bridge recalls the origin of the city's name (Bridgeport's name derives from the first drawbridge over the Pequonock River). The sailing ship represents maritime commerce (Bridgeport is a coastal city on Long Island Sound). Bridgeport was one of the first cities to manufacture sewing machines and has a monument to the inventor, Elias Howe.

HOW SELECTED: The flag was created for the city's centennial commemoration in 1936. Alderman Taft proposed a resolution to adopt this design as the civic flag, which the city council approved by a 15-1 vote.

DESIGNER: Unknown.

MORE ABOUT THE FLAG: Bridgeport has had two seals. The seal in use today on the civic flag was designed by Julian H. Sterling and adopted by the common council in 1873. It is a revision of the original seal.   JC

BUFFALO, NEW YORK

Population Rank: U.S. ..... # 58
New York ...... # 2

Proportions: 5:8 (official)

Adopted: 7 May 1924 (official)

DESIGN: The field of Buffalo's flag is dark blue with a central image in white. In the center is the city seal, from which emanate thirteen rays ("electric flashes") of three jagged sections each similar to the conventional depiction of lightning flashes. Between each pair of flashes is a five-pointed star, point outwards. The seal itself has a narrow ring around the outside edge. The seal's field is white with blue figures. In the upper half, from the hoist, are a lighthouse on a pier, a three-masted ship under full sail (bow toward the hoist), and a small sailboat. The top of the pier and the surface of the water on which the ship and boat are sailing (Lake Erie) form the bisecting line. The waters of the lake occupy about a third of the top of the seal's lower half. The remainder shows a shoreline, below which the old Erie Canal is seen, with a canal boat (also headed toward the hoist) being drawn by two horses or donkeys, one ahead of the other. The rear animal has a human figure riding it. The lower edge of the canal has a fence running along it, and below are shrubs, filling in the remainder of the seal.

The Charter and Code of the City of Buffalo (1974) specifies the official dimensions:

Said flag in dimensions shall be five (5) feet wide by eight (8) feet long, or a flag of other dimensions may be used if the width and length and the following elements are of similar proportions. The inner and outer circles above indicated on a flag of five by eight (5x8) feet shall be, respectively, eighteen (18) inches and twenty-two (22) inches in diameter. The electric flashes shall be sixteen (16) inches long and approximately one and one-half inches wide at the base, which base shall be separated from the outer circle by a space of one-fourth (1/4) inch. The stars shall be four (4) inches tip to tip, and the center of each star shall be sixteen (16) inches distant from the center of the circle.

SYMBOLISM: The 13 stars symbolize that New York was one of the thirteen original colonies of the United States. The flashes recall the fact that Buffalo was one of the first cities to install electricity widely. The ship and lighthouse on the seal show that Buffalo is an important commercial port on Lake Erie, and the boat suggests that the lake is also a center for recreation. Buffalo was the terminus of the Erie Canal, which helped to develop the city commercially.

HOW SELECTED: By the city planning committee, which held a citywide contest.

DESIGNER: Louis Greenstein, president of the local chapter of the American Institute of Architects.

MORE ABOUT THE FLAG: The designer was awarded $250 as winner of the contest. The prize was presented to him by the mayor on 14 June 1924, Flag Day, which was declared a holiday for the occasion. Greenstein had designed a similar flag in 1907 for the Old Home Week celebration that was chosen by a committee at that time as the best design.

FORMER FLAG: On 3 June 1912, Mayor L. P. Fuhrmann and the commissioner of public works, Francis G. Ward, proposed a flag to the city council that was apparently not adopted officially. This flag has a "Continental buff" field with the coat of arms of New York in its center. Superimposed on the shield of the arms is the city's seal. Both arms and seal are all in blue. While Fuhrmann and Ward asserted in their letter to the council that it was common in other cities to use the city seal superimposed on the arms of the state, no such practice was in fact observed.   JP

BURLINGTON, VERMONT

Population Rank: U.S... # 918
Vermont...... # 1

Proportions: 2:3 (unofficial)

Adopted: Circa 1991 (unofficial)

DESIGN: The flag of Burlington is divided horizontally. The upper section is medium blue, with a curved scroll in yellow with **BURLINGTON** in red. In the top half of the lower section is a mountain range in dark and medium green. Below it is a lake in light blue with four medium-green islands near the hoist. In the center of the flag is a quartered shield. The first quarter is royal blue with a white dove flying toward the hoist; the second is red with a yellow "lamp of knowledge" with a white flame; the third is yellow with seven dark green pine trees placed from top to bottom 2,2,2,1; the fourth is royal blue with five white narrow horizontal stripes charged with thin black stripes; overall are the two masks of the theater, tragedy and comedy, in white and outlined in black. In the center of the shield is a white globe centered in the mid-Atlantic Ocean (depicted in light blue) with the edges of North and South America, Greenland, and Europe and Africa depicted in dark green. Between the first and second quarters, above the globe and emanating above the shield into the center of the scroll, is a city hall image in white, outlined in black, with a yellow dome atop a tower (the new city hall is shown, as opposed to the image of the old city hall that appears on the city seal). The tower overlaps a yellow half-disk with four red conjoined triangles in a semi-circle touching its top on either side of the tower; the dome overlaps the scroll below the "N" of the city's name.

SYMBOLISM: The medium blue represents the sky, while the light blue symbolizes Lake Champlain, one of the largest lakes in the United States, on which Burlington is located. The mountain range is New York's Adirondack Mountains, the view from Burlington westward across Lake Champlain. The islands are the Four Brother Islands, with Juniper Island farthest from the hoist.

The first quarter's dove symbolizes peace and Burlington's connections to its sister cities: Yaroslavl, Russia; Puerto Cabezas, Nicaragua; Burlington, Ontario, Canada; and, since the introduction of the flag, both Arab and Israeli Bethlehem, Israel. The second quarter's lamp of knowledge represents the colleges and universities in Burlington: The University of Vermont, Champlain College, Burlington College, and Trinity College (which closed in 2001). It also represents the city's commitment to education and in particular its public schools.

The third quarter's pine trees represent the city's commitment to the environment and conservation. According to the flag's official description, the pine tree was chosen because it is "the state tree of Vermont", although the sugar maple is actually the state tree. However, the pine tree does prominently figure on the Vermont state seal and on the Vermont coat of arms. Two pine boughs flank the arms and are referred to as the "Vermonter's badge", as troops from Vermont wore such a badge in 1814 at the Battle of Plattsburgh. The fourth quarter's theater masks reflect the city's love of the arts. The globe represents the theme of "we are one world".

HOW SELECTED: A group of students in the Paradise Project at Edmunds Middle School developed the flag. The project was conceived and led by Cara Wick, an eighth grader.

DESIGNER: Students at the Edmunds Middle School in Burlington, Vermont.   JC 🏴

CARSON CITY, NEVADA ✪

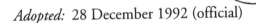

Population Rank: U.S... # 566
Nevada...... # 6

Proportions: 2:3 (official)

Adopted: 28 December 1992 (official)

DESIGN: The specifications of Carson City's flag are established in detail by ordinance, based on a field that is 4 by 6 feet. The flag is a horizontal tribar of white, blue, and white stripes, each one foot, four inches wide. The blue stripe is "process blue" and has two narrow white horizontal stripes one inch wide running across it, two and one-half inches from the top and bottom edges of the blue stripe. Over the blue stripe is a modified version of the circular city seal, 20 inches in diameter, its center one foot, seven inches from the hoist edge. A white line one inch wide encircles the seal on the portion that rests on the blue stripe.

The seal itself is enclosed in a narrow blue ring and depicts in its center the dome of the state capitol. Over the capitol fly (on the same pole) the United States flag, and below it, and slightly smaller, the Nevada state flag, both in full color. The white capitol is centered on a silhouette of the state in blue. In the upper hoist quadrant of the seal is a very large brown golden eagle (*Aquila chrysaetos*), in flight toward the fly; about half of its right wing extends beyond the seal onto the blue stripe and its left wing arches over the capitol, but behind the flagpole. Behind the eagle and capitol are blue sky and white clouds. Just above the center on both sides of the seal are snow-capped mountains. The remainder of the seal's background is white. A narrow black line, passing behind the base of the capitol dome, divides the upper and lower half of the seal.

Dominating the lower hoist quadrant is a Pony Express rider on a horse in full gallop, facing the fly. The rider's hat is white; his scarf, yellow; his shirt, "process magenta"; his vest, brown; his trousers, blue; his boots, black. The horse is a dark brown. Above the rider's head is a white five-pointed star on the state silhouette, marking the location of Carson City as the state's capital. Dominating the lower fly quadrant is an 1875 Virginia & Truckee Railroad steam locomotive (No. 22, *The Inyo*) and its tender, in three-quarter profile, shaded in black and white, headed toward the viewer. Most of its smokestack extends into the upper fly quadrant. Steam is emitting from the train's whistle, behind the smokestack. Below the rider and locomotive, in the center in black lettering, is **FOUNDED** in Casio Open Face font, and immediately below, in the same font, but twice as large, is **1858**, followed by two smaller letters, **CC**, all in black.

Curved above the seal, within a radius of 14 inches from the seal's center, is **CARSON CITY**, and below, within the same radius, **NEVADA**, all in blue letters in Helvetica Condensed bold type.

SYMBOLISM: Blue and white are the city's official colors. The inner ring of the seal represents the city's sphere of influence as the hub of government in northwest Nevada. The mountains are the Sierra Nevada and Carson ranges that surround Eagle Valley where Carson City is located.

The eagle recalls that the first permanent settlers hung a stuffed eagle over the doorway of their log cabin in November 1851 and suggests the courage, strength, perseverance, and stability of Carson City over the decades. The Pony Express came through Carson City in 1860 and was important to the territory's development into a state. The Virginia & Truckee Railroad united Carson City with the rest of the United States and was the city's largest employer for several decades. Carson City was named and surveyed as a town in 1858. The **CC** on the seal is for the United States Mint that was established there (all coins minted in the city bore the mint mark "CC" for Carson City).

HOW SELECTED: The Carson City Historical Commission developed the design and submitted it to the board of supervisors.

DESIGNER: Verne R. Horton, a commercial artist, created the flag based on the elements suggested by the historical commission.   JP

CASPER, WYOMING

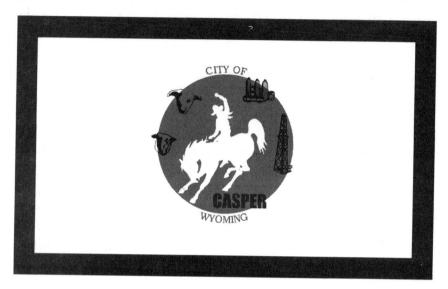

Population Rank: U.S... # 698
Wyoming...... # 2

Proportions: 3:5 (usage)

Adopted: Unknown

DESIGN: The field of Casper's flag is white, with a blue border one-quarter unit wide on a field of 3 by 5 units. In the center is the inner portion of the city's seal, which has a circular red field of 1.5 units in diameter. In its center is a large white silhouette of a cowboy astride a bucking horse that faces the hoist. Running from the bronco's left fore-leg is **CASPER** in blue, running along the lower portion of the red disk with the final letter extending on to the white field. On the seal at 9 o'clock is the head of a sheep; at 11 o'clock, a steer's head; at 1 o'clock, three oil-treating tanks; and at 3 o'clock, an oil derrick; all in blue. Curved above the seal is **CITY OF**, and curved below is **WYOMING**, all in small red letters.

SYMBOLISM: The "bronco rider" and horse represent Wyoming, the oil derrick and treating tanks symbolize the energy industry, and the sheep and steer are for the ranching industry of the region.

HOW SELECTED: Unknown.

DESIGNER: Unknown.

MORE ABOUT THE FLAG: The city's seal has additional elements not used on the flag's seal: a rising sun and city outline, to symbolize the bright future of the growing city of Casper; plowed fields, suggesting the agriculture of the area; and a mountain, representing Casper Mountain. A rope design, also omitted on the flag, encircles the outer edge of the seal. The border on Wyoming's state flag, although a different color, perhaps inspired the border on Casper's flag.   JP

CEDAR RAPIDS, IOWA

Population Rank: U.S... # 180
Iowa...... # 2

Proportions: 3:5 (usage)

Adopted: 8 October 1962 (official status uncertain)

DESIGN: The field of the flag of Cedar Rapids is white. Across approximately the central third of the field horizontally, extending seven-eighths of the flag's length, is a symbolic city skyline in blue. Beginning at the hoist side is a historic mill, separated from the church with a steeple that follows it by three corn stalks. In the center is a representation of the city's Memorial Coliseum. On the fly side is a factory with two smokestacks, then three more stalks of corn, and finally the girders of an unfinished rectangular building. Above the mill is a cloud; another is behind the upper part of the Coliseum; and smoke wafts from the smokestacks toward the fly. The scene is enclosed on the sides and above by three curved lines with the first indentation at the church steeple and the second at the factory smokestacks. The scene rests on a blue heraldic ribbon on which the city's motto appears in white (with quotation marks): "**PROUD of YESTERDAY** [below the mill and church] **PROGRESSIVE TODAY** [below the Coliseum] **PROMIS-ING TOMORROW**" [below the factory and unfinished building]. Above the scene, running across the field nearly the same length as the scene is **CEDAR RAPIDS**; below, centered below the central segment of the scene is **IOWA**, all in large red letters.

SYMBOLISM: In 1963 the city administration explained the flag's symbolism:

Red, white, and blue are the three basic colors because they are the basic colors of both the American flag and the flag of Iowa. The ribbon on which the slogan of Cedar Rapids appears represents the Cedar River which has been and probably always will be an important part of Cedar Rapids. The structure on the left [hoist] represents the first mill built in Cedar Rapids along the river in 1842. The role of agriculture is represented by the stalks of corn on both the left [hoist] and right [fly] of the design. The church pictured represents the many churches for which Cedar Rapids is famous and proud. The Memorial Coliseum is symbolic of the progressive city which Cedar Rapids is today. This building houses both our city government and the Chamber of Commerce. The factory illustrates the role of industry in Cedar Rapids today and in the future. The steel girders of an unfinished building represent the promising future of our great city.

HOW SELECTED: A contest was held among the four high schools of the city.

DESIGNER: Fred Easker, Jr.

MORE ABOUT THE FLAG: After the flag was adopted, 114 were made. Two were kept for the mayor's office and council chambers; the remainder sold for $3.35 each.   JP 🛡️

CHARLESTON, SOUTH CAROLINA

Population Rank: U.S... # 243
South Carolina...... # 2

Proportions: 3:5 (usage)

Adopted: mid-1990s (unofficial)

DESIGN: The flag of Charleston is dark blue on which is centered the embellished city seal in white and dark blue. On a flag with a ratio of 3 by 5 units, it has a diameter of 1.6 units. The seal is described officially in the ordinance of adoption: *On the right in the foreground is a female figure seated, her right arm raised and forefinger pointing, her left arm down and left hand holding a scepter; on the left is a ship under full sail; in the background is a water view of the city, with the steeples towering; immediately below the female figure are the words,* "**Carolopolis Condita A.D. 1670**", *(Charleston founded in the year of our Lord 1670). Encircling the whole are the following inscriptions in Roman capitals:* "**Aedes mores juraque curat**" *(She cares for her temples, customs, and rights) and* "**Civitatis Regimine Donata A.D. 1783**" *(Pre-*

sented with the government of a body politic in the year of our Lord 1783)". The seal was first authorized on 13 August 1783. The current design is based on a version of the seal introduced in 1882 by Mayor William A. Courtney. There are palmetto branches below the seal and books stacked along its sides. At the top is a scroll, quill pen, and oil lamp.

SYMBOLISM: Of the city seal, Historian David C. R. Hesser writes *Tradition identifies the woman as the personification of the city itself, and the design evokes an image of Charleston deriving its livelihood from the sea and prepared to defend itself.* (A 'Warrior Queen of Ocean': The Story of Charleston and Its Seal, *South Carolina Historical Magazine* 93 (1992): 167.

HOW SELECTED: In the mid-1990s Mayor Joseph P. Riley changed the existing flag, although no legal authorization for the new design can be found.

DESIGNER: Unknown.

FORMER FLAGS: Mayor Courtenay first unfurled a Charleston city flag in 1882, but the exact design is unknown. For many years, an unofficial flag of dark blue with a large white central disk bearing the unembellished seal was used.   JP

CHARLESTON, WEST VIRGINIA ✪

Population Rank: U.S... # 559
West Virginia...... # 1

Proportions: 7:12 (usage)

Adopted: 1970 (unofficial)

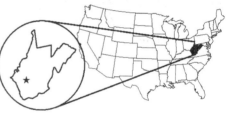

DESIGN: Charleston's flag has a border of blue with a coat of arms in the center on a light field, perhaps in imitation of the West Virginia state flag. However, the field in Charleston's flag is bright yellow instead of white and the shade of the blue border is lighter than on the state flag. Above the shield of the arms is a red scroll with **CHARLESTON** in black. Surrounding the lower half of the shield are various green leaves, predominantly oak leaf clusters. The shield is set on a decorative framework of descending lines, creating the effect of a fringed trumpet banner. In the topmost part of the shield appears the dome of the state capitol in blue and yellow with **MDCCXCIV** (1794 in Roman numerals) in blue. The arms are quartered. In the first quarter (upper hoist corner), a crossed rifle and arrow appear in yellow on a green field. In the second quarter is a sternwheeler in yellow on blue.

The third quarter shows a pick and shovel, yellow on black. The fourth quarter contains a yellow cog, looking very much like a flower, on a red field.

SYMBOLISM: The capitol dome refers to Charleston's status as the capital of West Virginia. The crossed rifle and arrow recall the city's frontier heritage and its beginnings as a fort in the French and Indian War. The paddleboat represents the role of shipping in Charleston's economy and its location at the juncture of two rivers. The pick and shovel are those of a coal miner, emphasizing the importance of mining to West Virginia. The black color further stresses the role of coal in the Charleston economy. The cogwheel reflects the city's industries as well as its former nickname as "the Cog City". The leaves surrounding the lower half of the shield may be for the love of nature of the city's inhabitants.

HOW SELECTED: The city's flag was the result of a competition organized by the *Charleston Gazette* on the occasion of Charleston's 175th anniversary in 1969. A panel of judges headed by the mayor selected the winner.

DESIGNER: Gilbert Bayless, a 35-year-old analyst from the city of Bancroft, won the $500 prize out of a field of 1,236 entries.

MORE ABOUT THE FLAG: Charleston has its own "Betsy Ross". Mrs. William O. Arden researched and designed the first West Virginia state flag. She had the further honor of creating the first official Charleston flag.   RM

CHARLOTTE, NORTH CAROLINA

Population Rank: U.S. ..... # 26
North Carolina ...... # 1

Proportions: 3:5 (usage)

Adopted: 6 May 1929 (official)

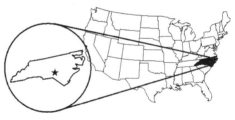

DESIGN: Charlotte's flag has the city seal centered on a white saltire on a light blue field. The seal depicts a tree in the center. To the left, a hornet's nest hangs on the tree. On the right, a liberty cap bearing the word **LIBERTY** hangs on one of the tree's branches. Rays radiate behind the tree. Below the tree, two hands clasp, with **1775** below. Enclosing this design, **CITY OF CHARLOTTE MECKLENBURG COUNTY** curves clockwise over the top of the seal and **NORTH CAROLINA** curves counterclockwise below. Between these inscriptions are two stars. The seal appears in blue outline on a white field surrounded by blue inner and outer lines. A white fimbriation separates the seal from the field.

SYMBOLISM: The flag closely resembles Scotland's saltire (St. Andrew's Cross), although it may instead be a conscious or unconscious adaptation of a Confederate battle flag. Blue and white are Charlotte's official colors. The tree represents growth. The hornet's nest is a symbol for the city dating from Revolutionary times. In the words of a city pamphlet, *... in the American Revolution, her citizens fought so fiercely that a British general compared being in Charlotte to being in a hornet's nest.* The Liberty Cap is another reference to the Revolution, showing the desire of Charlotte's citizens for freedom. A further reminder of the American Revolution is the date 1775, when the Mecklenburg Declaration of Independence was adopted (the year before the Continental Congress adopted one for all the colonies). Overall, the seal and flag suggest a sense of history and, as a tree can grow from a sapling to a mighty oak, hope for a grand future is further emphasized by the rays radiating from behind the tree.

The historical authenticity of the "Mecklenberg Declaration of Independence" has been challenged by most scholars who have investigated the subject.

HOW SELECTED: Adopted by the city council.

DESIGNER: Information unavailable.

MORE ABOUT THE FLAG: Charlotte has another flag, adopted in 1985. It may be considered a government service flag, since it is flown outside the Government Center and its central charge appears on government vehicles. It consists of a stylized white crown centered on a green field occupying about the central three-fifths of the flag overall. Its center forms an "M". The crown is for unity—all city agencies cooperating for the good of Charlotte's citizens.   RM 🛡

CHESAPEAKE, VIRGINIA

Population Rank: U.S..... # 90
Virginia...... # 3

Proportions: 3:5 (usage)

Adopted: 23 December 1975 (official status uncertain)

DESIGN: Chesapeake's flag has a dark red field with the city seal in color in the center. Six gold five-pointed stars surround the seal at 9, 11, 1, 3, 5, and 7 o'clock. The seal has a diameter of 1.6 units on a field of 3 by 5 units. A narrow double ring of gold encircles the seal, forming an outer edge that appears as a single gold ring when reduced in size or seen from a distance. Another gold ring, this one beveled, 1.2 units in diameter, lies within the outer rings. In the space between on a dark red field appears, curved clockwise from 9 o'clock to 3 o'clock, • CITY • OF • CHESAPEAKE • VIRGINIA • 1963 • and curved below, counterclockwise, in smaller letters, **NORFOLK COUNTY 1636 • SOUTH NORFOLK 1921**, all in gold.

The center of the seal shows two male figures, facing each other and shaking hands. Their shirts, sleeves rolled up to the elbow, are white; their trousers, dark gray. The fly figure holds a large wrench in his left hand. In front of the hoist figure is an old-fashioned gray hand plow with red handles. The ground on which they are standing, which extends to the horizon line bisecting the seal horizontally, appears to be a plowed field, in gray. On the horizon line, on the hoist side, between the beveled ring and the figure with the plow, is a small white house surrounded by tall green trees. On the fly side is a gray factory with two smokeless smoke stacks, in front of which is a gray truck, facing the hoist. Between the two men is a gray freighter, moving toward the hoist, its stern hidden behind the fly figure. Above, and centered between the two men, is a small golden yellow sun, with 27 rays emanating from it out to the edge of the beveled ring. The sun shines in a light blue sky that fills the upper half of the seal. In very small dark blue letters curved and centered above the sun is **ONE INCREASING PURPOSE**.

SYMBOLISM: The city describes the symbolism of the flag's seal: *The man's figure on the left* [hoist] *represents the rural population, with a background of fields, trees, and a home. The plow beside him represents agriculture. On the right* [fly] *is the man representing industry, with a factory in the background. The rising sun symbolizes the bright future that will result from the joined hands. The motto above the figures, 'One increasing purpose' is a phrase from* [Alfred Lord] *Tennyson's Locksley Hall, a poem that deals with the promising future of man.* The red color of the flag stands for the valor at the Battle of Great Bridge (December 9, 1775, in which the British were completely defeated in the Virginia Colony), and the six gold stars are for the six boroughs of Norfolk County.

HOW SELECTED: The seal was selected by a special meeting of the governing bodies of the City of South Norfolk and Norfolk County, which combined formed the new city of Chesapeake. The flag was proposed later by the new city's mayor, Marian Whitehurst. The seal was officially adopted 2 January 1963.

DESIGNER: Kenneth Harris, a Norfolk artist, who designed both the seal and flag.   JP

CHEYENNE, WYOMING ✪

Population Rank: U.S... # 565
Wyoming...... # 1

Proportions: 3:5 (usage)

Adopted: Circa 1985 (unofficial)

DESIGN: The flag of Cheyenne has a white field with a brown border and the city's emblem in the center. On a flag of 3 by 5 feet, the border is 4 inches wide. The emblem, which resembles a seal, is 25 inches in diameter and consists of an outer ring in white edged in brown, and an inner ring in brown, edged in white. In the outer ring appears in brown **CITY OF**, centered and curved clockwise above, and **CHEYENNE**, centered and curved counterclockwise below, all 2.5 inches high. In the inner ring appears **THE EQUALITY STATE**, centered and curved clockwise above and **WYOMING**, centered and curved counterclockwise below, all in yellow letters 1 inch high. Separating the phrases in the inner ring are two sets of three white stars, the middle star larger than the others. Occupying most of the center of the emblem is a brown bull bison on white, standing in three-quarter profile, facing the hoist with its left shoulder at the center. In the center, below the grass below the bison's feet, is **1867** in brown, perhaps three-quarters of an inch high.

SYMBOLISM: The bison appears on the Wyoming state flag, although depicted differently. The first charter for the government of the city of Cheyenne was adopted in 1867, in what was then a part of the Dakota Territory. Wyoming is called "The Equality State" because of the rights women have traditionally held here. In 1869 Wyoming's territorial legislature enacted a bill granting women the right to vote, the first government in the world to do so.

HOW SELECTED: Mayor Don Erickson asked his staff to develop a city flag.

DESIGNER: Central Services Superintendent Ron Harnish.

MORE ABOUT THE FLAG: The city emblem was adopted officially on 11 July 1994 by the city council, but without the date, 1867, which still appears on the flag. The border on Wyoming's state flag, although a different color, may have inspired the border on the Cheyenne flag.

FORMER FLAG: Cheyenne used a flag for its centennial commemoration in 1967. This flag has a red field with a narrow white border  inside a wider blue border. In the center of the flag is a bucking horse, head down and tossing a cowboy in the air toward the hoist, all in white. Around this figure, in white letters forming a circle, is • CHEYENNE • WYOMING • over the top and CENTENNIAL • 1867 • 1967 below. The figure evidently recalls a true incident, the famous bronco, known as Muggins, throwing the rider Albert (Stub) Farlow; it is a common Wyoming emblem. JP

CHICAGO, ILLINOIS

Population Rank: U.S. ...... # 3
Illinois ...... # 1

Proportions: 2:3 or 3:5
(both official)

Adopted: 21 December 1939 (official)

DESIGN: Chicago's flag has a white field with two blue horizontal stripes, each about one-sixth of the width of the hoist, and set slightly less than one-sixth of the way from the top and bottom. Between the two blue stripes are four bright red six-pointed stars, spaced evenly across the center horizontally.

SYMBOLISM: The Chicago flag is replete with symbolism. Probably no other city attaches so much symbolism to the various parts of its flag. The three white horizontal stripes represent, from the top, the North, West, and South sides of the city. The upper blue stripe represents Lake Michigan and the North Branch of the Chicago River; the lower blue stripe, the South Branch of the Chicago River and the Great Canal. Each of the red stars symbolizes an important event in the city's history, and the points of each of the stars, in turn, represent civic virtues and history. From the hoist, the symbolism is:

First star: Fort Dearborn. The points of this star represent transportation, labor, commerce, finance, populousness, and salubrity.

Second star: The Chicago Fire of 8-10 October 1871. Its points symbolize religion, education, esthetics, justice, beneficence, and civic pride.

Third star: The World's Columbian Exposition of 1893. The points of the third star signify historical periods of the area. The dates represent the end of those periods: France, 1693; Great Britain, 1763; Virginia, 1778; Northwest Territory, 1798; Indian Territory, 1802; and Illinois Statehood, 1818.

Fourth star: The Century of Progress Exposition of 1933. Its points represent the World's Third Largest City (in 1933); the city's Latin motto, Urbs in Horto ("City in a Garden"); the city's English motto, "I will"; the Great Central Market; and Wonder City (the first and last two are nicknames).

HOW SELECTED: In 1915, Alderman James A. Kearns proposed to the city council that Chicago have a civic flag. The council agreed and established the Chicago Flag Commission, which held a contest and offered a prize for the winning design. This design was submitted on 28 March 1917 and adopted by the city council in the summer of 1917.

DESIGNER: The winner of the competition was Mr. Wallace Rice, an author and editor, who had been interested in flags since his boyhood. He worked on his design for approximately six weeks.

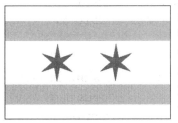

MORE ABOUT THE FLAG: Rice's design was the same as the current flag, except that it had only two stars, representing two major events that had occurred up to that time. While no special significance was then attributed to their points, Rice explained that the stars were given six points to avoid confusion with the five-pointed stars on the national flag. Possibly to reinforce this distinction, the first stars had long and rather sharp points; their form persisted for several decades.

In 1933, a city ordinance placed a third star on the flag for the Chicago world's fair, the Century of Progress International Exposition. The ordinance also directed that the municipal flag be displayed on all municipal buildings whenever the national flag was displayed, but subordinate to it. The flag was authorized to be pointed or notched when suspended vertically from windows or over a street, reflecting the fashion of the time. In the same ordinance, the council created a municipal pennant described as *a long streamer showing the three stars on white at the staff, the fly being equally divided, blue and white*, with proportions of 2:15 or 2:20, and a municipal badge, described as *on a silver ground three red stars with sharp points, six in number, between two blue bars*.

In 1939, the fourth star was added to the flag, together with the additional symbolism ascribed to the points of the stars. Although no mention was made of changes to the pennant or badge, in practice the fourth star would presumably be added to them as well.

Currently the points of the flag's stars are shortened and not as exaggerated as earlier versions. The shade of the blue color is not specified, but in practice tends to be a medium blue.

Probably because of the requirement that municipal buildings fly the city flag, Chicago's flag flies widely throughout the city on police stations, fire stations, libraries and schools, and no doubt is among the most recognized civic flags in the nation. It is certainly well known by the citizens of Chicago. When a police officer or firefighter dies, the Chicago flag drapes the casket. The flag's four-star motif has come to characterize the city, painted on its street signs, appearing on uniforms of police and firefighters, and even imprinted in concrete railings, sidewalks, and bridge abutments.   JP

CINCINNATI, OHIO

Population Rank: U.S. ..... # 54

Ohio ...... # 3

Proportions: 2:3 (usage)

Adopted: 15 June 1940 (official), 1895 (unofficial)

DESIGN: According to the ordinance of adoption:
The flag of the City of Cincinnati shall be rectangular in shape. It shall have a white ground work. In the center shall be a red letter 'C'. Extending horizontally from either side of the letter 'C' shall be three wavy parallel lines of navy blue. Within the letter 'C' shall be the seal of the City of Cincinnati in blue. Extending upward from a point at the top of the letter 'C' and spaced equally from its center line shall be a cluster of five buckeye leaves in red. The proportional dimensions of the flag and of its various parts shall be according to the official design thereof on file in the Council Chamber of the City of Cincinnati. The wavy blue lines occupy approximately the center horizontal third of the field. The seal is described

officially as having *in the center, a representation of a winged rod entwined with two serpents crossed by a sword, above which shall appear the scales of justice, which shall be surmounted with the words "Juncta Juvant".*

SYMBOLISM: The red "C" is for Cincinnati. The red buckeye leaves above it represent Ohio, the "Buckeye State". The wavy blue lines symbolize the Ohio River, on which Cincinnati is situated. In the seal, the winged rod signifies commerce; the serpents, wisdom; the sword, authority and power; and the scales, justice. The motto *Juncta Juvant* is translated variously as "United They Assist", "Things Joined Together Are Helpful", and, more freely, "Growth through Unity".

HOW SELECTED: The *Cincinnati Times-Star* ran an editorial on 23 November 1895, offering a prize of $50 for a distinctive flag for the "Queen City". Mayor John A. Caldwell named a panel of prominent citizens to judge the over 100 entries. The seal had been authorized 19 May 1819.

DESIGNER: The winner, who signed his entry as "Zero of Burnet Woods" (a neighborhood of the city), was later identified as Emil Rothengater, a foreman at Russell Morgan Lithograph Co. (later the U.S. Printing Co.).

MORE ABOUT THE FLAG: After the winning design was selected, Charles P. Taft, editor of the *Times-Star* and a U.S. congressman, had Congress give Cincinnati exclusive rights to the design on 24 January 1896. The flag's selection, however, was controversial due to a strong sentiment of the time that the national flag was the only one the city needed, so Cincinnati's flag remained unofficial and largely unseen until its 1940 adoption.   JP 🏴

CLEVELAND, OHIO

Population Rank: U.S...... # 33
Ohio ...... # 2

Proportions: 2:3 (usage)

Adopted: 24 February 1896 (official)

DESIGN: Cleveland has a vertical tribar of red, white, and blue stripes, with a shield with the city's coat of arms centered on the white stripe. According to the ordinance of adoption: *The middle stripe shall bear the American shield with the word* **Cleveland** *in blue, across its center, and the figures 1796 in red, at its base encircled by a* [green] *laurel wreath. The outline of the lower half of the shield shall be in red and the upper in blue. In the upper left-hand corner* [as seen by the viewer] *shall stand an anvil, hammer and wheel, and in the upper right-hand corner an anchor, windlass and oars. Under the shield, in black letters, shall be placed the words* **Progress and Prosperity.**

SYMBOLISM: The colors are those of the United States flag. (Cleveland's flag predates the Ohio state flag, adopted in 1902, which uses the same colors.) The devices on the shield represent Cleveland's status as an industrial city and a commercial port on Lake Erie. Moses Cleaveland founded the city in 1796. It was named for him, although the spelling has been altered.

HOW SELECTED: The Cleveland *Plain Dealer* sponsored a contest to commemorate the city's centennial in 1896. After a great deal of deliberation, a committee of the city council selected the winning entry from among a large number of designs because of its "dignity, simplicity, and appropriateness".

DESIGNER: Susie Hepburn, an 18-year-old art student.

MORE ABOUT THE FLAG: Miss Hepburn later married the *Plain Dealer's* reporter, Robert Beach, who had delivered the winning prize of 50 silver dollars to her. Initially some citizens opposed to the idea of a city flag, believing it would compete with the revered national flag, so to dispel any controversy the city council referred to the flag as the "city banner" in the ordinance of adoption.

Manufactured versions of the flag evidently rarely follow the ordinance's specifications for the motto under the shield. The letters are often shown in blue (likely to save expense), and the word "and" between "Progress and Prosperity" is sometimes shown as an ampersand or even a large dot. Some versions of the flag also make the white center bar wider, to accommodate the shield more comfortably. Cleveland police officers wear the flag as an arm patch and it appears on the logo of police cars.

OTHER FLAG: Cleveland is one of the few U.S. cities with a sub-municipal flag, in this case, the area known as Ohio City, which was an independent city from 1836 until its annexation to Cleveland in 1854. Although there was no flag for the independent Ohio City, there was a city seal. In October 1983 John Nosek, a resident of the area, thought a distinctive flag would be a source of neighborhood pride, and he persuaded a business associate, Leon Stevens, to design a flag based on the old Ohio City seal. The flag is pennant-shaped, in proportions of 1:2, and has a blue field with a red canton shaped like a pie slice, the curved edge next to the blue field. One large white five-pointed star, pointed toward the upper hoist corner, is in the hoist corner of the canton. Along the canton's inner edge, and curved to match it, is **OHIO CITY** in white. On the blue field are 25 white five-pointed stars arranged in rows of 3, 3, 3, 3, 6, and 7. The stars represent the 25 states of the Union when Ohio City was incorporated. The flag has become popular in the area, and metal versions of it grace the street signs.

JP

COLORADO SPRINGS, COLORADO

Population Rank: U.S...... # 48
         Colorado ...... # 2

Proportions: 3:5 (usage)

Adopted: 26 July 1912 (official)

DESIGN: The white field of the Colorado Springs flag is 22 by 46 units, with a blue border 4 units wide on all sides except the hoist, making overall a flag of 30 by 50 units. Indented 8 units from the hoist is a six-sided lozenge (called a "shield" in official descriptions) 20 units from top to bottom, and 11 units across, placed on the field equidistant from top and bottom of the flag. The hoist and fly sides of the lozenge are 12 units from top to bottom parallel to the flag's width; the four remaining sides (two above and below) are 7 units each. The lozenge has a narrow green border of .8 units. The lower half of the lozenge's field, a royal blue, is itself a lozenge, resulting in a chevron shape for the top half, which has a white field. In the top third of the blue portion are two gold trapezoidal ingots, placed on either side of the field. Below, in the lower third of the field, is another gold ingot, in the center. In the upper part of the lozenge is a gold sun rising, with five rays equidistant from each other. The sun is partially obscured by the upper point of the blue lozenge, which represents a mountain peak.

SYMBOLISM: According to the resolution of adoption:

The White Field is intended to represent the cleanliness and health of the City, and the Blue Border our Blue Skies; the Shield carries the Sun, of which we're justly proud; the Mountain stands for Pikes Peak, and on it are pictured the gold ingots of our mining industries; the Green Band about the Shield represents the Park System surrounding the city.

HOW SELECTED: Presented to council by the Civic League.

DESIGNER: Dr. Caroline Spencer and the Civic League.

MORE ABOUT THE FLAG: When the flag was presented to city council, some council members suggested that "C. S.", the city's initials, be included in the design. The Civic League, ahead of its time with respect to flag design, opposed the idea, and it was dropped. However, when the flag was first flown, shortly after adoption, it caused so much comment and consternation that the administration folded the flag and stored it away. It did not fly again for nearly 70 years.   JP

COLUMBIA, SOUTH CAROLINA ✪

Population Rank: U.S... # 191
South Carolina...... # 1

Proportions: 2:3 (usage)

Adopted: 1912 (official)

DESIGN: The flag of Columbia has a dark blue field. In its center is the city's seal with a diameter of 3 units on a field of 6:9. The seal has two concentric yellow circles around its outer circumference, one inside the other, forming a ring with a dark blue field. **CITY of COLUMBIA** S.C. curves clockwise over the top and **JUSTITIA VIRTUTUM REGINA** curves below, counterclockwise, all in white. In the center of the seal, facing outward, is a female figure, Justice. Blindfolded, she holds the scales of justice in her left hand, which is slightly raised; in her right hand she holds an unsheathed sword, point on the ground. Her gown is white, with a brown lining visible at her feet and in the drape on her left side. She stands on yellow ground, the background behind her is sky blue. In the field curving on either side of the seal are a stalk of corn on the hoist side and a cotton plant on the fly side. The corn plant has green leaves, two yellow ears of corn with brown tassels, and a third ear of corn at the top with only the brown tassel. The cotton plant has green leaves, a brown stem, and four white cotton tufts. Both plants are large, and occupy about 4.5 units of the field, top to bottom.

SYMBOLISM: The seal shows Justice reigning symbolically. Corn and cotton were the principal crops in the Columbia area when the flag was adopted.

HOW SELECTED: A contest was held, with a $25 prize going to the winner.

DESIGNER: A local schoolteacher, whose name has been lost in official records.

MORE ABOUT THE FLAG: The flag was developed as a memento for the men and women from Columbia who have served in the United States Armed Forces.   JP

COLUMBUS, OHIO

Population Rank: U.S. ..... # 15
Ohio ...... # 1

Proportions: 3:5 (usage);
10:19 (official)

Adopted: 28 January 1929 (official)

DESIGN: The flag of Columbus has three vertical stripes, in approximate proportions of 1:2:1. In the manufactured version the center stripe is actually closer to 2.3, no doubt to accommodate the large central device. The ordinance of adoption specifies the colors of the stripes as *chrome yellow at the left* [hoist]; *scarlet red at the right* [fly]; *and white at the center.* The seal and coat of arms of the city appear on the center of the white stripe. The 1912 resolution adopting the original flag and seal describes the device:

On a blue field a half-wreath of buckeye leaves, green, and a half-circle of 16 stars, the whole enclosing a national shield bearing a gilt circle in which appears a galley, or vessel, of the fleet of Christopher Columbus, after whom said city is named, said shield and vessel to be in proper colors, above and clutching the shield to be an eagle, with outspread wings, proper, guarding a golden yellow star, making the seventeenth and representing Ohio. Above and between the wings of the eagle to appear the cupola of the state capitol, surmounted by the lettering Columbus, Ohio, *gilt, in old English letters.*

Due to confusion over the years about the seal and the coat of arms in the device described, on 9 December 1958 the entire emblem was designated as Columbus' official seal. Because the wording describing the seal allows some latitude for an artistic interpretation, several different versions have been used.

SYMBOLISM: Christopher Columbus's ship recalls the city's name. The shield and eagle are traditional American symbols. The capitol building shows that Columbus is Ohio's capital city. The 17 golden yellow stars commemorate Ohio as the 17th state to join the Union (in 1803). The yellow and red colors of the flag suggest the colors of Spain, Columbus's patron on his voyage to the New World.

HOW SELECTED: By resolution of the city council.

DESIGNER: Unknown.

MORE ABOUT THE FLAG: Few city flags have had such a convoluted history as the Columbus flag. It is not known whether the flag legislated in 1929 ever flew. By at least as early as 1965, however, the city flag on display in council chambers was very different from the one adopted, having three vertical stripes of red, white, and blue, with the seal in the center stripe.

In 1975 when the discrepancy was finally noticed, the wrong flag had been displayed for at least ten years. The proportions of the stripes on this flag were ostensibly 1:1:1, but the center stripe was closer to 1.3.

In 1976, for the United States bicentennial, the correct flag was made and installed in city hall. The stripes on this flag were approximately 1:1.4:1. These stripe proportions were in use until about 1985, when the current proportions came into use. The flag's official proportions of 10:19 are the same as the United States flag.

FORMER FLAGS: The first flag of Columbus, adopted 12 February 1912, was the seal/coat of arms on a blue field. A committee convened by city council had chosen it. Although the 1912 council clearly stated that the flag, not the seal, had a blue field, a modern literal interpretation of the language gave the seal a blue field in the 1976 version of the flag.   JP

CONCORD, NEW HAMPSHIRE ✪

Population Rank: U.S... # 848
New Hampshire ...... # 3

Proportions: 3:5 (official)

Adopted: 10 December 1979 (official)

DESIGN: *The City flag shall be of the design indicated below with or without the words CONCORDand NEW HAMPSHIREas they appear thereon. The official design and color scheme of the flag will be on file with the City Clerk.* (Section 1-2-3 of the *Concord City Code*)

The flag has three vertical stripes of dark blue, white, and dark blue, with the center stripe being twice as wide as the other two stripes. On the center white stripe is a Concord Coach in red with a black outline and with yellow wheels, with **CONCORD** above the coach and **NEW HAMPSHIRE** below it, all in dark blue block letters. The alternative official version omits the words.

SYMBOLISM: Concord, New Hampshire, was the birthplace of the famous Concord Coach. In 1827 Lewis Downing, who owned a wagon wheel shop in Concord, formed a partnership with J. Stephen Abbott and developed their famous coach, which provided a smoother ride than its predecessors. Their company, Abbott, Downing & Company, and its successors produced thousands of stagecoaches until it was dissolved and the name acquired by Wells Fargo in 1927.

HOW SELECTED: Unknown.

DESIGNER: Unknown.

MORE ABOUT THE FLAG: A flag different from the 1979 code currently hangs in the city manager's office. It has a dark blue vertical hoist stripe, one-third the width of the flag. On the remaining white field is a Concord Coach with **CONCORD** above and **NEW HAMPSHIRE** below, as in the official version adopted in 1979. While these inscriptions read correctly on the reverse of the flag, the coach runs the opposite direction. In addition, the red Concord Coach's body has black ornamentation on it.

FORMER FLAGS: Concord has had at least four other flags, some *de facto*. About 1950 a *de facto* city flag had three equal vertical stripes of white, dark blue, and white. On the center stripe is the city seal in color with a dove holding a red scroll inscribed with **NEW HAMPSHIRE** in gold over the top. **CITY OF** appears on the hoist stripe and **CONCORD** on the fly stripe, all in gold.

An article in the *Concord Monitor* of 22 October 1979, illustrates a civic flag proposal. It has a dark blue vertical hoist stripe, one-third the width of the flag. On the top section of this stripe is a white dove holding an olive branch in its beak, flying toward the right or fly of the flag. Below the dove is a white five-pointed star. It shows the Concord Coach, as in the official version, with **CITY OF CONCORD, N.H.** in dark blue letters arched over the top of the coach, and **1853** in white on a dark blue scroll below the coach. The article explains the symbols: *A dove holding an olive branch for peace, which in Latin is "concord"* [*concord* actually means "agreement". The Latin word for "peace" is *pax*.]. *A star shows that Concord is the state capital. The blue is the color of New Hampshire. The Concord Coach represents Concord; the city was incorporated in 1853.* This design was the result of an eight-month search by a council committee, and combined the best features of "five or six designs" submitted. Wendell and Ralph Holt, who owned a flag and home furnishings shop in Concord, assisted with the design.

This article also states there were two other existing city flags. The first, described in the October 1979 city code as official, had three equal vertical stripes of white, dark blue, and white, with the city seal in color at the top of the hoist stripe. In the center, on the blue stripe, is a white dove with an olive branch in its beak flying downward toward the hoist.

Another flag was designed in 1951 by a high school student. It has three equal vertical stripes of dark blue, white, and dark blue, with the city seal in color in the center stripe. Below it in block letters is **CITY OF CON-CORD.**

JC

CORPUS CHRISTI, TEXAS

Population Rank: U.S..... # 60
              Texas...... # 8

Proportions: 2:3 (official)

Adopted: 10 March 1953 (official)

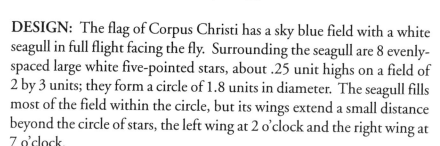

DESIGN: The flag of Corpus Christi has a sky blue field with a white seagull in full flight facing the fly. Surrounding the seagull are 8 evenly-spaced large white five-pointed stars, about .25 unit highs on a field of 2 by 3 units; they form a circle of 1.8 units in diameter. The seagull fills most of the field within the circle, but its wings extend a small distance beyond the circle of stars, the left wing at 2 o'clock and the right wing at 7 o'clock.

SYMBOLISM: The ordinance of adoption details the symbolism: *The sky blue field, or background, in such flag represents the Corpus Christi Bay on which the world's largest Naval Air Station is located, and the sea gull superim-*

posed thereon represents the people of Corpus Christi, both those who were born and raised here and those who have come as visitors and friends to become residents, and the eight (8) stars superimposed thereon and surrounding the white sea gull symbolize the eight major industries of the City of Corpus Christi, being that of Agriculture, Commerce, Oil, Chemicals, Grains, Sea Foods, Metals and Ore Refining, and Tourist Trade.

HOW SELECTED: In 1952, the city council sponsored a contest for a new city flag in all junior and senior high schools in the city.

DESIGNER: The winner of the contest was 16-year-old Barbara Hesse.

JP 🛡

DALLAS, TEXAS

Population Rank: U.S. ...... # 8
            Texas ...... # 3

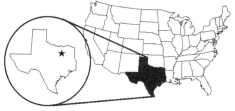

Proportions: 2:3 (official)

Adopted: 13 February 1967 (official); amended 24 July 1967.

DESIGN: The flag of Dallas is described in the amended ordinance of adoption:

The official flag of the City of Dallas is an emblem of four sides, and four angles of ninety degrees each. The background or field shall consist of two stripes or bars of equal size, the upper stripe or upper bar being red in color and the lower stripe or bar being blue. The two stripes or bars shall be separated in the center by a small white bar or line. There shall be superimposed upon this field a white star of five points, three points of which rest in the red bar; the top point rests in a vertical line drawn through the exact center of the flag. The two lower points of the star rest in the blue bar. In the exact center of the star shall appear the seal of the City of Dallas with a field or background of gold; the detail and lettering in the seal shall be of blue.

The proportions of the elements are carefully delineated in a diagram of the flag. The field is .666 by 1 unit. The star's top point is exactly in the center of the field, .052 of a unit from the top. Each side of the star's points is .229 of a unit. The seal's diameter is .220 of a unit.

The seal has two concentric outer rings enclosing **CITY OF DALLAS** curved clockwise, above, and **TEXAS**, curved counterclockwise, below. An interior ring of 44 dots encloses a large five-pointed star, within which is a smaller five-pointed star subdivided into ten sections giving it a three-dimensional appearance.

SYMBOLISM: The red, white, and blue of the flag reflect the colors of both the Texas state flag and the flag of the United States. The single star for Texas' nickname, "The Lone Star State", is characteristic of many Texan city flags.

HOW SELECTED: A committee headed by Councilman Millard Dilg solicited designs for a new city flag from 20 Dallas artists, who submitted 42 proposals. A six-person committee headed by Councilwoman Sibyl Hamilton selected the winning entry.

DESIGNER: Mr. E. L. Gilchrist.

MORE ABOUT THE FLAG: The ordinance of adoption originally included two adjectives describing the colors as "blood" red and "azure" blue that were subsequently omitted in the later amendment. The flag's colors are now a dark red and dark blue. The ordinance of adoption also specifies 25 regulations on the display of the flag, as well as a section providing for prosecution as a misdemeanor if some of these rules are violated or the flag is desecrated willfully, provisions very unusual for civic flags.

FORMER FLAG: The first flag of Dallas was officially adopted on 20 March 1916, the result of a contest suggested by Mayor Henry D. Lindley and administered by the Dallas *Evening Journal.* The winner was Jane Malone, who won a prize of $25; her design was chosen by the city commissioners. The flag is swallow-tailed with a dark blue field and proportions of 3 units at the hoist (tapering to 2.5 units at the fly) by 5 units long. In the center of the field is a large silhouette map of the state of Texas, in white, approximately 2 units high and wide. A red five-pointed star marks the position of Dallas on the map, and below it, in large red block letters stretching about 1.75 units, is **DALLAS**. The framed design hung on the wall of the city secretary for years, but no flag was ever manufactured. In 1935, in order to celebrate the state's centennial, plans were put forth to manufacture the flag, but nothing came of them. In 1954, students at Southern Methodist University made a flag for the city that closely resembled the official design, but it was not until the 1960s that three flags with the official design were made, shortly before the adoption of the new design.   JP

DENVER, COLORADO

Population Rank: U.S..... # 24
Colorado...... # 1

Proportions: 4:7 (usage)

Adopted: 1926 (official)

DESIGN: Denver's flag has a wide white zigzag stripe resembling an outspread 'M' running from hoist to fly and separating an upper field of dark blue from a lower field of red. Centered in the upper field is a yellow disk. On a field of 4 by 7 units, the stripe is .67 units wide, its top edge starting at 1.25 units above the base of the field and ascending to 2.75 units at its apices. The disk is 1.5 units in diameter.

SYMBOLISM: A brochure from the city describes the symbolism:

A yellow circle in the center symbolizes the gold in Colorado's hills as well as the sun. The circle's position indicates Denver's central location in the state. The blue field in which the sun rides is for 'Colorado's unmatched skies'. A white jagged line refers to the mountains which form Denver's backdrop 'indicative of the wealth of silver in the hills'. It also is symbolic of the Indian background in the state's history. The foreground under the mountains in red is in reference to the red earth from which Colorado gained its name. Others have suggested that the white portion suggests snow on the mountains of the region. The colors match those of the Colorado flag, as do the symbols: a white stripe and a yellow disk.

HOW SELECTED: The Sons of the American Revolution sponsored a contest with a prize of $25 for the winning entry. The city council added another $25 for a total of $50. More than 150 entries were received. The Denver Art Commission judged the contest.

DESIGNER: The winner was Margaret Overbeck, a North Denver High School student.

MORE ABOUT THE FLAG: Denver's flag is flown widely and appears on street signs throughout the city.   JP

DES MOINES, IOWA ✪

Population Rank: U.S. ..... # 92
      Iowa ...... # 1

Proportions: 1:2 (usage)

Adopted: 15 April 1974 (official)

DESIGN: The flag of Des Moines has a dark blue field with a red trapezoid at the hoist, its top not quite 3 times the width of its base. On a field of 12:24 units, the trapezoid's top would be 5.5 units and its base 2.3 units. Three arched bridges in white, each 2.7 units high, extend from the trapezoid to the fly edge, with one unit between each, and at top and bottom. They also increase in width from top to bottom, such that although each has 3 complete arches, a fourth arch is only partially shown, each progressively a bit wider. The arches of the top and center bridges are staggered over the bridge below it parallel to the trapezoid.

SYMBOLISM: The three bridges represent the row of bridges across the Des Moines River, easily recognized landmarks of the city that unify the east and west sections of the city. The colors of the flag recall those of the United States flag.

HOW SELECTED: At the suggestion of seventh-grade students from Callanan Junior High School that the city adopt a flag, the Greater Des Moines Chamber of Commerce conducted a contest during March 1974. There were 383 entries from residents ranging from three months old to octogenarians.

DESIGNER: The contest winner was Walter T. Proctor, editor, publisher, and founder of *American Host*, a hotel-motel-resort industry magazine.

MORE ABOUT THE FLAG: The first official flag-raising ceremony for the new city flag was held on 31 March 1975, nearly a year after the flag was adopted. Proctor received a framed letter of appreciation from the Des Moines City Council, a certificate from the chamber of commerce, and a framed facsimile of the finished flag design.   JP ▨

DETROIT, MICHIGAN

Population Rank: U.S. ..... # 10
Michigan ...... # 1

Proportions: 3:5 (usage)

Adopted: 20 April 1948 (official); 1907 (unofficial)

DESIGN: Detroit's flag resembles an armorial banner, divided into quarters with the city seal overlaying the flag's center. The first quarter is blue with 13 white stars, placed horizontally in three rows of 5, 4, 4. The second quarter is red with three gold lions, "passant guardant" (walking by with head to the viewer), one over the other, placed so that the middle lion is in the center of the quarter's field, the top lion slightly toward the hoist, and the lower lion slightly toward the fly. The third quarter has a white field with five gold *fleurs-de-lis*, two centered above three below. The remaining quarter has 13 stripes, 7 red and 6 white, running diagonally toward the lower fly. A gold line separates the quarters and outlines the seal.

The seal, with a white background and bordered in gold, is circular and shows two female figures of classic Greek style, standing side by side facing the hoist. The hoist figure is dressed in a long red *chiton*. A long light blue drape covers her head, left shoulder, and right arm, and extends to the ground. Her head is inclined, as if in sorrow, her right arm points to her right, her left arm is stretched toward the ground. The second figure stands somewhat behind the first, with her right arm on the left shoulder of the other, as if comforting her. She is dressed in a blue *chiton*, with a red outer drape, a *himation*, over her right shoulder and tucked into her girdle under her left arm, which points behind her, to her left. Her head is uncovered, her brown hair swept up in classic fashion. Behind the women in the center are red flames; toward the hoist, some buildings on fire with orange flames; toward the fly, buildings untouched. Curved over the top half of the seal is **THE CITY OF DETROIT**, in black. Horizontally, below the female figures, is **MICHIGAN**, also in black. In somewhat smaller black letters to either side of the figures at about their knee-level are two Latin mottoes, each of two words, one over the other. The hoist motto is **SPERAMVS MELIORA**; the fly motto, **RESVRGET CINERIBVS**, after the Roman fashion of using "V" for the contemporary "U". The seal was officially adopted 26 March 1827.

SYMBOLISM: The flag recalls Detroit's early history. The seal commemorates the great fire of 1805, which destroyed Detroit. The hoist figure weeps at the loss of the city, echoed by the motto, *Speramus Meliora* ("We hope for better things"). The other figure points toward the future, symbolized by the motto, *Resurget Cineribus* ("It shall rise again from the ashes"). The first and fourth quarters of the flag represent Detroit governed by the United States (1796-1812 and 1813 to the present) using components of the United States flag. The second quarter symbolizes the British control of the city (1760-1796 and 1812-1813) using the English symbol of three lions (ultimately deriving from Richard Lion-Heart). The third quarter indicates the French founding of Detroit (1701-1760) using the *fleur-de-lis* symbols of the French monarchy.

HOW SELECTED: Presented to the city by the designer in 1907.

DESIGNER: David E. Heineman. The seal was designed by a Native American artist, J. O. Lewis.

MORE ABOUT THE FLAG: Soon after the flag was designed in 1907, the city had a flag made. The original proportions were 21:31. It was first flown on 12 June 1908 for "Pennant Day", in honor of the Detroit Baseball Club. For years, most people assumed that the flag was official, since it was used by the city at civic functions. However, as a result of a 1948 inquiry from an advertising firm requesting a copy of the official flag, the city determined that the flag had never been adopted by ordinance, so the common council made the flag official on 20 April 1948.

Heineman's original design shows the seal in an oval shape without the name of the city and state, and the mottoes in black on white heraldic ribbons, **SPERAMUS MELIORA** curved above and **RESERGET CINERIBUS** curved below. The female figures are shown slightly differently; the hoist figure has her right arm to her brow, and does not wear the drape; the other figure has her right arm about her companion's waist. A gold band surrounds the oval. The circular seal replaced the oval rendition about 1974, and has continued in use.　　JP 🏳️

DOVER, DELAWARE ✪

Population Rank: U.S. #1,127
             Delaware...... # 2

Proportions: 13:21 (usage)

Adopted: 29 May 1972 (official)

DESIGN: The flag of Dover has a white field; in its center is an elongated rhombus with a gold field and narrow dark blue border. On a field of 13 by 21 units, the rhombus is 9 by 15 units. The city's intricate seal, 5 units in diameter, is centered in the rhombus. The outer circle of the seal is yellow. A smaller concentric yellow circle forms the inner edge of a ring with a dark green field on which is inscribed **The City of Dover** over the top, and **Delaware** below, all in yellow Old English letters. The interior of the seal has the same form as the arms of the town of Dover, Kent, U.K., a trefoil (cloverleaf shape) on an inverted equilateral triangle. The field behind the trefoil/triangle is a dark aquamarine; within the trefoil is a dark orange. The trefoil has a dark aquamarine border, edged on both sides in yellow, and studded with 13 yellow-edged red dots around it. The top lobe of the trefoil, according to the ordinance adopting the seal, *represents the coat of arms of William Penn,* [as adapted by] *Kent County, Delaware,* the county in which Dover is located. Those arms have a shield divided vertically, the dexter side dark aquamarine and the sinister side dark green.

The shield has a red horizontal bar across its center, charged with three yellow disks, and an inverted crescent above. Three yellow spear tips bristle from the shield's top. The hoist lobe of the trefoil bears the great seal of the state of Delaware in miniature, without the words "Great Seal of the State of Delaware", as it appears on the state flag. The remaining lobe of the trefoil, toward the fly, imitates the lobe in the same position of the Dover, U.K., arms, showing St. Martin (the patron saint of Dover, U.K.) astride a brown horse facing the hoist, in front of a dark aquamarine turreted castle. Where the triangle's points appear at the indentations of the lobes, they have a red field edged in yellow. The hoist point displays a white dogwood flower; the fly point, a green holly leaf; and the bottom point, **1603** in yellow. Immediately below the bottom point on a white heraldic ribbon appears, in tiny red letters, **CAPITAL OF THE FIRST STATE.** The seal was adopted 12 January 1959.

SYMBOLISM: The rhombus also appears on the Delaware state flag, and the gold and blue echo the buff and blue of that flag. The trefoil of the seal represents three geographical areas linked to the city: Kent County; the state of Delaware; and the town of Dover, U.K., which provided the city's name. Delaware's nickname is "The First State", as the first state to ratify the U.S. constitution on December 7, 1787.

HOW SELECTED: City employees began working on a design in September 1969. After much trial and error, they submitted several designs to the city council for comment. In 1972, a basic design was chosen.

DESIGNER: City employees.

MORE ABOUT THE FLAG: Mrs. Shirley Slater made the first flag, with the design hand-painted on silk.   JP

El Paso, Texas

Population Rank: U.S. ..... # 22

Texas ...... # 4

Proportions: 3:5 (official)

Adopted: 29 March 1962 (official)

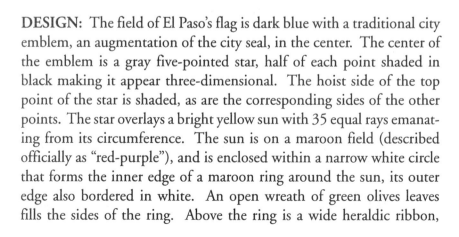

DESIGN: The field of El Paso's flag is dark blue with a traditional city emblem, an augmentation of the city seal, in the center. The center of the emblem is a gray five-pointed star, half of each point shaded in black making it appear three-dimensional. The hoist side of the top point of the star is shaded, as are the corresponding sides of the other points. The star overlays a bright yellow sun with 35 equal rays emanating from its circumference. The sun is on a maroon field (described officially as "red-purple"), and is enclosed within a narrow white circle that forms the inner edge of a maroon ring around the sun, its outer edge also bordered in white. An open wreath of green olives leaves fills the sides of the ring. Above the ring is a wide heraldic ribbon, white on the front and maroon on the back. The ribbon is folded so that the front shows from about 10 to 2 o'clock, and its back ends hang down to 8 and 4 o'clock. On the ribbon appears **CITY OF EL PASO** in maroon in an Arial-type font. A shorter ribbon covers the lower central part of the ring, with **TEXAS** in the same letters.

The drawing accompanying the ordinance of adoption shows a flag of 3 by 5 feet. The emblem is positioned 17 inches from the edge of the hoist and the fly, and 6 inches from the top and bottom. The emblem measures 26 inches horizontally, and 24 inches vertically.

SYMBOLISM: The star is identical to the star on the city's official seal, as well as on the official seal of the state of Texas. The radiant sun echoes the city's nickname, "The City of the Sun". An informational document accompanying the ordinance of adoption also specifies the symbolism of each of the colors:

(1) Golden-yellow: Richness of a sunny climate.
(2) Yellow-green: Hope, good fortune, fertile land and vitality.
(3) Silver: Faith
(4) White: Purity
(5) Blue: Sincerity
(6) Red-purple (two shades): Fellowship, warmth, and shelter.

No real distinction is made between white and silver on the flag, and the red-purple portions appear as one color, although the intention was to make the field around the sun a darker purple than the other maroon areas. The ordinance of adoption mentions only "red-purple" and does not specify two shades. Similarly, only "green" is mentioned, not "yellow-green".

HOW SELECTED: In 1960, a group of Girl Scouts wanted to embroider a city flag, and as the project proceeded, they learned that the city flag in council chambers had an incorrect city seal. The city administration decided to re-design the flag and ultimately came up with a new flag design deemed more authentic historically.

DESIGNER: The city planning department, for the administration.

MORE ABOUT THE FLAG: The emblem on the flag dates to about 1880; it was enclosed in a cornerstone of a new city hall built in 1899. When that city hall was demolished in 1958 to make way for a replacement, the emblem was recovered. In addition to the star and radiant sun, it also shows a spray of wheat on its dexter side and grapes and grape leaves on its sinister side.

FORMER FLAGS: El Paso adopted its first flag on 17 June 1948. The ordinance of adoption specifies its design:

Now therefore, be it resolved that the official flag of the city of El Paso shall be a light blue field with the seal of the City in gold in or near the center thereof.

The flag was manufactured in a 5:8 ratio, but instead of the official seal of the city, the manufacturer used what was termed a city "crest", which was really the seal of the State of Texas with the city's name on a ring around it.

The official city seal does not have the olive and oak branches that wreathe the state seal, on the one hand, and on the other, the city seal has the name of the state spelled out around the star, one letter between each set of points. Since the "crest" was widely used (and still is) on city stationery, the difference went noticed until 1960 when the Girl Scouts examined the flag more closely, thinking to embroider a new one. Thus, with the adoption of a new flag, the 1948 version was never actually made.   JP 🏴

FORT SMITH, ARKANSAS

Population Rank: U.S... # 323
Arkansas...... # 2

Proportions: 4:7 (usage)

Adopted: Circa 1912-1913 (official status uncertain)

DESIGN: The flag of Fort Smith is a horizontal tribar of equal dark blue, white, and red stripes, with a gold canton. The canton overlays the top two stripes at the hoist. In the center of the canton is the city's seal, blue letters and figures on white. On a flag of 12 by 21 units, the canton is 8 units square and the seal's diameter is 4.7 units. Around the seal's edge is a narrow beveled ring that encloses another ring on which appears **CITY OF FORT SMITH ARK.** in a Times Roman font, arched clockwise around the seal from 9 o'clock to 3 o'clock. Curved below in an Arial font, counterclockwise, is **INCORPORATED A.D. 1842.** The inner edge of this ring is made up of dots. In the seal's center, occupying most of the field, is a large bald eagle, with wings outstretched, facing the fly. From the eagle's neck to the bottom of the seal, thus covering most of its body, is a heraldic shield divided horizontally into three parts. The top segment shows a paddle-wheel river-boat, steaming toward the hoist. The center segment depicts a plow on the hoist side and a beehive on the fly side. A shock of wheat occupies the bottom segment. On the eagle's hoist wing rests a winged angel on a laurel bough, looking toward the fly, arms outstretched as if to steady the shield, legs extended along the hoist edge of the shield to the bottom.

On the eagle's fly side are two elements, a ribbon issuing from its beak with two visible sections bearing **REGNANT POPULUS** ("The People Rule"); and below the ribbon, an unsheathed sword, slanted along the shield's edge so the point of the sword is toward the hoist, and the hilt toward the fly. In the center above the eagle's head is a small Goddess of Liberty standing on what appears to be a cloud. Facing the hoist, her left hand holds a staff surmounted by a liberty cap, and her right hand gestures toward the hoist holding a wreath. Curved next to the goddess's right hand on the hoist side are three tiny five-pointed stars enclosed in squares, and beyond her left hand are five more. Without the light stars, this design essentially reproduces the state seal of Arkansas.

SYMBOLISM: The red, white, and blue are colors in the United States and Arkansas flags. Gold suggests the value placed by the citizenry on its city. The eagle on the seal is said to represent speed and wisdom, as well as generosity and forgiveness. The three stars on the hoist side above the eagle reputedly represent the three nations that ruled Arkansas before the United States (France, Spain, and the United Kingdom). The five stars on the fly side symbolize the five Native American tribes who once occupied Western Arkansas (presumably the Caddo, Cherokee, Choctaw, Osage, and Quapaw). The angel on the hoist side represents Mercy; the sword on the fly side, Justice. The riverboat on the shield stands for commerce on the Arkansas River; the plow and beehive symbolize agriculture; and the wheat represents the fertile lands of the Arkansas Valley.

HOW SELECTED: Information unavailable.

DESIGNER: Information unavailable.

MORE ABOUT THE FLAG: The flag is believed to have been adopted around 1912-1913 when the city adopted a new commission form of government.

FORMER FLAGS: Fort Smith may have had a previous flag, with a somewhat different city seal. An additional outer ring surrounds the seal, with a five-pointed star on either side at the midpoints horizontally. Curved above in an Arial font is **ALL FOR ONE**; and below, **ONE FOR ALL**. This ring was later omitted from the seal, perhaps in the 1912-1913 civic government transition. JP

FORT WAYNE, INDIANA

Population Rank: U.S. .... # 84
Indiana ...... # 2

Proportions: 2:3 (usage)

Adopted: 1934 (official)

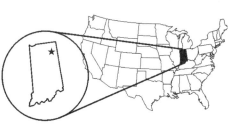

DESIGN: The flag of Fort Wayne has a dark blue field trisected by a white Y-shaped figure positioned horizontally. The top of the "Y" extends to both corners of the hoist, and its bottom bisects the fly. Overlaying the center of the "Y" is a white circle with a blockhouse in red. Curved above the blockhouse is **FORT WAYNE**, below is **INDIANA**, on the hoist side **17**, and on the fly side **94**, all in dark blue. A silhouette of a male Native American head is centered in the hoist field, in red, with two feathers and in profile facing the fly. In the top fly field is a red *fleur-de-lis* and in the lower fly field, is an upright red lion, facing the fly.

SYMBOLISM: The white "Y" represents the confluence of three rivers in the center of Fort Wayne: the St. Joseph (top hoist), the St. Mary's (bottom hoist), and the Maumee (fly). The blockhouse symbolizes the original Fort Wayne, established in 1794 by General Anthony Wayne, for whom the city is named. The Indian head recalls the early settlement of the Miami Indians near the city's current site. The *fleur-de-lis* recognizes the contribution of the French, who organized Fort Miami, the first fort on the site, as a trading post in the 1680s. The lion symbolizes the British, who captured Fort Miami in 1760 and occupied it until 1763, when the Indians reoccupied the site during Pontiac's Rebellion. Indians held the area until Gen. Wayne secured the land in 1794 for the fledgling United States.

HOW SELECTED: Through a contest, in 1916.

DESIGNER: Guy Drewitt, whose 1916 design is described (no picture is extant) as a blue field with a white Y and two small white stars, position unspecified, to recognize Fort Wayne's position as the second largest city in Indiana.

MORE ABOUT THE FLAG: Drewitt's original design was apparently used until 1934, when at the suggestion of a local citizen he modified the flag to its current design.   JP

FORT WORTH, TEXAS

Population Rank: U.S..... # 27
Texas...... # 6

Proportions: 4:7 (usage)

Adopted: 4 September 1968 (official)

DESIGN: The Fort Worth flag is a horizontal tribar of light blue, white, and green stripes in proportions of 2:3:2. Across the top stripe, in black block letters, is **FORT WORTH**, occupying most of the stripe. Centered on the green stripe, in similar letters, is **TEXAS**. The white stripe displays a frontal silhouette of a stylized black "Texas Longhorn" head stretching nearly the entire length of the flag.

SYMBOLISM: The blue stripe represents the space age to come (as foreseen in 1968). The white stripe depicts the Trinity River channel, and the green stripe symbolizes the green of the prairie. The longhorn head suggests one of the city's nicknames, "Cowtown", recalling Fort

Worth's early years, after railroads arrived, as a major center for the shipment of cattle.

HOW SELECTED: The city council and the art commission co-sponsored a contest for a city flag, the winner to receive $250.

DESIGNER: Winner of the prize for his design was Richard Pruitt, a commercial advertising artist and Fort Worth resident.

MORE ABOUT THE FLAG: Of the 153 entries submitted in the flag contest, 42 finalists were displayed in the Fort Worth Art Center. The public voted for a favorite flag, but the judges chose a different design, since they were not bound by the public vote. The judges were Dr. Richard Fargo Brown, curator for the Kimbell Museum; Jack T. Holmes, a public relations executive; and Mrs. Edwin R. Hudson, Sr., president of the Tarrant County Historical Society.

In November 1969, a Fort Worth flag was taken to the moon on the Apollo 12 flight by Cmdr. Alan L. Bean, a former Fort Worth resident and a graduate of a high school there.

FORMER FLAG: The earlier flag of Fort Worth was apparently unofficial. A flag maker, J. J. Langever, designed it in 1912. Also with proportions of 4:7 units, the flag has a white field with three horizontal red stripes placed across its center creating alternating white and red stripes in proportions of 1.25/.3/.3/.3/.3/.3/1.25. Superimposed on the center of the field over the red stripes is an elaborate design in light blue (perhaps faded from an earlier darker blue). Centered above the lowest red stripe is a city skyline, its narrow sky filled with industrial smoke depicted over it. Resting on this portion is a sort of pillar on which a panther crouches, facing the hoist. A horse and a sheep support the pillar. Over the panther curves **THE PANTHER CITY** in blue. Centered above all is a five-pointed star, with half of each point shaded to give the appearance of three dimensions, and a halo of radiant lines around it. Below the skyline is a white rectangle bordered in blue, announcing "WE'RE FOR SMOKE", also in blue. All this is supported by what appears to be a winged sphinx, an image popular at the time. Curved counter-clockwise below the image is another legend, ALL ROADS LEAD TO FT. WORTH, in blue. To illustrate this motto, 17 blue lines, apparently representing actual, individually labeled roads, emanate from behind the design in all directions.

The panther recalls another of the city's nicknames, "The Panther City", reportedly given to the city by travelers who had seen panthers in the brush near there, and even asleep on a city street, though no one seems to be certain about the name's origin. The "We're for Smoke" legend refers to the time before air pollution was a concern, when the city was courting heavy industry and factories with smoke stacks were common images of progress.   JP

FRANKFORT, KENTUCKY ✪

Population Rank: U.S. # 1,362
Kentucky ...... # 7

Proportions: 2:3 (usage)

Adopted: 14 September 1959 (official)

DESIGN: The field of Frankfort's flag is white. Centered on the field is a disk with a yellow field, one-fourth the length of the flag in the diameter. Bisecting the disk is an S-shaped blue line, about one-fourteenth the circle's diameter in width, forming a 'yin-yang'-type figure. In the top half of the disk is the old state capitol and in the lower half is the new state capitol, both in blue outline. Surrounding the disk is a wreath, in blue, open at the top. The diameter of the wreath is about three-eighths of the field's length. In the white space between the wreath and the disk appears **FRANKFORT**, arched clockwise over the top of the circle, and **KENTUCKY**, counterclockwise below, all in blue block letters. Midway between the two words are five-pointed stars: gray on the hoist side and blue on the fly side. Centered below the wreath, midway between the wreath's edge and the edge of the field, appears 1786 in large blue numerals.

In the upper hoist corner is a circular figure resembling a medallion, the outer edge of which is a blue line, with a narrow yellow band immediately within. In the center in yellow with blue shading is a profile of Daniel Boone, facing the fly. The field of the medallion is white. In the upper fly corner is a similar medallion with a three-quarter profile of a Boy Scout, in the same colors, facing the hoist.

SYMBOLISM: The flag was designed to be a reverse of the Kentucky state flag, with yellow and white on blue. The horizontal S-figure in the center of the flag represents the S-curve of the Kentucky River that divides the city. The old capitol symbolizes the past; the new capitol, the present. The blue wreath represents the famed bluegrass of Kentucky. The gray and blue stars signify, respectively, Frankfort's status as a city in both the Confederate States of America (1862-1863) and the United States (from 1792). Frankfort was first settled in 1786.

The hoist medallion with Daniel Boone commemorates him as the discoverer in 1767 of "the fair land of Kentucke", as he described it. The fly medallion recognizes that the first Boy Scout troop in the United States was formed in Frankfort in 1908.

HOW SELECTED: A committee of five local prominent citizens, appointed by the mayor and city commissioners. The committee solicited designs from the community.

DESIGNER: None of the designs had all the elements that the committee had in mind, so the committee itself undertook to design the flag. Hence the designers are Col. George M. Chinn (USMC, ret.), of the Kentucky Historical Society; Ermina Jett Darnell, an artist; Eudora Lindsay South, a music teacher; Margaret Brown Sullivan, an artist; and Allan M. Trout, a journalist.

MORE ABOUT THE FLAG: The decision to adopt a city flag came about in 1959 because the city had erected a new municipal building,

and the city manager, Russell Marshall, thought it would be appropriate to fly a civic emblem from the new flagpole in front of the building.
The idea for a city flag was something of a novelty at the time, since
only three other Kentucky cities—Louisville, Newport, and
Prestonsburg—had adopted flags.   JP 🛡

FREMONT, CALIFORNIA

Population Rank: U.S..... # 85
California.... # 13

Proportions: 2:3 (usage)

Adopted: 1970s (unofficial)

DESIGN: Fremont's flag is a variation on the design of the United States flag. It has 13 stripes of red and white and in the center of the blue canton is a white eagle in flight toward the hoist, looking back toward the fly, and clutching nine white arrows and a peace pipe in its talons. Above and below the eagle are undulating rows of 13 white stars each.

SYMBOLISM: This is a popular version of the flag of Capt. John C. Frémont, who led U.S. Army exploratory expeditions into the far West in the 1840s. At the time his flag was made (1842), there were 26 states in the Union, hence the 26 stars. Frémont is said to have used the peace pipe in the eagle's talons in the belief that Native Americans seeing the flag would understand it better than another traditional European symbol such as an olive branch.

HOW SELECTED: The "Fremont Flag" was logical for the city named for Frémont to use in the absence of an official flag. The city of Fremont itself is very young: it came into being in 1956 when five cities on the southeastern edge of the San Francisco Bay consolidated into one.

DESIGNER: Jessie Benton Frémont, the explorer's wife and devoted publicist, designed and sewed the original version as a substitute for the national flag, as her husband prepared to explore in Mexican territory not (yet) belonging to the United States. She combined design elements from the United States national flag and U.S. Army regimental flags. The original is now in the Southwest Museum of the American Indian in Los Angeles, California. Its dimensions are 47 by 83 inches. The actual flag has a white canton, with the eagle painted in blue and white stars outlined in blue. The peace pipe has a red bowl. The reverse side has a different design.

MORE ABOUT THE FLAG: Although the city has no official flag, long-time flag retailer James J. Ferrigan III writes: *In the 1970s they* [Fremont city officials] *did fly a flag which they both identified and purchased as the 'Fremont City Flag', and as such was supplied by the Paramount Flag Co. and by the Weeks, Howe, Emerson Co., both of San Francisco. This was the so-called blue canton Fremont flag.*

Another flag, considered by some to be the city flag, hangs in the mayor's office. It places the city seal on a solid background.

Historically, the "blue canton Frémont Flag" is simply an error. Jessie Frémont's flag with a white canton was "corrected" by some 20th century flag book authors, who assumed it was a mistake and depicted the flag with a blue canton. That misrepresentation has even led some to assume that there were actually two Frémont flags. JP 🛡

FRESNO, CALIFORNIA

Population Rank: U.S. ..... # 37
California ...... # 6

Proportions: 3:4 (usage)

Adopted: 10 May 1962 (official)

DESIGN: Fresno's flag is a vertical tribar of equal brown, light blue, and light olive-green stripes. Centered on the brown stripe is a circular white gear, 24 teeth on a narrow white band facing outward. On the blue stripe is the compound leaf of the ash tree: in light olive-green, a long stem extending from near the center bottom and branching out to show two pairs of leaves culminating in a single leaf at top center. FRESNO appears in an Arial-type font in brown across the bottom of the center stripe, three letters on either side of the stem of the ash leaf. On the green stripe is a golden yellow sunburst, 24 short rays curved clockwise on a narrow white circular background, corresponding in size and position to the gear of the first stripe.

SYMBOLISM: Brown represents the productive, fertile soil of the Central Valley of California. Light blue symbolizes the clear blue skies of Fresno's year-round mild climate. Light olive-green (called "sunny green" by the city) is for the green fields and trees that abound in and around Fresno. The geared wheel of industry symbolizes Fresno's status as the agribusiness leader of the nation, as well as the great industrial future of the city. The ash leaf recalls the source of the city's name, the Spanish *fresno* ("ash tree"). The city's name in brown reflects its agricultural heritage; the stem of the ash leaf grows out of, but does not divide, its namesake city. The sunburst denotes the giver of life to the fields and orchards that surround Fresno. It is also a reminder of the endless sunny days typical of the city. The white of the gear and sun's field symbolizes the snow of the Sierra Nevada, from which the city derives its water.

HOW SELECTED: In 1962, the Downtown Association of Fresno sponsored a contest open to the public to create a city flag with a prize of $250 to the winner. Judges for the contest included Mayor Arthur L. Selland; Edwin M. Eaton, President of the Fresno Historical Society; Councilman Paul G. Wasemiller; Floyd Hyde, President of the Fresno Arts Center; and Karney Hodge, President of the Downtown Association. Judging was based on design simplicity, inclusion of an appropriate theme, harmonization of colors, and artistic presentation. The contest received over 600 entries.

DESIGNER: The winner of the $250 prize was Lanson H. Crawford, a local resident.

MORE ABOUT THE FLAG: The Fresno City School District has developed a curriculum for elementary students that includes a detailed description of the flag and its symbolism, as well as two flags in outline that the students can color according to directions.   JP

GARLAND, TEXAS

Population Rank: U.S..... # 90
Texas.... # 10

Proportions: 10:19 (official)
2:3 (usage)

Adopted: 12 October 1971 (official)

DESIGN: Garland's flag has a dark blue field with a narrow gold border. In the center of the flag is the circular city seal with a diameter of about 5 units on a field of 6 by 9 units. The seal also has a gold border, slightly narrower than the field's border. The field of the seal is a light blue on which appears a large gold silhouette of Texas that, from top to bottom, covers about three-fourths of the field. Overlaying the state map is a very large dark blue ovoid **G**, bordered in gold, extending nearly the full width of the seal. Curved across the top part of the "**G**" is **CITY OF GARLAND**, and centered on the lower part is **TEXAS**, all in gold and an Arial-type font. A medium-size gold five-pointed star, edged in dark blue, is positioned over the center bar of the

"G", marking the city's location on the state map.

SYMBOLISM: The two shades of blue (PMS 291 and PMS 285) and metallic gold are the official colors of the city. The large "G", of course, is the initial letter of the city's name, and the star, aside from denoting the geographic location of the city, suggests the nickname of Texas, "The Lone Star State". The official 10:19 proportions are the same as the United States flag.

HOW SELECTED: Chosen by the city council.

DESIGNER: Jesse Green, a local graphic artist, designed the flag and seal.

MORE ABOUT THE FLAG: The official flag, while still in use in Garland, has been supplanted by the city's "logo flag", adopted in January 1994 apparently in an effort to present a more modern image. The city's logo, designed by Dallas design firm Arthur Eisenberg & Associates, was gradually phased in to replace the city seal on letterheads, vehicles, signage, and flags used by the city. Today the logo flag is seen more often than the official flag.

The logo flag is a horizontal tribar of red, white, and blue stripes in proportions of 1:1.5:1. Centered horizontally on the center stripe is GARLAND in blue and an Arial-type font, about .375 units high on a field of 2 by 3 units. The first letter "A" in the name is without its cross-bar—in its place are two thin blue curved lines sweeping up to the top of the next letter, "R", where a small five-pointed red star is perched as if shot from a fireworks rocket. Below the city's name is a thin red horizontal line. Below the red line, beginning at the base of the "R", and terminating below the final "D", is CITY OF GARLAND, TEXAS, in small blue letters. The blue is a medium blue, in between the shades of the two official blue colors adopted in 1971. As a result, the city's name appears twice on this flag.   JP 📛

GLENDALE, ARIZONA

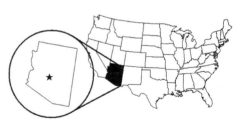

Population Rank: U.S. ..... # 80
                     Arizona .... # 5

Proportions: 2:3 and 5:8 (usage)

Adopted: 1990 (official)

DESIGN: Glendale's flag places the city logo on a white field. The logo incorporates lettering below three stylized, overlapping shapes representing pillars. The lettering reads **GLENDALE** in a Times Roman-style font in teal (turquoise), except the **A** joins with a **Z** below it, in a script-like font in copper, representing "Arizona". Parts of the **A** and **Z** overlap the adjoining letters. The pillar shapes, all copper-colored, are each a rectangle divided into quadrants just above its horizontal center, with a circular section (whose diameter is one-half the width of the rectangle) centered around the quadrants' intersection point removed and one of the two lower quadrants removed. On a field of 4 by 6 units, the teal lettering extends 4.2 units wide and 0.6 units high. The pillars range from 1 unit wide and 1.25 units high to .75 units wide and .85 units high. The largest pillar is in the center; the others flank and overlap it on the left and right. The copper and teal colors are officially PMS 173c (876) and PMS 328.

SYMBOLISM: According to the city: *In 1990 a new contemporary logo was designed and officially adopted for use by the city. The new logo replaced the city seal and is characterized by three stylistic pillars adapted from a strong architectural element in city hall … The purpose of the logo was to provide a symbol and combination of color that can be easily identified by both citizens and businesses. The pillars represent three key elements of community—the citizens, the business sector, and the government that serves them.* Turquoise and copper are the city's colors. Turquoise may represent the gemstone common in the area and frequently used in local jewelry; copper may represent the mineral wealth of the region.

HOW SELECTED: The flag and logo were developed and adopted in anticipation of the 1991 centennial of the founding of Glendale.

DESIGNER: The Marketing and Communications Department of the city, with help from an outside firm.

MORE ABOUT THE FLAG: The Glendale city warehouse orders about 8 flags every year in 4 by 6 feet and 5 by 8 feet sizes. The flag flies on one of three poles in front of the city office building. In order to ensure preservation of its flags for future generations, the city donated full-size versions of the current and former flags to the Glendale Historical Society in 1998.

FORMER FLAG: Glendale's previous flag bears the city seal approved by ordinance #1083 on June 12, 1979. The seal is depicted in copper, centered on a white background, with a diameter of 2.5 units on a field of 4 by 6 units. According to city code, *The city seal shall*

be of circular design. Across the top portion the word "Glendale" is shown. The word "Arizona" is across the bottom portion. Off center to the left on the inside of the seal is an outline map of the state. Across the same portion is a silhouette of a "family" looking over the horizon, the city, and its sur- roundings. The rays emanate from the center of the city upward. Below the family is shown the date of incorporation (1910). (Code 1963, § 1-6) Design One/Attention Getters, represented by Don Hasulak, designed the seal.

The city's original seal, adopted when Glendale was incorporated on June 18, 1910, featured a sugar beet to honor the engine of local economic recovery after the disastrous 1895 flood, the beet sugar factory built in 1906.   Ted Kaye

GLENDALE, CALIFORNIA

Population Rank: U.S. ..... # 98
California .... # 14

Proportions: 2:3 (usage)

Adopted: 10 November 1970 (apparently unofficial)

DESIGN: Glendale's flag has a bright yellow field with the city seal slightly above the center. Below the seal appears **CITY OF GLEN-DALE** in blue block letters. On a field of 4:6 units, the letters are half of a unit in height, and stretch across the field for 5 units, centered horizontally. The diameter of the seal is 2.3 units. It is divided into four equal quarters on a yellow field by a slender four-pointed star, its arms divided vertically into light blue and dark blue. Beginning with the top ray, the blue colors alternate, beginning with light blue on the hoist side of the ray, so opposing rays are exactly opposite in coloration. Overlaid on the star's center is a small, angular shield bordered in yellow. On it is a dark blue peacock on a light blue field, seen from behind, its head in profile toward the fly, and its tail reposing on the ground behind it. Perched atop the shield is a highly stylized American eagle all in yellow, wings outspread, and head lowered, peering toward the fly. The first quarter shows Glendale's city hall, white shadowed in blue, with green bushes around it. The second quarter shows a yellow California bear, outlined in blue and standing on green grass, a single five-pointed star over its head, in imitation of the same figures on the state flag. The third quarter shows a water pump in white, outlined in brown, with blue water pouring from it, and enclosed in a blue ring. A white fist clutches three blue bolts of lightning at 2 o'clock on the ring above the water. The fourth quarter depicts the historic Casa Adobe in blue with a yellow roof and green trees and shrubs around it and blue mountains in the background.

SYMBOLISM: The yellow suggests sunshine; blue, the folded hills. The peacock on the seal recalls Glendale's winning float in the shape of a peacock in the 1924 Tournament of Roses parade, when the city was the first ever to win a Sweepstakes Prize. The American eagle over the shield represents the United States. The depiction of city hall represents city government; the bear and star, the state of California. The water pump and lightning bolts suggest hydroelectric power. Casa Adobe is a historic home originally built for Tomás Sánchez, first sheriff of Los Angeles County, and his wife, Marìa Sepálveda de Sánchez. It was restored in 1932 and is now a museum. The mountains are the region's Verdugo Mountains.

HOW SELECTED: Chosen by Mayor Perkins.

DESIGNER: Unknown.

FORMER FLAG: The first flag of Glendale features only the shield element of the city seal on a pale yellow field, described as buff in old records, and bordered on all sides except the hoist with a border, described as "amethyst blue", although more likely sapphire blue was meant. The distinctive angular shield is bordered in a pattern of yellow, blue, yellow. The shield's field is a light blue; the peacock, in natural

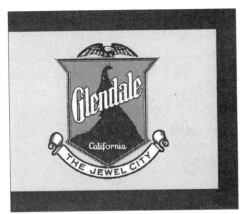

colors. On a field of 3 units by 3.5 units, the shield is 1 unit across, horizontally, in its center. Written in white, linked, calligraphic letters that vary between .5 and .25 units high, depending on the size of the letter, is **Glendale**, slanted from the mid-section of the shield to its upper quarter; centered across the bottom, in white script letters about one-fifth as high as the others, is **California**. The eagle perched on the shield's top has patriotic wings, with 8 five-pointed white stars on blue over 6 red and 5 white stripes on its hoist wing, and 6 stars and an equal number of stripes on its fly wing. Below the shield is a heraldic ribbon in white, outlined in blue, with **THE JEWEL CITY** across it in dark blue.

This flag was designed by Hugh A. Maron, who won $100 in a contest sponsored by Charles L. Peckham and business associates. It was officially adopted by the city council on 18 September 1924, amid enthusiasm for the city's winning peacock float at the Tournament of Roses that same year. (There is no indication that this ordinance has ever been repealed officially.) The city seal was changed in the same legislation so that the central portion of the previous seal, a star, would be replaced by the new shield-and-peacock design, as on the current flag.   JP

GRAND FORKS, NORTH DAKOTA

Population Rank: U.S.... # 741
North Dakota .... # 3

Proportions: 2:3 (usage)

Adopted: 5 December 1994 (official)

DESIGN: The flag of Grand Forks has a white field. Two irregular horizontal stripes, green over dark blue, with a white fimbriation between them, fill the lower three-eighths of the field. The green stripe is divided into three sections: two trapezoids on either side, wider at the hoist and fly and narrower in the center, where a green diamond-shaped section joins the two trapezoids to depict sloping river banks. The blue stripe is narrower at the hoist and fly and widens to the center, where a narrow "V" shape extends along the base of the green diamond, to depict two river forks forming one larger river that flows outwards. Centered immediately above the green diamond figure is **1870** in black. Centered above that date is an abstract notched stalk of yellow vegetation, crossed over a red feather with a black tip and quill. Over these, in a semi-circle arching clockwise from the midpoint of the hoist side to the midpoint of the fly side, is **Grand Forks, North Dakota** in black.

SYMBOLISM: The flag represents the spirit of the city and the region. The white background symbolizes the fresh, clean air and open environment of the area. The dark blue represents the river forks that give the city its name, and symbolizes their role in the foundation of the community. The green river banks stand for life and future growth along the river. The red feather recognizes the city's Native American heritage. The yellow stalk represents the area's reliance on agriculture. The date, 1870, marks the naming of the area, "Grand Forks," reputedly by Sanford C. Cady, the first postmaster, at the confluence of the Red River and the Red Lake River.

HOW SELECTED: A contest was held, with a city-wide vote on the entries.

DESIGNER: Scott Telle and Craig Silvernagel, owners of Ad Monkeys, an advertising firm, designed the winning entry.   JP ▨

GRAND RAPIDS, MICHIGAN

Population Rank: U.S. ..... # 93
            Michigan ...... # 2

Proportions: 2:3 (usage)

Adopted: 26 July 1915 (official)

DESIGN: The flag of Grand Rapids is a vertical tribar of equal dark blue, white, and dark blue stripes. Centered on the white stripe is the city seal, consisting of a white field bordered by two concentric circles of dark blue dots, forming solid rings. On a field of 2 units by 3, the seal is about 1 unit in diameter. In the ring, curved over the top clockwise from 9 o'clock to 3 o'clock is **CITY OF GRAND RAPIDS MICH.** in dark blue. Curved below from 7 to 5 o'clock counterclockwise is the Latin motto, **MOTU VIGET.** ("Strength in Activity"). In the center of the seal is a bald eagle, in flight toward the hoist, bearing an American shield, and clutching several arrows, all in dark blue and white. Centered over the eagle are Scales of Justice, held by a hand reaching down from the clouds, all in dark blue and white. Nine separate "bundles" of three gray rays each are spaced evenly behind the eagle and scales, emanating outward from a baseline that forms the horizontal midpoint of the seal. Centered below the eagle, resting on the inner beaded ring, is **1850** in dark blue.

SYMBOLISM: The seal suggests that divine justice guides the American spirit. The rays represent light. The seal was adopted in 1850.

HOW SELECTED: Joseph Penney, a member of the common council in 1850, suggested the design of the seal.

DESIGNER: Aaron B. Turner, the city clerk in 1850, designed the seal. The designer of the flag is not known.

MORE ABOUT THE FLAG: Grand Rapids uses a "city banner" more often than the official flag. The Grand Rapids banner has a field of blue with the city's logo in the center. The logo is oval, wider than high, and measures about 1.5 units across its horizontal center on a field of 2 by 3 units. The field of the logo is yellow, representing the sun. Across the lower third of the field is a narrow, blue undulating stripe representing the Grand River that courses through the city. Resting on this stripe is a horizontal figure, .5 units at its widest and slightly more than a unit in length, that begins about one-fourth of the way from the oval's hoist edge and extends to its fly edge. The figure represents the Alexander Calder sculpture in the city, *La Grande Vitesse*, which on the logo resembles a large chess pawn lying on its side. The logo was designed by Joseph Kennebrew, a sculptor and painter.

FORMER FLAG: The city's first flag was officially adopted on 8 March 1896. It is described only as having red, white, and blue stripes with the inscription **Furniture City**. JP 🏴

GREENSBORO, NORTH CAROLINA

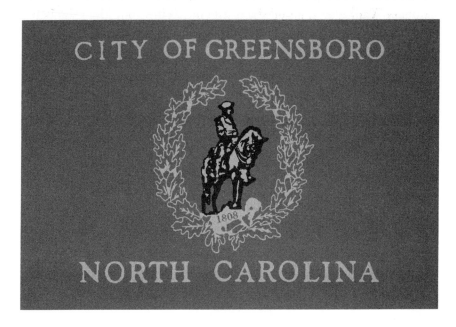

Population Rank: U.S. ..... # 77
North Carolina ...... # 3

Proportions: 2:3 (usage)

Adopted: 5 April 1965 (official)

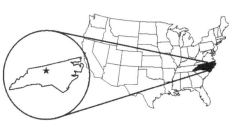

DESIGN: The field of Greensboro's flag is, not surprisingly, dark green. In the center of the field is a depiction, in yellow with dark green shadings, of Major General Nathanael Greene on horseback, in three-quarter profile, facing toward the fly. The horse, at rest, stands on a yellow base with **1808** on it in dark green. Surrounding the entire figure is an open wreath of dark green oak leaves detailed in yellow. The wreath is about 1.125 units in diameter on a field of 2 by 3 units. Centered horizontally across the top of the field is **CITY OF GREENSBORO**, centered across the bottom is **NORTH CAROLINA**, all in large yellow letters.

SYMBOLISM: Major General Nathanael Greene, for whom the city was named, was George Washington's second in command and a Revolutionary War hero. It is said that when he led his troops into the Battle of Guilford Court House (a decisive battle on March 15, 1781, that took place in what is today northwest Greensboro), the flag at the head of his troops was green. The oak leaf wreath symbolizes sturdiness and durability. The date, 1808, is the year of the city's incorporation.

HOW SELECTED: The Rotary Club of Greensboro initiated the idea of a city flag and solicited designs from the public. A. Earl Weatherly chaired the committee from the club that selected the favorite.

DESIGNER: Charles L. Hodgin, a member of the planning department at city hall.

MORE ABOUT THE FLAG: The Rotary Club had the first flags made, and presented one to the city on the date of its adoption.

JP

GULFPORT, MISSISSIPPI

Population Rank: U.S... # 378
               Mississippi...... # 2

Proportions: 2:3 (usage)

Adopted: Between 1977 and 1981 (unofficial)

DESIGN: Gulfport's flag has a blue field with the city's seal in the center, consisting of 1 unit in diameter on a field of 2 by 3 units. Horizontally across the center of the seal, about .125 units high, is a yellow stripe with **GULFPORT** in blue letters. Immediately below, in letters about one-fourth as high, is **WHERE YOUR SHIP COMES IN**. The portion above and below the yellow stripe is divided in half with a narrow, vertical yellow line, giving the entire seal the appearance of being quartered. In the upper hoist quarter is a commercial ship, yellow shaded in blue, sailing on a green ocean toward the hoist, with a blue sky and a yellow cloud, above it near the hoist edge of the seal. The upper fly quarter has a yellow skyline of the city in its lower part, with green foliage at its base, and, in a blue sky above, a yellow airplane in a landing approach toward the hoist. In the lower hoist quarter is a yellow house with two rows of blue windows, four in each row, a blue sky, and some greenery to the hoist side and below the house. The lower fly quarter shows a yellow sailboat on green water headed toward the fly, with a circular yellow sun near the fly edge of the seal in a blue sky. The entire seal is edged in yellow.

SYMBOLISM: The ship refers to Gulfport's shipping industry. The airplane over the skyline shows that the city is connected to the world by air as well. The house suggests Gulfport's history as a city of homes, and the sailboat symbolizes its tourist industry.

HOW SELECTED: Mayor John H. "Jack" Barnett held a contest to design the flag, sometime between 1977 and 1981.

DESIGNER: The winner was a Mr. Sneed (first name unavailable).

MORE ABOUT THE FLAG: The first flag was made by Josephine Alfonso. JP 🏴

HARRISBURG, PENNSYLVANIA ✪

Population Rank: U.S.... # 709
       Pennsylvania.... # 12

Proportions: 3:4 (official)

Adopted: April 1907 (official)

DESIGN: The ordinance of adoption describes Harrisburg's flag:

A field of dark blue rectangular in form, of which the length shall be 1 1/3 times its width, with a narrow gold or yellow border, in the middle of the field and slightly above the center a large white keystone, having thereon, outlined in blue, the dome of the State Capitol rising from clouds; above the dome at the dexter or right side a roundel or disk of gold or yellow, and at the left a fleur-de-lis of gold or yellow; below the dome, three crescents, two above one, of gold or yellow, and beneath the keystone the word Harrisburg in gold or yellow slightly curving upward.

SYMBOLISM: The white keystone refers to the state's nickname, "The Keystone State". The new capitol dome represents Harrisburg as the state's capital. The crescents are from the arms of John Harris, for whom the city is named. The *fleur-de-lis* symbolizes the County of Dauphin, of which Harrisburg is the county seat, named for the eldest son of the king of France. The roundels (disks) are prominent on the arms of William Penn, for whom the state is named.

HOW SELECTED: Chosen by the common council, with the select council concurring.

DESIGNER: Unknown.   JP 🛡

HARTFORD, CONNECTICUT ✪

Population Rank: U.S.... # 179
Connecticut...... # 2

Proportions: 4:7 (usage)

Adopted: 12 September 1983 (official)

DESIGN: The flag of Hartford bears a white disk, a modified version of the city seal, centered on a blue field. Surrounding the disk is a wide blue ring reading **CITY OF HARTFORD** at the top and **CONNECTI-CUT** at the base, separated by two five-pointed stars, all in white. A thin white ring outlines the circumference of the blue ring. In the center of the disk is the coat of arms of the city: On a white shield is a hart fording a stream, facing the hoist; in the background is a landscape and in the foreground a single grapevine, all in blue. The outline of the shield, along with mantling of leaves across the top and sides of the shield, the American eagle with spread wings at the top of the shield facing the hoist, and the scroll with the motto **POST NUBILA PHOEBUS** below the shield, are in gold outlined in blue.

Note: The difference between the city seal and the one on the flag is the seal on the flag does not have SEAL OF THE in its inscription before CITY OF HARTFORD around the top of the disk.

SYMBOLISM: The city was named for Hertford, England, and the hart fording a stream is a symbolic play on the name "Hartford". In the forefront is a grapevine, a reference to the state of Connecticut, of which Hartford is the capital, as the state seal bears three grapevines. The American eagle used in the crest was a popular motif in American seals in the 1800s (the city seal was adopted on 19 April 1852). The Latin motto *Post Nubila Phoebus* means "After the Clouds, the Sun".

HOW SELECTED: Unknown.

DESIGNER: Unknown.

MORE ABOUT THE FLAG: A part of the preamble to the adoption of the city flag states: *At the Court of Common Council meeting of 14 February 1983 a resolution was passed stating that the Court of Common Council wishes to recognize the old flag as the basis for the official City of Hartford Flag.*

Later, the Traveler's Insurance Company (Hartford is sometimes referred to as the Insurance Capital of America, with so many insurance companies which have been headquartered there or nearby) donated a royal blue flag with the seal of the city of Hartford at a special ceremony held in the court of common council.

On 12 September 1983, the mayor and the court of common council requested a resolution to *accept this flag as the official flag of the City of Hartford and request that the Administration of the City of Hartford and Corporation Counsel take whatever steps necessary for the adoption and protection thereof; and be it further resolved, That the Mayor and Court of Common Council congratulate the Travelers Insurance Company for providing the City of Hartford with its first official flag* ... Since the mayor and court of common council requested a resolution to make the design the official flag on 12 September 1983, it appears that this, rather than 14 February 1983, is the official adoption date.

FORMER FLAGS: There was no prior official flag used by the city. However, there must have been at least one prior unofficial flag, as the language of one of the resolutions above refers to "the old flag as a basis for the official City of Hartford flag".   JC 🛡

HELENA, MONTANA ✪

Population Rank: U.S. #1,500
              Montana ...... # 6

Proportions: 5:9 (usage)

Adopted: Unknown (apparently unofficial)

DESIGN: The flag of Helena has a blue field with a large white disk in the center, bordered in gold. On a field of 5 by 9 units, the disk is 3 units in diameter. On the disk is the depiction of an old fire watch-tower, in black, in the center, 2 units high, and 1.25 units wide at the base. Around the tower is a sparse green landscape, its upper edge slanting from about 9:30 o'clock to about 3:30 o'clock. Arched over the top of the disk in large gold letters is **GUARDIAN OF THE GULCH**. Centered below the disk, in gold numerals the same size, is **1881**.

SYMBOLISM: The symbolism is explained by the city:

Helena is graced with one of the most significant historic structures in the west. This structure is a symbol of both devastation and pride. Before Helena was 10 years old, she experienced nine fires that ravaged the downtown area. Three of those fires were considered 'great fires', the most destructive occurring on 9 January 1874. The community that night was experiencing a typical Montana winter. Temperatures were around 15 below [zero, Fahrenheit] *and the winds were raging with hurricane force. History tells us that the disaster was started by a … cook who started a fire in the chimney pipe of his wood-fired stove. In an attempt to put out the fire, he picked up a bucket of what he thought was water, instead it turned out to be cooking oil. A large explosion occurred that night, every single business in the downtown area burnt to the ground and 150 homes were lost.*

That next year citizens came together and erected a fire tower, completed with … a shiny new bell. To this day the fire tower graces the downtown area. In 1982 the Helena City Commission proclaimed the fire tower and the words 'Guardian of the Gulch' the official symbol and motto for the City of Helena.

The city incorporated in 1881. The gulch in the motto is the "Last Chance Gulch", where four prospectors discovered gold in 1864, leading to the founding of Helena.

HOW SELECTED: Likely designed as a result of the city commission's 1982 proclamation.

DESIGNER: Unknown.   JP

HIALEAH, FLORIDA

Population Rank: U.S. ..... # 75
Florida ...... # 5

Proportions: 2:3 (usage)

Adopted: 2001 (official status uncertain)

DESIGN: Hialeah's flag has a white field of 2 units by 3, with the city seal in the center .8 units in diameter. Curved above the seal and extending from near the hoist to near the fly is CITY OF HIALEAH in blue letters one-fourth of a unit high. Below the seal, in similar letters, but centered and horizontal, is FLORIDA, also in blue. The seal is edged in yellow. Concentric to this circle is a smaller one composed of blue beads. Between the two circles, on a white background, • SEAL • CITY OF HIALEAH • 1925 • curves clockwise above and INCOR-PORATED curves counter-clockwise below, all in blue. The seal's center shows Chief Tiger Tail in ceremonial dress, standing slightly to the fly side of the seal, facing the viewer, and pointing toward the hoist with his right arm. The chief is barefoot and wears a full long-sleeved robe that comes down to his calves, suggesting the famous coat-of-many-colors of the Biblical Joseph, with horizontal stripes of red, yellow, green, white, and purple. There is a button row down the front of the top half of his robe, and a white collar at his neck. Four palm fronds frame the chief, two on either side. He stands on a field of lush grass, and behind him dawn is breaking into a blue sky. Two pink flamingos, facing the fly, stand in the background under the chief's right arm.

SYMBOLISM: Chief Tiger Tail, a Muskogee chief, resisted the incursion of the U.S. Army into the area of south Florida in 1841. He is said to be pointing to the place that many years later would become the city of Hialeah.

HOW SELECTED: The flag was altered when the seal was changed in late 2001. The flag is a revision of an earlier design.

DESIGNER: City hall personnel.

MORE ABOUT THE FLAG: The original seal was designed in 1925. By 2001, it was thought to be too colorless, so it was reworked to give it a more interesting appearance.

FORMER FLAG: The first flag of Hialeah was designed in 1960 by Phyllis Adams, a city employee. It is similar to the current flag except that the seal is entirely in blue and shows only Chief Tiger Tail without the palm fronds, sunrise, or flamingos. Above the seal, also blue, is **CITY OF HIALEAH**, with "OF" much smaller than the rest. Below in blue letters about half the size of the words above is **HIALEAH, FLORIDA**, such that the city's name appears three times on the flag.   JP

HONOLULU, HAWAII

Population Rank: U.S...... # 41
Hawaii...... # 1

Proportions: 3:4 (usage)

Adopted: 13 December 1960 (official)

DESIGN: The field of Honolulu's flag is dark yellow, with the city seal in the center. On a field of 3 by 4 units, the seal's diameter is 2 units. Its outer edge is also dark yellow and beveled to resemble a rope, detailed in black. Immediately within the outer edge is a white ring, the inner edge of which is red, bordered yellow and beaded in white. On the band thus formed between the two edges, arched over the top half from midpoint to midpoint is **CITY AND COUNTY OF HONO-LULU** in black block letters. Centered below and curved counterclockwise, is **STATE OF HAWAII** in the same letters. On each side between the upper and lower legends is a small five-pointed yellow star.

In the center vertical half of the seal is a baroque-style heraldic shield with a narrow border, colored like the seal's edges, that conforms to the shield's rounded edges with extra curlicues. The shield is divided quarterly, the first and fourth quarters being 8 horizontal stripes of white, red, and blue, beginning with white at the top. The second and third quarters have a yellow field charged with a black stick with a white ball on top, a *pūlo'ulo'u*, also called a *kapu* or *tabu* stick. A small escutcheon of green charged with a small yellow five-pointed star, overlays the shield's center point. Above the shield, filling the space between the shield and the inner circle of the seal, is a yellow rising sun. The dexter supporter is Nuuanu Pali; the sinister supporter, Diamond Head, both in brown. The sky of both and the sea in front of Diamond Head are light blue while the canyon running down from Nuuanu Pali is green.

SYMBOLISM: The yellow field is the color of Oahu's flower, the *ilima*. The shield of the seal was originally designed for the Republic of Hawaii in 1895. The red, white, and blue stripes of the first and fourth quarters come from the Hawaiian national flag (now the state flag). The eight stripes in each quarter represent the eight inhabited islands under one rule. The *pūlo'ulo'u* are markers used in ancient times and during the monarchy, composed of a ball-like object, often cloth-covered, that was pierced by a stick and stuck in the ground to mark off areas reserved for nobility and royalty and beyond which commoners were forbidden to pass. The early balls were white, and later they were sometimes gold. These *kapu* markers symbolize authority and protection. The star in the center is the Star of Hawaii, and the rising sun symbolizes a new era dawning on Hawaii.

HOW SELECTED: In 1960 the new Ala Moana Shopping Center opened with 102 flagpoles. Ala Moana officials wanted to fly "meaningful" flags from the poles, and thought that the city flag should be among them. When they learned the city had no flag, shopping center staff asked a local commercial artist to design one, after which they presented it to city council for approval.

DESIGNER: Tom Neiman, a commercial artist, working from ideas supplied by Charles Tyng, manager of Ala Moana's public relations and advertising department.

MORE ABOUT THE FLAG: Some confusion has resulted among various artists depicting the *pūlo'ulo'u* on the seal, apparently due to the phrase, "a white ball pierced on a staff". "Pierced" was sometimes interpreted to mean a hole horizontally through the ball, thus giving it the appearance of a stick with a loop, or a key-like object. Recent research into their shape has determined that they were ball-like objects that were stuck onto a stick, much like a tennis ball would look if it had been pushed onto a sharp stick, and the seal has been modified to show that on city stationery and other documents. In the past, the staff mentioned in the ordinance was shown variously as black or white.

FORMER FLAG: For many years the existence of a flag was apparently forgotten and most city hall staff believed that there was no city flag. Not long ago, the old flag was rediscovered in a corner of a conference room. That flag had a lighter yellow field and variations in the colors of the emblems in the seal. It showed the old form of the *kapu* sticks, white with a yellow center in the "loop". The lettering was blue, as were the silhouettes of Nuuanu Pali and Diamond Head. The two stars on the ring of the seal were outlined in blue like a pentagram and the outer ring was depicted in yellow. The shield in the center was yellow with a blue star. JP

HOUSTON, TEXAS

Population Rank: U.S. ...... # 4
　　　　　　　　Texas ..... # 1

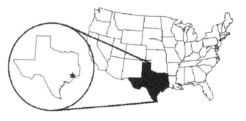

Proportions: 1:2 (official)
　　　　　　　17:30 (usage)

Adopted: 13 September 1915 (official)

DESIGN: Houston's flag has a field of medium blue with a large white five-pointed star taking up about the center third of the flag. On a field of 17 by 30 units, the two upper points of the star are equidistant from the flag's edges at 6 units each, and the distance between the two points from each other is therefore 18 units. In the center of the star is the circular city seal with a diameter of 6 units. The seal has a golden yellow, braided edge. Within it is a smaller, concentric golden yellow beaded circle. Between these two circles is a blue field on which **CITY OF HOUSTON** is inscribed, curved over the top half in golden yellow letters running clockwise. Curved below, and centered with a small cluster of three golden yellow leaves at either side, is **TEXAS**, in golden yellow letters running counter-clockwise. In the seal's center, on a white field, is a golden yellow locomotive of 1840s vintage, smoke rising from its funnel-shaped smoke stack, and steam escaping from its whistle as it heads toward the hoist. Centered above it is a golden yellow five-pointed star, and below, an old-fashioned field plow, headed toward the fly. The shadings on the golden yellow elements are in red.

SYMBOLISM: Characteristic of many cities in the Lone Star State of Texas, Houston's flag bears a single large star, as well as a single star on the seal. The seal was adopted 24 February 1840. The locomotive on the seal, modern in its day, antici-pates by about a decade the first railroad (Hous-ton and Brazos Rail Road Company) in Houston  and in Texas. The plow is said to represent the cultivation of fields for the important cash crop of cotton, which the railroads shipped to buy-ers.

HOW SELECTED: On 24 May 1915, the city council authorized Mayor Ben Campbell to appoint a six-person committee to select a flag from submitted suggestions. Besides the mayor, who served *ex officio*, the others on the committee were Major F. Charles Hume, Judge E. P. Hamblen, and Mesdames Charles Stewart, M. Looscan, and Gentry Waldo.

DESIGNER: W. A. Wheeldon. (No honorific is supplied, so one as-sumes that it is "Mr." Wheeldon; ladies of the day were always referred to by an honorific.)

MORE ABOUT THE FLAG: At some point in the 1990s, several artistic alterations were made in the seal, apparently unofficially, and the blue of the field was lightened slightly. When the flag was first adopted, the seal was depicted according to the specifications of the ordinance of adoption with a navy blue ring around it. The seal's outer ring was white, and the lettering, with a small star on either side of **TEXAS** instead of the leaves that were on the original seal, was black.

The inner edge of the white ring had a smaller, narrow red circle within it around the field of the seal in white. The locomotive, star, and plow were also black. The flag's field was navy blue.   JP ▨

HUNTINGTON, WEST VIRGINIA

Population Rank: U.S... # 538
West Virginia...... # 2

Proportions: 4:7 (usage)

Adopted: 5 November 1976 (official status uncertain)

DESIGN: Huntington's flag has a white field and proportions of 4 by 7 units. HUNTINGTON runs across the field horizontally for about 5.5 units, 1.5 units below the top edge. The initial letter "H" is composed of four interlocking rectangles outlined in yellow, twice the size of the remaining letters, which are black. These letters appear to be on a white strip overlaid on a blue circular gear 2 units in diameter, with 7 teeth visible above and 7 below the letters. Above the "TO" in HUNTINGTON is 1871, in black, about half the height of the other letters. Immediately below the city's name, on the hoist side of the gear, is WEST, and on the fly side, VIRGINIA, in black letters the same height as the date. Centered below the lower edge of the gear is another, smaller blue gear, about .75 units in diameter, with 9 teeth, which appears to intermesh with the larger gear above. The smaller gear is encircled with a narrow white space from which extends, on either side, a shape resembling wings made up of red, white, and blue horizontal stripes, top to bottom. From tip to tip across the entire figure, the red stripe extends about 3 units; the white stripe, about 2.5 units, and the blue stripe, 2.25 units. Below that figure, about .5 units from the bottom edge of the flag, is **GEARED FOR PROGRESS**, centered in black letters the same height as the name of the state above.

SYMBOLISM: The gears and motto, "Geared for Progress", are meant to show that Huntington is a thriving city commercially. The city was incorporated in 1871.

HOW SELECTED: Information unavailable.

DESIGNER: Gordon P. Chain, a retired draftsman from the city.

MORE ABOUT THE FLAG: The date of introduction suggests that the flag may have been designed during the United States bicentennial commemoration.   JP

INDIANAPOLIS, INDIANA ✪

Population Rank: U.S...... # 12
Indiana...... # 1

Proportions: 2:3 (usage)

Adopted: 20 May 1963 (official)

DESIGN: The flag of Indianapolis has a dark blue field with a white five-pointed star pointing upwards in the center. Around the star is a circular field in red. Surrounding the red field is a white ring, from which extend four white stripes from top to bottom and from hoist to fly, thus creating four equal quadrants in the field. The stripes are about one-seventh the width of the flag, with the white ring the same width as the stripes. The diameter of the red circle is about two-ninths the width of the flag.

SYMBOLISM: The large white star represents the Soldiers and Sailors Monument, a landmark in the city's center, as well as the status of Indianapolis as the state capital. The white circle and the red field within it depict the Monument Circle area of the city. The color red also signifies, according to the ordinance of adoption, *the driving energy and urge for progress that has made the City of Indianapolis race ahead.* The four white stripes, each at a ninety-degree angle to the circle, represent North and South Meridian Streets, vertically, and East and West Market Streets, horizontally. The four quadrants of dark blue symbolize the residential areas of the city. The colors of the flag—red, white, and blue, also the colors in the United States flag—symbolize the citizens' patriotism.

The city flag assumed a new role as the *de facto*, though not *de jure*, symbol of Marion County on 1 January 1970, when the city and county merged their governments into "Unigov". Marion is the only one of Indiana's 92 counties to adopt this form of government.

HOW SELECTED: A contest was held by the John Herron Art Institute in 1962.

DESIGNER: The winner was Roger Gohl, a student at the Institute.

FORMER FLAG: Gohl's design reworked the best elements of the city's first flag, adopted on 21 June 1915. Ironically, no flag of the 1915 version was made until 1960, when Mrs. Norma Gribler sewed one, just two years before a new flag was adopted. The earlier flag, designed by Harry B. Dynes, a city resident, is divided vertically into two sections, the first of which is two-fifths of the flag's length. On a blue field is depicted a white circle, about 3/18ths the width of the section, with four spokes radiating diagonally to each of the four corners of the section, thus forming four quadrants. In the top and bottom quadrants, there are two large white stars, one superimposed vertically over the other in the quadrant's center. In the hoist and fly quadrants, the stars are placed similarly, but smaller and farther apart so that there is a star at each of the spokes' intersections. One large white star, also on a blue field, is in the center of the inner circle; superimposed on it is the corporate seal of the city in gold. Nine alternating red and white horizontal stripes occupy the remaining three-fifths of the flag.

The white circle in the blue field represented the city's center, Monument Place (now called Monument Circle), and the four diagonal spokes represented the four major avenues radiating from the Circle: Kentucky, Massachusetts, Indiana, and Virginia. The large white star symbolized the city's mayor, whose power was denoted by the corporate seal. The four large stars in the top and bottom quadrants stood for the city clerk, city controller, city police judge, and the school board; the four smaller stars represented the board of public works, board of safety, board of health, and park board. Lastly, the nine stripes symbolized the nine city councilmen.   JP 🛡

IRVING, TEXAS

Population Rank: U.S. ... # 100
Texas .... # 12

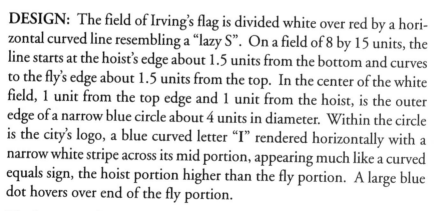

Proportions: 8:15 (usage)

Adopted: 16 October 1975 (official)

DESIGN: The field of Irving's flag is divided white over red by a horizontal curved line resembling a "lazy S". On a field of 8 by 15 units, the line starts at the hoist's edge about 1.5 units from the bottom and curves to the fly's edge about 1.5 units from the top. In the center of the white field, 1 unit from the top edge and 1 unit from the hoist, is the outer edge of a narrow blue circle about 4 units in diameter. Within the circle is the city's logo, a blue curved letter "I" rendered horizontally with a narrow white stripe across its mid portion, appearing much like a curved equals sign, the hoist portion higher than the fly portion. A large blue dot hovers over end of the fly portion.

The logo was officially adopted on 16 October 1975 and by extension, the flag was as well. While the flag is not specifically mentioned in the ordinance, it does state that the logo shall be "approved for all City of

Irving purposes". In a council meeting on October 1, the use of the logo on the city's checks, stationery, and new city flag was specifically mentioned as examples of how the logo would be employed.

SYMBOLISM: The "I" is an innovative way to use the city's initial. (It was not universally well received when presented to the city council, however.) The large dot of the logo symbolizes the Civic Center Complex; the wavy lines below represent Irving Boulevard (State Highway 356) that runs in front of city hall. The colors and their arrangement are said to echo the design of the Texas state flag. Irving is one of the few Texas cities without the "Lone Star" motif on its flag, although a small white star does appear on the logo's blue dot on city stationery.

HOW SELECTED: The logo's development came about with the building of the new civic center that opened in 1976. It was felt that a new design was needed to represent the new space.

DESIGNER: Jim Scoggins, of the architectural firm of Grogan-Scoggins Associates, the architect of the new city hall.   JP

JACKSON, MISSISSIPPI

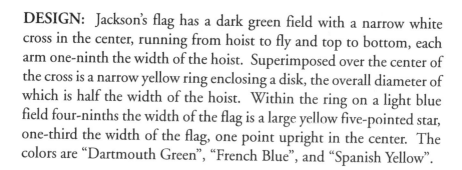

Population Rank: U.S... # 109
                    Mississippi...... # 1

Proportions: 2:3 (usage)

Adopted: 12 January 1993 (official)

DESIGN: Jackson's flag has a dark green field with a narrow white cross in the center, running from hoist to fly and top to bottom, each arm one-ninth the width of the hoist. Superimposed over the center of the cross is a narrow yellow ring enclosing a disk, the overall diameter of which is half the width of the hoist. Within the ring on a light blue field four-ninths the width of the flag is a large yellow five-pointed star, one-third the width of the flag, one point upright in the center. The colors are "Dartmouth Green", "French Blue", and "Spanish Yellow".

SYMBOLISM: The star represents Jackson's status as the capital of Mississippi. The blue field behind the star denotes the city's position on the Pearl River. The white cross symbolizes Jackson as the "Crossroads of the South".

HOW SELECTED: A contest, apparently sponsored by the city, and open to all city residents, was held in 1992.

DESIGNER: The flag is a combination of the similar themes of 25 entries among the 167 who submitted designs, blended by the six judges of the contest, and assisted by vexillologist Clay Moss. The only entrant named in contemporary newspaper accounts is 11-year old Tiffany Dennis.

MORE ABOUT THE FLAG: The first flag cost $270, provided by Metro Jackson Convention and Visitor's Bureau.

FORMER FLAG: The former flag of Jackson was apparently unofficial, developed by city officials and representatives of the Metrocenter Mall when mall officials, who wanted to fly city flags at the mall, learned that Jackson had no city flag. William Hobson, manager of the mall, presented the first flag to the city council on 14 February 1978.

The flag has a white field. In the center is a depiction in red of the head and shoulders of President Andrew Jackson (for whom the city was named) in three-quarter profile facing toward the fly, with the collar of his coat buttoned under his chin. Centered immediately below the collar, in small white figures, is 1822, commemorating the founding of the city. The figure is about 1.25 units high by 1.25 units wide at its widest point on a flag of 3 by 5 units. **JACKSON** is centered above the figure and **MISSISSIPPI** centered below, all in dark blue letters one-half unit high.
JP 🏴

JACKSONVILLE, FLORIDA

Population Rank: U.S. ..... # 14
Florida ...... # 1

Proportions: 2:3 (official)

Adopted: 9 March 1976 (official)

DESIGN: Jacksonville's flag is described in the ordinance of adoption: *The official flag of the city shall be a rectangle having the dimensions in the ratio of one (hoist) to one and one-half (fly), divided horizontally into two equal panels: The upper panel has a rampant equestrian statue of Andrew Jackson in silhouette over a sunburst; the lower panel has a silhouette of Duval County and the words* CITY OF JACKSONVILLE, FLORIDA *in a recumbent concave arc thereunder, all on a solid field. The rays of the sunburst, silhouette of Duval County and the words* CITY OF JACKSON-VILLE, FLORIDA *are gold; the equestrian statue of Andrew Jackson is dark brown, the upper panel background is white and the lower panel field is orange.* The statue of Jackson faces the hoist; the sunburst has 30 gold rays that extend from the midpoint of the flag behind the statue and extend to the edges of the flag on the top three sides.

SYMBOLISM: The top half of the flag shows the statue of Andrew Jackson, the 6th president of the United States, for whom the city was named. The image, taken from the official seal, is an exact depiction of the statue in Jackson Park in New Orleans, Louisiana. (The city seal was first adopted 7 August 1888.) The map of Duval County on the lower part indicates that the city and county are now conterminous. The sunburst suggests Florida's nickname, "The Sunshine State".

HOW SELECTED: A city council committee, dissatisfied with the previous flag, wanted a new city flag that would suggest Jackson's new image as the "Bold New City of the South". A contest was held through the auspices of the Bold CityFest Committee, a group organizing a civic celebration with the same name. The local chapter of the American Institute of Architects judged the 148 entries and sent five semifinalists to a committee comprising four city councilmen, the Jacksonville Area Planning Board director, the information services officer, and Mayor Hans Tanzler.

DESIGNER: Don Bozeman, an employee of the Seaboard Coast Line, who won the $500 prize for best design.

MORE ABOUT THE FLAG: The flag was raised at city hall for the first time in a ceremony on 1 October 1976. Although the ordinance of adoption clearly states that the figure of Andrew Jackson on the flag is brown, and the lower stripe is orange, the city has at least one flag showing the statue as black and the lower stripe as red, possibly a manufacturing error.

FORMER FLAG: The dimensions of Jacksonville's previous flag were not specified and varied somewhat according to the manufacturer, but were generally 3:5. The field of the flag is white. In the upper hoist corner are two red gateposts with rounded tops. Coming from behind the post closest to the hoist and curving across the bottom of the second post and extending in a flowing fashion across the field diagonally to-

ward the lower fly is a wide dark green ribbon, notched on both ends. Across the ribbon in large white block letters is **JACKSONVILLE**. Behind the ribbon, and occupying most of the center portion of the field are two long-stemmed red poinsettias in full bloom. In the lower hoist corner is a variation of the city seal, showing Jackson's statue in black facing the fly and surrounded by a red-edged white ring on which **CITY OF JACKSONVILLE** arches over the top and **FLORIDA** curves counterclockwise below, all in red. The gateposts and ribbon recall the former motto of Jacksonville, "The Gateway to Florida". The poinsettias represent Florida.

A number of incorrect facts concerning the adoption and designer of the flag were quoted for a number of years in various sources, evidently originating in a 1925 book by T. Frederick Davis, *History of Jacksonville, Florida and Vicinity, 1513 to 1924*. Davis wrote that the flag was designed by G. D. Ackerly and adopted by council on 15 January 1914. However, later research reveals that the flag was adopted on 21 January 1914, and the designer was, in fact, Edmund Jackson, whom Ackerly (then the city recorder) instructed with this colorful admonition: "I don't want no snakes, I don't want no alligators, and I don't want no coconuts." What he got, of course, were poinsettias!   JP 🏴

JEFFERSON CITY, MISSOURI ✪

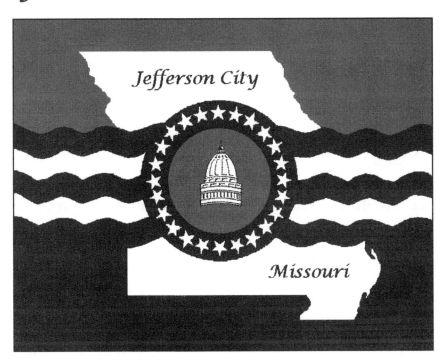

Population Rank: U.S... # 901
            Missouri .... # 13

Proportions: 3:4 (usage)

Adopted: 5 March 1990 (official)

DESIGN: The flag of Jefferson City is essentially a horizontal tribar: top, red; bottom, dark blue; and the center divided into five wavy stripes, three dark blue alternating with two white. Superimposed on these wavy stripes in the center of the flag is a circle, its top and bottom extending approximately one-eighth of its diameter above and below the top and bottom blue wavy stripes. The circle has a red field, on which the capitol dome is centered in white with dark blue shadings. Surrounding the red field is a blue ring with 24 white five-pointed stars, points outward. The entire center bar with stripes and circle overlays a large white silhouette map of the state of Missouri occupying, in the upper third of the field, about seven-fifteenths of the width, beginning about one-sixth of the distance from the hoist. In the lower third of the flag, the map occupies about three-fifths of the width, beginning about one-fifth of the distance from the hoist. Thus, only the northern and southern thirds of the state are visible, with the remainder covered by the central device. In a dark blue Calligraphy-421 BT-type font, **Jefferson City** is centered on the white portion of the map on the top bar, and **Missouri** is centered on the fly half of the white portion of the map in the bottom bar.

SYMBOLISM: The dome of the state capitol identifies Jefferson City as the capital of Missouri. The 24 stars on the blue ring represent Missouri's rank as the twenty-fourth state to join the Union. The wavy blue and white stripes symbolize the Missouri River. The colors are explained in the ordinance: *The official flag of the City shall have a color scheme of red, white and blue inspired by the flags of both the State of Missouri and the United States.*

HOW SELECTED: A committee of three councilmen and three citizens selected the winning entry in a contest held in early 1990. Cash prizes were awarded for first, second, and third places.

DESIGNER: David Woodside won the contest.   JP

JERSEY CITY, NEW JERSEY

Population Rank: U.S...... # 72
New Jersey...... # 2

Proportions: 2:3 (usage)

Adopted: 19 July 1938 (official)

DESIGN: The flag of Jersey City has three equal vertical stripes of blue, white, and yellow, with the city's seal set slightly above center on the white stripe. The seal has a gold field edged in brown, and bears a shield divided in half horizontally, white over light brown. In the top center of the shield is a large sailing ship, brown with gold sails mostly furled, as if at anchor, its prow facing the fly. To the hoist side of the ship, on the landed horizon, is a brown steam locomotive and coal tender, smoke chugging from its smokestack toward the fly. On the fly side of the ship, also on the horizon, is a historic city skyline in white with black shadings and prominent church steeples. A white seagull floats over the ship's stern. In the lower half of the shield, on the upper hoist side, is a small white sailboat. In the lower center is a two-masted ocean steamer with brown smokestacks and yellow smoke billowing from them, coming into dock at a burnt-sienna-colored wharf that slants across the bottom hoist portion of the shield. Above the shield is a brown-edged gold scroll with an inscription, **LET JERSEY PROSPER** , in brown letters. Surrounding the shield is a brown-edged gold ring with **CORPORATION OF JERSEY CITY** curving clockwise over the top, in brown.

SYMBOLISM: The three stripes of blue, white, and yellow are supposed to commemorate the colors of the Dutch, as Jersey City was located in the province of New Netherlands. However, the color yellow would more appropriately be orange, as blue, white, and orange were the colors in the Dutch national flag and its trading companies in the early 1600s.

The sailing ship is the *Half Moon*, in which the explorer Henry Hudson sailed up the Hudson River in 1609. Jersey City is on the east side of this river, across from Manhattan Island. Today the ships represent the maritime commerce of the city. The pier heads in the background reflect the early Dutch settlement established here in 1630 as Communipaw.

HOW SELECTED: William J. McGovern, director of parks and public property, asked that Mr. Hugh Clarke design the flag.

DESIGNER: Hugh "Buz" Clarke, a city engineer.

MORE ABOUT THE FLAG: The flag was adopted by a city resolution introduced by William J. McGovern, city commissioner. The original resolution states that *the official seal of the City of Jersey City be included and affixed to the white on this flag, with the numerals 1630 placed below the seal.* This original seal was not enclosed in a circle as it is today, but was just the

heraldic ribbon and shield. Moreover, as is frequently the case in rendering of city seals by different artists
over the years, the elements of the seal
are pictured differently. The field of
the shield is not divided by colors, although we do not know what the
original colors may have been, if any.
No locomotive appears on this shield,
just primitive buildings on either side
of the sailing ship, and the steamboat
is under way toward the lower hoist corner, no wharf in sight. The
date, 1630, does appear at the lower center on the city's seal today in a
circular band around the edge, but has not been carried over to the
current flag.   JC 🏴

JUNEAU, ALASKA ✪

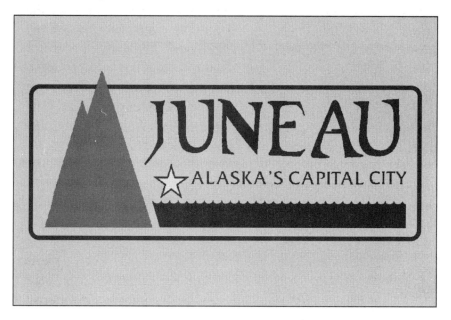

Population Rank: U.S. #1,193
Alaska...... # 2

Proportions: 2:3 (usage)

Adopted: Not known

DESIGN: The field of Juneau's flag is light blue. The central figure on the flag is contained in a rectangle with a narrow darker blue outline and rounded corners. On a field of 2 by 3 units, the rectangle is approximately 1.25 units high and 2.5 units wide. Occupying about the first third of the space within the rectangle from the hoist is a green silhouette of perhaps two mountain peaks or pine trees. The figure is almost a pyramid with two points, the one on the hoist side slightly lower than the other, the tip of which extends slightly beyond the top of the rectangle. The top half of the remaining space within the rectangle contains **JUNEAU** in large slender letters of the darker blue. Immediately below this name is a medium-sized five-pointed gold star, outlined in the darker blue and positioned directly between the "J" and the "U". To the fly side of the star is **ALASKA'S CAPITAL CITY** in much smaller letters of the same darker blue. Horizontally along the bottom of the space, even with the base of the pine tree pyramid, is a bar with a wavy top, again in the darker blue.

SYMBOLISM: Juneau can be reached only by air or water. The wavy blue bar represents the Pacific Ocean, on which the city is located. The gold star represents Juneau's status as the capital of Alaska. The green figures suggest the city's northerly clime and mountainous setting.

HOW SELECTED: Unknown.

DESIGNER: Unknown.

FORMER FLAG: There appears to have been an earlier flag, about which little is known. The city hall personnel speculate that it may have been the flag of the city before it unified with the surrounding borough (county) on 1 July 1970, when Juneau became known as the City and Borough of Juneau. This flag has proportions of 4:7 and a gold field. In the canton is an Alaska state flag with a white border on its bottom and fly sides. This border is itself edged in red. Centered on the field between the canton and the fly is a circular emblem. Its center is a light blue disk with a black totem-like figure with two bird heads. The head turned toward the hoist is dark and may be an eagle; the head turned toward the fly is a white goose or duck with a yellow bill. Around the disk is a white ring on which **JUNEAU** appears arched across the top, and **1880**, the date of Juneau's first settlement, below.   JP

KANSAS CITY, MISSOURI

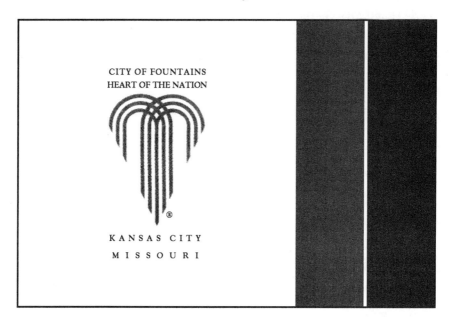

Population Rank: U.S. ..... # 36
Missouri ...... # 1

Proportions: 2:3 (official)

Adopted: 9 December 1992 (official); amended 25 May 1995

DESIGN: In the flag of Kansas City, the field is divided vertically so that the hoist two-thirds is white, and the remaining third consists of a red bar and a blue bar with a fimbriation of white between them. Centered on the white field is the city seal, composed of a fountain-like symbol whose outline suggests a heart. The symbol is red at the top, gradually fading through a pale purple to blue at the base, each of the colors occupying about one-third of the symbol horizontally.

According to the ordinance of adoption: *The official corporate flag is 135 units in width and 90 units in height with the official corporate seal 60 units in height centered on a white field 90 units square adjacent to the staff. There are vertical red and blue stripes 22 units each in width, with* the red stripe located adjacent to the white field and the blue stripe located adjacent to the red stripe. A vertical white stripe one unit in width separates the red and blue vertical stripes.

The official corporate seal is further described:

The official corporate seal of the city consists of the corporate symbol — surrounded with a two-line legend above reading **CITY OF FOUNTAINS** *and* **HEART OF THE NATION,** *and a two-line legend below reading* **KANSAS CITY** *and* **MISSOURI** *in goudy old style capital letters, such legend being in black if a white field is used and in white if a black field is used. The seal is rectangular ....*

The "corporate symbol" alluded to above is described in some detail:

The official corporate symbol of the city is formed within an implied rectangular space proportionately six units wide by eight units high. An imaginary base line drawn horizontally two units below the upper boundary divides the figure into vertical elements below, curved above. Imaginary lines drawn from the two ends of the base line to the center of the lower boundary serve as a cut line for vertical elements in the figure. The figure or symbol itself consists of five vertical lines separated by four vertical spaces, the line and space widths being equal and totaling two units in width, beginning at and centered from the lower border to the center point of the horizontal base line. From a point two units from the left boundary as center of arc, the center and two vertical lines in the right of center are extended in a 180-degree arc to the left, and then in a straight line to the cut line. From a point two units from the right boundary as center of arc, the center (used for both) and two vertical lines to the left of center are extended in a 180-degree arc to the left, and then in a straight line to the cut line. From a point two units from the right boundary as center of arc, the center (used for both) and two vertical lines to the left of center are extended in a 180-degree arc to the right, and then in a straight line to the cut line. The full color version displays the shape formed by the outline described in this subsection with color graduating uniformly from blue at the lowest point or tip of the symbol to red at the uppermost quadrant points of the arcs. Where used, the field is either white or black. When viewed in full color, the symbol appears as a fountain with the graduated color implying upward movement. The overall shape of the symbol reads transparently as a heart, symbolizing 'Heart of the Nation'.

SYMBOLISM: The city seal reflects the city's two nicknames: "City of Fountains" and "Heart of the Nation". The colors are found in the United States and Missouri flags as well.

HOW SELECTED: By Mayor Emanuel Cleaver II.

DESIGNER: Unknown.

MORE ABOUT THE FLAG: Despite the flag's detailed specifications, the city apparently uses a flag that does not follow them. A sketch received from city hall shows a vertical tribar of equal blue, white, and red stripes. The city seal is on the center bar. Nothing more is known about this version.

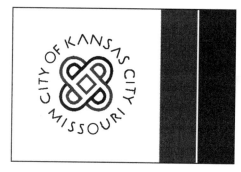

FORMER FLAGS: Kansas City has had four previous flags. The one in use from 7 January 1972 to 9 December 1992 was identical in form and proportions to the current flag, except that the seal was different, and is described:

The official corporate symbol of Kansas City shall be four double-lined interlocking hearts, forming a single shape with the four extremities congruent to a square, the colors of said symbol being red, white and blue. The official corporate seal of Kansas City shall consist of the aforesaid corporate symbol surrounded by a legend of **City of Kansas City, Missouri,** *in sans serif capital letters, said legend being black.*

The "interlocking hearts" symbol might be described as two paper clips in the shape of an "X", forming a diamond-shaped square in their center. The stroke of the "X "from hoist to fly as blue with red eyelets at its top and bottom, and the other stroke of the "X" from fly to hoist as red with blue eyelets, and a blue square in the center, and one has an approximation of the image that does, indeed, form hearts outlined half in blue and red, or red and blue, sequentially clockwise. The legend, in black letters, is circular in form. **CITY OF KANSAS CITY** is arched over the upper two-thirds of the circle; **MISSOURI** is curved and centered below. The "A"s in "**KANSAS**" lack the cross-stroke, so they appear as inverted "V"s. The entire symbol is on a white field.

The city's previous flag (its third) had been adopted on 26 December 1944, apparently as a result of Mayor Gage's request to the municipal art commission to design a new flag. The commission's members were Mrs. R. J. DeLano, Jo Zach Miller III (at that time in the U.S. Army), Alfred L. Benjamin, Harry L. Wagner, Keith Martin, and Mrs. Russell C. Comer. The flag has a blue field with a white horizontal stripe in the center; the top and bottom blue portions are 2.25 units wide and the white stripe is 1.5 units wide. Superimposed and centered on the flag is a large seal-like device (but not the city's seal of the period) with a white field and the diameter of 4.25 units.

In the circle's center is a large red heart, 2.5 units high and wide. A silhouette of a Native American on horseback, in blue, overlays most of the heart. The horse is 2 units from tail to nose; the distance from the top of the rider's head (omitting the feather) to the base of the image is 2 units. The horse and rider face the fly; the rider carries a bow and quiver, shading his eyes with one hand. The right front leg of the horse is raised slightly.

Surrounding the heart and silhouette is a blue ring; its width is 0.375 units and its overall diameter 3.25 units. Surrounding this blue ring is a white ring of a half unit in width, and an overall diameter of 4 units. Curved and centered over the top of the white ring is **KANSAS CITY**, and curved below, **MISSOURI**, all in blue in an Arial-like font. One blue star centered on each side of the ring separates the wording. The whole is enclosed in another blue ring identical to the first one, except that its diameter of 4.25 units forms the outer edge of the device. A very narrow fimbriation of white surrounds the entire circular device on the blue field. The colors (red and blue) and the proportions of the flag (10:19) were officially stated as those of the United States flag. The flag was in use until 7 January 1972.

Details of the second city flag's history are very sketchy. The flag was rediscovered in 1942 when Mayor Gage undertook his campaign for a new city flag. Evidently it had been displayed in 1936 at the dedication of the city's new municipal auditorium, and was used from time to time thereafter at that building. In 1942 when the mayor learned of the flag, nobody knew its official status, but he sent it to the municipal art commission for its consideration (The flag apparently did not meet with the members' approval, since the commission came up with a different flag two years later). The 1936 flag is a horizontal tribar of equal blue, white, and blue stripes, and overall proportions of 2:3. The city's then-current seal appears in the center in blue.

On the hoist side of the seal is **KANSAS**, on the fly side, **CITY**, all in blue. The seal has a white ring bordered in blue around its outside. On the ring, curving from 9 o'clock to 3 o'clock, is **SEAL OF KANSAS CITY**, and centered below, counterclockwise, is **MISSOURI**, all in blue. The center of the seal shows a stylized American shield, with its lower sides curved outwards and a narrow white border fimbriated on both edges in blue. The upper part is blue with 11 five-pointed white stars, 5 over 6. The rest of the field is white. Arched across the center of the field in small blue letters is **INCORPORATED**. Centered immediately below in small blue figures is **1850**. Arched immediately above the shield in the crest position is **JACKSON**, and below the shield, curved to match the curve of the seal, is **COUNTY**, all in small blue letters.

The city's first flag was officially adopted on 17 June 1913, as "the outward manifestation of civic pride due to the building of its new Union Station". The flag has a blue pennant-shaped field, with proportions of 7:18. At the hoist, the city seal in blue on white occupies the entire width of the flag. On the fly side of the seal, **KANSAS CITY** appears white capitals that grow progressively smaller as they approach the pennant's point. The seal is an earlier version than on the 1936 flag. In the white ring fimbriated in blue around the outside is **A GOOD PLACE TO LIVE** arched over the top half, in blue. In the corresponding space below is a pair of laurel branches joined at the center, in white outlined in blue. The American shield in the center of the seal has five white stars on the blue upper section above **INCORPORATED 1850**, displayed in the same fashion as the seal on the 1936 flag. However, in place of the county's name on that later seal, this one has **KANSAS** arched above and **CITY** centered below. During Mayor Gage's 1942 effort to develop a new city flag, the city clerk unearthed this flag, which had also been stored away and forgotten. When it was shown to the mayor, he declared the flag "a college boy's pennant", and rejected it out of hand.   JP

LANSING, MICHIGAN ✪

Population Rank: U.S... # 183
Michigan ...... # 8

Proportions: 2:3 (usage)

Adopted: 17 October 1994 (official)

DESIGN: Lansing's flag is white with the city seal in the center. On a field of 12 by 18 units, the seal is 9 units in diameter. Immediately within its outer circumference is another circle of 7 units, thus forming a ring around the central device. Curved and centered over the top in black is **LANSING**, and curved and centered below is **MICHIGAN**, also in black. The central device depicts the dome of the state capitol, the hoist side in white with black detail, and the fly half black with white detail. Behind the dome is a deep orange sun, whose rays stretch to the circle's edge against a purple sky. Green trees flank the dome on either side, and in front of the capitol flows the Grand River, shown smaller at the hoist and growing gradually larger as it undulates toward the fly.

SYMBOLISM: The capitol denotes Lansing's status as the capital of Michigan. The black and white of the capitol dome symbolize the diversity of the community. The orange sun represents hope and opportunity for the future. The sun and the purple sky symbolize the emotional warmth of the city. The green trees suggest Lansing's beautiful neighborhoods. The Grand River is shown in white to demonstrate the city's commitment to keep it clean and protect the environment.

HOW SELECTED: Mayor David Hollister charged the Lansing Image Task Force with developing a plan to improve the city's image. Among its recommendations was the adoption of a new city seal and flag.

DESIGNER: Unknown.

FORMER FLAG: The city's first flag was made in 1969. It consists of a dark blue field with the then-current city seal (which had been in use for more than 100 years) in the center. That seal also has an outer ring, but the edges of that ring are shown as beveled, in gold. In block gold letters curved and centered over the top of the ring is **CITY OF LANSING**, and below, **MICHIGAN.** Separating the upper and lower words is a gold star on either side at about 4 and 8 o'clock. The central device shows a brown log cabin with smoke rising from its chimney at the hoist side into a blue sky. In the center is a woodsman, felling a bare brown tree. Behind the tree, on the fly side, is an orange sun on the horizon. The base of the image is green, depicting grass. JP 🛡

LAS VEGAS, NEVADA

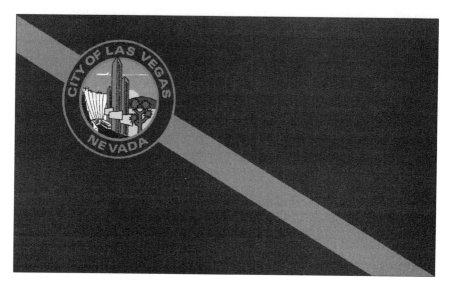

Population Rank: U.S...... # 32
Nevada...... # 1

Proportions: 3:5 (official)

Adopted: 2 October 1968 (official)

DESIGN: The ordinance of adoption sets forth the specifications for the flag of Las Vegas:

The flag for the City of Las Vegas shall be of cloth and three by five feet (3'x5') in size. Smaller or larger reproductions may be made provided all parts and portions are proportionate to the dimensions as shown.

In general, the flag shall have a Royal Blue background with a Silver diagonal stripe upon which a facsimile of the city seal shall be placed.

The silver stripe shall be four and five-eighths inches (4-5/8") in width. The upper edge of the stripe shall coincide with a line drawn diagonally from the upper left to the lower right corner.

*The facsimile of the city seal shall be as follows. The center picture portion shall be the same in color and shape as the actual seal, however, the outer ring shall carry only the words City of Las Vegas, Nevada in the following manner: The words **City of Las Vegas** shall be centered in the upper outer ring and the word **Nevada** shall be centered in the lower outer ring. The seal facsimile, sixteen and one-half inches (16-1/2") in diameter shall be placed in the center of the silver stripe. The center of the seal shall be exactly fifteen inches (15") from the left edge of the flag. All other portions or parts of the flag shall be Royal Blue in color.*

The "center picture" shows a cluster of three tall silvery buildings in the center, the middle building the tallest, the hoist building the shortest, and the fly building midway between the two in height. The buildings have yellow marquees framed in silver at their base. On the lower hoist side of the buildings is Hoover Dam (originally Boulder Dam) in white, at about the center of the seal horizontally, from which blue water of the Colorado River runs across the base of the seal to the center. A narrow portion of a brown cliff is on the hoist side of the dam. On the lower fly side, at about the same horizontal position as the top of the dam, is Sunrise Mountain, in brown with orange shadings. In the foreground in front of the mountain is a green Joshua bush with four limbs. The sun, in yellow with orange rays, rises behind the mountain where it joins the center buildings. The sky above is blue, from light to dark from the center to the edge of the scene. A jet plane flies in the distance near the hoist side, and heading in that direction, leaving a horizontal contrail. The outer ring around the seal has a royal blue field; the lettering on it and the edges of the ring are silver. The lettering above is clockwise and below, counterclockwise.

SYMBOLISM: Silver and blue were adopted as the city's official colors on the same date as the flag's adoption, representing *the silver state of Nevada under clear skies of blue and in a land filled with beautiful natural colors.* The buildings with their marquees suggest tourism, the city's most important industry. Manmade Hoover Dam, controlling the Colorado River to form Lake Mead, complements the ruggedness of the natural desert symbolized by the mountain and Joshua bush. The jet represents civil and military air traffic in the region.

HOW SELECTED: On 7 April 1965, the city council authorized a contest for a city flag design. The winning design was not officially adopted for 3 years.

DESIGNER: Kenneth A. Bouton, an administrative assistant to the city manager.

MORE ABOUT THE FLAG: When the flag was adopted, the city seal on it had been adopted two years earlier, on 19 October 1966. That seal was identical to the current seal except that in the lower half of the ring surrounding it, instead of just the name of the state, also appeared the name of the county, so that the lower portion of the ring read **CLARK COUNTY, NEVADA**, in silver letters on blue. On 7 November 1979, the seal was altered to remove the name of the county.   JP

LEXINGTON, KENTUCKY

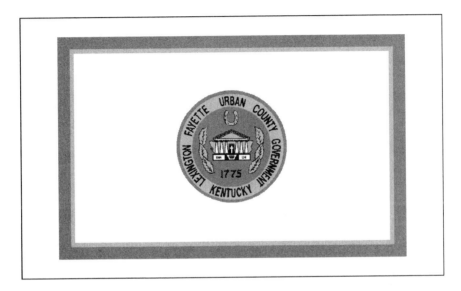

Population Rank: U.S. ... # 64
          Kentucky ...... # 1

Proportions: 4:7 (usage)

Adopted: November 1983 (official)

DESIGN: Lexington's flag consists of its seal centered on a white field, which is enclosed in a narrow, copper-gold inner border. This narrow border is set within a wider light blue border. To complete the flag, an even broader white strip surrounds the light blue border on all four sides. The white strip is broader at the hoist and fly. Details of the seal are set forth in the resolution of adoption:

... (H)enceforth the official Seal of the City of Lexington, Kentucky ... shall be a circle, in the center of which appears the front of Morrison Chapel of Transylvania College, bearing 1964 on the left cornerstone and the initials ENF on the right; an upright horseshoe thereover and overlapping burley tobacco leaves end to end on each side thereof [three on each side], *together with 1775, the date of Lexington's incorporation below, all of which shall be surrounded by a circle imprinted* **City of Lexington Common-**

wealth of Kentucky the outer edge of this circle being another smaller circle of smooth design. When depicted in color, said inner circle shall be of light blue background, with the chapel, tobacco leaves and horseshoe in gold with white shadows and 1775 in black; the circle containing the ... [legend] ... shall be of gold background, the lettering in white framed in black, and the outer circle of the same, light blue.

The legend now reads **LEXINGTON FAYETTE URBAN COUNTY GOVERNMENT** clockwise and **KENTUCKY** counterclockwise (at the lowest point in the circle). A narrow fimbriation of light blue forms the outer border of the seal. The seal on which the flag is based was adopted on 29 December 1964, superseding a 1916 version. The lettering on the 1964 seal changed in 1974 when the city and county governments merged.

SYMBOLISM: Morrison Chapel of Transylvania University symbolizes the history of the area. Transylvania University was the first college west of the Allegheny Mountains. The horseshoe above Morrison Hall represents the importance of horses in this area of Kentucky. The horseshoe is positioned with the open end upward, for good luck. The burley tobacco leaves stress the importance of tobacco to the economy of Lexington, the world's largest burley tobacco market. The blue in the background of the seal is for the bluegrass of Kentucky.

HOW SELECTED: The seal was adopted in a contest sponsored by the city of Lexington. According to local tradition, the designer used a piece of dry cleaner's cardboard she took out of one of her husband's shirts. Her husband happened to be the mayor of Lexington. He unwittingly chose his wife's design, in a blind contest. The flag itself was designed by a later mayor and his aides and adopted by the Urban County Council. It took only a month from conception to adoption.

DESIGNER: Elizabeth Nunn Fugazzi designed the seal. The design of the flag is attributed to Mayor Scotty Baesler and his aides.

MORE ABOUT THE FLAG: Elizabeth Fugazzi envisioned her seal as a model for the first city flag, but nearly twenty years passed before a design was adopted.   RM

LINCOLN, NEBRASKA ✪

Population Rank: U.S..... # 76
Nebraska...... # 2

Proportions: 2:3 (usage)

Adopted: 14 September 1931 (official)

DESIGN: Lincoln's flag has a medium blue field of 4 by 6 units. In its center appears the state capitol, a tower in white. The tower overlaps an incomplete red ring, 2.5 units in diameter, so that the ring appears to run behind it very near its top, and then continues in a circle on both sides until about 5 and 7 o'clock, where it is obscured by a yellow ear of corn with green leaves on either side and congruent to the circle. Between the ears of corn in the center at the base of the tower is a sheaf of yellow wheat. The distance from the top of the tower to the base of the wheat sheaf is 3.8 units. A second red ring, one unit in diameter, is within the larger ring, and placed behind the tower so that its top edge is about half way up the tower, and thus only a portion of the ring is visible. Extending from this ring to the larger ring are four red rays, one each at about 2, 4, 8 and 10 o'clock. In white block letters on the larger ring, following its curve clockwise, are **CITY OF** on the hoist side and **LINCOLN** on the fly side.

SYMBOLISM: The white tower represents Lincoln's role as the capital of Nebraska. The red circles come from the insignia of the University of Nebraska, and represent education and culture; the corn and wheat symbolize Lincoln as an agricultural center.

HOW SELECTED: A flag design competition was sponsored by the chamber of commerce, restricted to residents of the city. The prize was $50. Five judges chose the final design from among more than 50 entries.

DESIGNER: Winner of the competition on 2 September 1931, Mrs. J. E. Fiselman.

MORE ABOUT THE FLAG: The contest for a flag design was inspired by a gift from members of the Rotary Club of Lincoln, England, who presented a flag of their city to Lincoln, Nebraska, during a visit in May 1928. Various groups in the city discussed the need to have a similar emblem, which resulted in the chamber of commerce competition. Frank D. Tomson, chairman of the chamber's flag committee, presented the flag to Acting Mayor Blair in a ceremony at city hall on 29 October 1932. In his remarks, Tomson said that a new Lincoln flag had also been presented to the city of Lincoln, England. In a further burst of grandiloquent rhetoric, Tomson exhorted, "It should find a place in every home within this city and be displayed as a hospitable welcome whenever visitors in numbers from other parts enter our gates."

JP

LITTLE ROCK, ARKANSAS ✪

Population Rank: U.S... # 110
 Arkansas...... # 1

Proportions: 3:5 (official)

Adopted: 18 October 1988 (official)

DESIGN: The flag of Little Rock has a white field, with a horizontal royal blue stripe and a vertical forest green stripe, both fimbriated in golden yellow, converging as in a Scandinavian cross upon a modified representation of the city seal in golden yellow. Each stripe is in turn fimbriated again in its own color. The image on the seal is a mound or rock pile against a level background. Suspended above the mound is a red silhouette of Arkansas with a golden yellow five-pointed star marking the geographical location of the city. These images are enclosed in a double ring. Surrounding the double ring are • **CITY OF LITTLE ROCK** •, clockwise around the top and • **ARKANSAS** •, counterclockwise around the bottom. An oak leaf on either side separates the two legends, beginning below the midpoint of the flag's height. Another double ring completes the seal design. The lettering and detailing on the images are in black.

SYMBOLISM: *The clean white background of the banner represents the optimism and open potential that the City has to offer. The royal blue horizontal stripe symbolizes the Arkansas River which borders Little Rock, and has served as an economical and historical emblem since the City's beginning. The ... cross ... symbolizes the location and stature of Little Rock ... a city serving not only as the crossroads of Arkansas, but a crossroad of the mid-southern ...States as well. The strong forest green color depicts the fields, parks and forests which contribute to the natural beauty of the City. The razorback red silhouette of the ...State of Arkansas shows her capital, the City of Little Rock, represented by the centered star. The star rises di-*rectly above 'The Little Rock' [the mound or rock pile] ... *protruding cliff along the Arkansas River ... The Arkansas River* [the level background] *behind the rock and the symmetrical oak leaves in the border of the seal are a stylized illustration of what the flag's stripes represent... the natural beauty of the City. Finally, the golden yellow color of the seal and bordering stripes symbolize the superior economic history, and the future economic potential that is available in the City of Little Rock...* (from the ordinance of adoption, Ordinance No. 15,566).

HOW SELECTED: The flag was selected through a contest sponsored by the city's board of directors and the City Beautiful Commission.

DESIGNER: David Wilson, a law clerk, won the $1,000 contest prize.

MORE ABOUT THE FLAG: Craig Rains won second place in the contest and a prize of $500, David Tullis won third place and $250.

RM

AMERICAN
CITY FLAGS

150 Flags
From Akron
to Yonkers

Color Plates

A JOURNAL OF VEXILLOLOGY

North American Vexillological Association
Volume 9/10 — 2002/2003

AMERICAN CITY FLAGS

Akron, Ohio

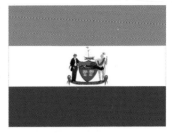

Albany, New York

Albuquerque, New Mexico

Anaheim, California

Anchorage, Alaska

Annapolis, Maryland

Arlington, Texas

Atlanta, Georgia

Augusta, Georgia

Augusta, Maine

AMERICAN CITY FLAGS

Aurora, Colorado

Austin, Texas

Bakersfield, California

Baltimore, Maryland

Baton Rouge, Louisiana

Billings, Montana

Birmingham, Alabama

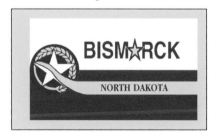

Bismarck, North Dakota

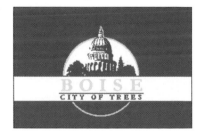

Boise, Idaho

Boston, Massachusetts

AMERICAN CITY FLAGS

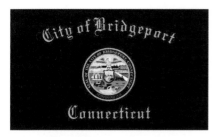

Bridgeport, Connecticut

Buffalo, New York

Burlington, Vermont

Carson City, Nevada

Casper, Wyoming

Cedar Rapids, Iowa

Charleston, South Carolina

Charleston, West Virginia

Charlotte, North Carolina

Chesapeake, Virginia

AMERICAN CITY FLAGS

Cheyenne, Wyoming

Chicago, Illinois

Cincinnati, Ohio

Cleveland, Ohio

Colorado Springs, Colorado

Columbia, South Carolina

Columbus, Ohio

Concord, New Hampshire

Corpus Christi, Texas

Dallas, Texas

AMERICAN CITY FLAGS

Denver, Colorado

Des Moines, Iowa

Detroit, Michigan

Dover, Delaware

El Paso, Texas

Fort Smith, Arkansas

Fort Wayne, Indiana

Fort Worth, Texas

Frankfort, Kentucky

Fremont, California

AMERICAN CITY FLAGS

Fresno, California

Garland, Texas

Glendale, Arizona

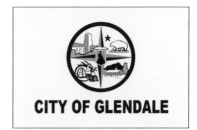

Glendale, California

Grand Forks, North Dakota

Grand Rapids, Michigan

Greensboro, North Carolina

Gulfport, Mississippi

Harrisburg, Pennsylvania

Hartford, Connecticut

AMERICAN CITY FLAGS

Helena, Montana

Hialeah, Florida

Honolulu, Hawaii

Houston, Texas

Huntington, West Virginia

Indianapolis, Indiana

Irving, Texas

Jackson, Mississippi

Jacksonville, Florida

Jefferson City, Missouri

AMERICAN CITY FLAGS

Jersey City, New Jersey

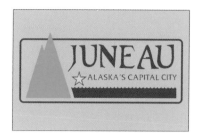

Juneau, Alaska

Kansas City, Missouri

Lansing, Michigan

Las Vegas, Nevada

Lexington, Kentucky

Lincoln, Nebraska

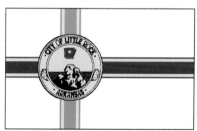

Little Rock, Arkansas

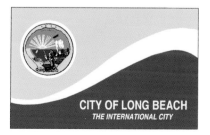

Long Beach, California

Los Angeles, California

AMERICAN CITY FLAGS

Louisville, Kentucky

Lubbock, Texas

Madison, Wisconsin

Manchester, New Hampshire

Maui County, Hawaii

Memphis, Tennessee

Mesa, Arizona

Miami, Florida

Milwaukee, Wisconsin

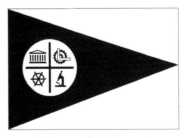

Minneapolis, Minnesota

AMERICAN CITY FLAGS

Mobile, Alabama

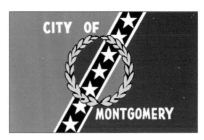

Montgomery, Alabama

Montpelier, Vermont

Nashville, Tennessee

New Orleans, Louisiana

New York, New York

Newark, New Jersey

Norfolk, Virginia

Oakland, California

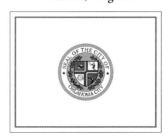

Oklahoma City, Oklahoma

AMERICAN CITY FLAGS

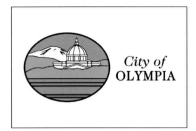

Olympia, Washington

Omaha, Nebraska

Philadelphia, Pennsylvania

Phoenix, Arizona

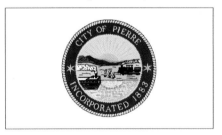

Pierre, South Dakota

Pittsburgh, Pennsylvania

Plano, Texas

Pocatello, Idaho

Portland, Maine

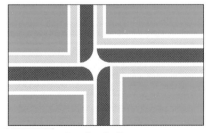

Portland, Oregon

AMERICAN CITY FLAGS

Providence, Rhode Island

Provo, Utah

Raleigh, North Carolina

Rapid City, South Dakota

Richmond, Virginia

Riverside, California

Rochester, New York

Sacramento, California

St. Louis, Missouri

St. Paul, Minnesota

AMERICAN CITY FLAGS

St. Petersburg, Florida

Salem, Oregon

Salt Lake City, Utah

San Antonio, Texas

San Diego, California

San Francisco, California

San Jose, California

Santa Ana, California

Santa Fe, New Mexico

Scottsdale, Arizona

AMERICAN CITY FLAGS

Seattle, Washington

Shreveport, Louisiana

Spokane, Washington

Springfield, Illinois

Stockton, California

Tacoma, Washington

Tallahassee, Florida

Tampa, Florida

Toledo, Ohio

Topeka, Kansas

AMERICAN CITY FLAGS

Trenton, New Jersey

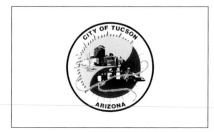

Tucson, Arizona

Tulsa, Oklahoma

Virginia Beach, Virginia

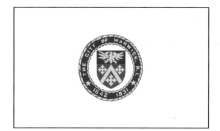

Warwick, Rhode Island

Washington, District of Columbia

Wichita, Kansas

Wilmington, Delaware

Worcester, Massachusetts

Yonkers, New York

LONG BEACH, CALIFORNIA

Population Rank: U.S. ..... # 34
California ...... # 5

Proportions: 3:5 (usage)

Adopted: 5 July 1967 (official)

DESIGN: The field of the flag of Long Beach is divided horizontally into three unequal sections of gold, white, and blue. The central section swirls in an "S" from the lower hoist to the upper fly, widening as it goes, giving the effect of an undulating wave moving toward a beach. On a field of 3 by 5 units, the gold portion is 2.25 units wide at the hoist and narrows to .5 units at the fly. The white portion is .25 units wide at the hoist and .75 units wide at the fly. The blue portion is .5 units wide at the hoist and widens to 1.75 units wide at the fly. Along the lower part of the blue portion, beginning about one-third of the distance from the hoist, is **CITY OF LONG BEACH** in a blue Arial font, and immediately below, in smaller italics of the same font, *THE*

INTERNATIONAL CITY. In the upper hoist is the inner portion of the city's seal (without the ring around it that has the city's name and date of incorporation, 1897), with a diameter of 1.5 units. Around the blue outside edge of the seal is a narrow, white circular band. On the seal's field of gold appears a large scallop shell in outline. Within the shell is a fanciful beach scene. According to the official description (colors, not mentioned in the description, are indicated in brackets):

The Seal of the City shall consist of a circular disk with a design cut thereon showing the 'Queen of the Beaches' [black robe, dark green apron, with a Minerva-like gold crested helmet] *seated on her throne in the foreground, scepter in hand, with the* [brown] *California 'Golden Bear' at her feet with the* [gold] *horn of plenty pouring forth agricultural and manufactured products while perpetual sunshine* [rising from the horizon, yellow, with white rays] *lights the heavens where an airplane* [dark red] *soars. There are also shown the* [green] *mountains and the* [blue] *sea, and a* [black] *ship, the* [gold] *auditorium, the* [gold] *Rainbow Pier and* [white] *yachts offshore, as well as a* [white] *light-house, breakwater and docks* [in red, white, and brown], *together with a* [brown] *railroad locomotive,* [red, white, and black] *factories, refineries and oil wells. Also included are a* [gold and white] *beach, the* [red] *book of knowledge and a* [gold] *lamp of wisdom.*

The queen's gold scepter is held in her right hand; her left hand rests on a gold circular shield between her and the small bear. The sky is aqua-colored with tinges of blue around the edges where it meets the edge of the shell. Curved across the center of the sky, next to the shell's edge, is

the Latin motto **URBS AMICITIAE** ("The Friendly City") in small blue letters. Centered, and curved across the portion of the gold field visible between the shell's edge and that of the seal, are four tiny black five-pointed stars.

SYMBOLISM: The gold color is for the sand of the city's eight-mile beach; the white represents the city's clear, clean air; and the blue is for the ocean. The seal uses the metaphor of a goddess blessing and protecting the arts, recreation, commerce, and industry of the city.

HOW SELECTED: The city held several contests for a city flag, but never found an acceptable design. Someone in the administration suggested adopting an adaptation of the popular Port of Long Beach flag, identical to the current city flag, except that Port's logo appears in the canton, and the legend across the bottom reads **PORT OF LONG BEACH**. The Port's logo is an oval globe showing the continents of the Western Hemisphere in white on blue oceans that extend to the rim of the Eastern Hemisphere land masses.

DESIGNER: Al Maddy, Director of Administration for the Harbor Department, designed the port's flag in 1964 or 1965. The seal was designed by Roland S. Gielow, a draftsman in the Engineering Department. The seal was adopted on 23 September 1930.

MORE ABOUT THE FLAG: The flag was displayed on the RMS Queen Mary on her final cruise from England to Long Beach in 1967, where she remains docked. The city flag was then flown daily from the ship's prow.   JP

LOS ANGELES, CALIFORNIA

Population Rank: U.S. .... # 2
　　　　　　 California ...... # 1

Proportions: 2:3 and 3:5 (usage)

Adopted: 22 July 1931 (official)

DESIGN: The field of the flag of Los Angeles has three vertical stripes of green, yellow, and red divided by zigzag lines (known heraldically as "dancetty") on each side of the center stripe. On a field 26 units wide, the stripes have a proportion to each other of 6:12:8 at the top and 8:12:6 at the bottom. Centered on the yellow stripe is the city seal, 7 units in diameter. A white (or silver) ring surrounds the seal, its outer edge beaded in white with black circumferences, its inner edge beaded with 77 solid black beads, alternating one large to ten small. Centered on the top half of the ring clockwise from 10 to 2 o'clock is **CITY OF LOS ANGELES**; centered below, running counterclockwise from 7 to 5 o'clock is **FOUNDED 1781**, all in black.

The field of the seal is a yellow disk with a quartered heraldic shield. The first quarter is an American shield (6 over 7 white stars on a blue chief, and 7 white and 6 red vertical stripes below). The second quarter is the California bear flag without any lettering. The third quarter is a bald eagle, facing the fly, but otherwise in the pose of the Mexican eagle with a serpent in its beak, perched on a *nopal* cactus. The fourth quarter are the arms of Castile and León, a gold castle on red on the hoist side, a red lion on white on the fly side, divided vertically so that León's portion of the field is slightly wider than Castile's. In the position of the dexter supporter is a spray of olives; above in the crest position, a spray of grapes; and in the sinister supporter position, a spray of oranges, all in natural colors.

SYMBOLISM: The colors of the stripes suggest the city's Mexican and Spanish heritage: Green and red from Mexico, and yellow and red from Spain. The seal is explained by the city:

The lion of León and the castle of Castile are from the Arms of Spain and represent Los Angeles under Spanish control from 1542 to 1821.

The eagle holding a serpent is from the Arms of Mexico and represents the period of Mexican sovereignty from 1822 to 1846.

The Bear Flag typifies the California Republic of 1846.

The Stars and Stripes indicate the present status of Los Angeles as an American City.

The sprays of Olive, Grape and Orange suggest the location of Los Angeles as a City set in a garden.

The beaded circle surrounding the shield represents a Rosary suggesting the part played by the Mission Padres in founding the city.

HOW SELECTED: The flag was presented to the city by the La Fiesta Association in preparation for the city's sesquicentennial anniversary celebration. The seal had been officially adopted on 27 March 1905.

DESIGNERS: Roy E. Silent and E. S. Jones, residents of the city.

JP

LOUISVILLE, KENTUCKY

Population Rank: U.S. .... # 66*
             Kentucky ...... # 2

Proportions: 3:5 (usage)

Adopted: 1927-1934 (official)

DESIGN: Louisville's flag is described by the ordinance of adoption:

The following described flag is hereby adopted as the official flag of the City. A flag which shall have thirteen silver stars and three gold fleurs-de-lis placed upon a field of blue. The stars shall be arranged in a circle in the first quarter after the manner of the thirteen stars of the American flag as adopted by Congress, June 14, 1777. Two gold fleurs-de-lis shall be placed in the second quarter and one gold fleur-de-lis shall be placed in the fourth quarter so that the three form a triangle with the point at the bottom and the base at the top.

---

* 66 is Louisville's rank as of the 2000 Census. As of January 1, 2003, Louisville merged with Jefferson County into one metropolitan government and jumped in national rank to 16. In so doing, Louisville reclaimed title to the largest city of Kentucky (lost in 1974 when Lexington merged with Fayette County).

The form of the fleurs-de-lis shall be the same as the 'Middle Ages' fleurs-de-lis form shown in the eleventh edition of the Encyclopedia Britannica, Volume 10, page 499. The blue of the flag shall be the same shade of blue as is in the field of the American flag.

SYMBOLISM: The circle of stars honors the thirteen original colonies, and of course, is only one of the arrangements of stars found in early United States flags and was not actually specified by the Continental Congress in 1777. Later generations, however, have come to favor this form for 18th-century United States flags, and so it is more frequently used. The *fleurs-de-lis*, according to the city, show the "continuing good will between our people and the people of France". The city was named for Louis XVI, the king of France at the time of the city's founding in 1778, to commemorate the help the French were giving to the colonists in their struggle for independence.

HOW SELECTED: Reportedly by a committee.

DESIGNER: The designer's name is lost, but there is some indication that a committee designed the flag, so that no single person was credited.

MORE ABOUT THE FLAG: The flag is widely seen in the city. Its adoption date is variously cited as 1927 and 1934, although it may have been designed earlier, if the reference in the ordinance to the Encyclopedia Britannica's eleventh edition (published in 1910-1911) is any indication.

A new flag recently appeared on the Internet for the Louisville-Jefferson County Metropolitan Government. The flag is blue with a gold-bordered white disk bearing in the center a gold *fleur-de-lis*, two gold stars, and the date 1778 in blue over some very thin gold horizontal lines. These devices are surrounded by a thin blue circle; at its base is a blue panel with **METRO** in white. Surrounding this is **LOUISVILLE • JEFFERSON COUNTY** in gold. JP 🏴

LUBBOCK, TEXAS

Population Rank: U.S. .... # 89
                          Texas .... # 11

Proportions: Not specified;
                   probably about 2:3

Adopted: 1999 (unofficial)

DESIGN: Lubbock's logo fills most of the white field of the city's flag. The logo is a large semi-circle atop a horizontal base, a thin blue rectangle fimbriated in gold over red that stretches from one edge of the logo to the other. On the rectangle is **Music Crossroads of Texas**, in white. Above this bar are two arches, the inner about two and one-half times the width of the outer, which has a blue area that shimmers from light to dark to nearly purple and back again, from about 10 to 2 o'clock. The remaining space on either side (9 to 10 and 2 to 3 o'clock) is filled with two vertical gold bars, a thin blue line between them, curved to conform to the borders of the arch, which is also fimbriated in gold.

On the blue portion of the area across the top of the arch, in white letters shaded in black and spaced evenly across the field, is **LEGEND-ARY**. A narrow white space, little more than a stripe, separates the top arch from the lower one, which has a narrow white border edged in black on both sides. The area of the arch is shaded a shimmering red, from dark to light to dark again from side to side. A black-edged gold five-pointed star sits on the base of the field on either side of the arch. In between is **LUBBOCK**, in very large white letters edged in dark blue. In the remaining space below this arch is a shimmering gold silhouette map of Texas, bordered in gold, with a white star showing the city's location in the northwest portion of the state. A small part of the top of the map extends onto the arch above it, so that the "BB" in the city's name rests on top of the map. Filling in the area behind the silhouette is a purple area on which a number of thin white rays in the fashion of a sunburst emanate upward to the edge of the arch from the center base point.

SYMBOLISM: The logo is meant to be eye-catching. Whether the symbolism was intended or not, the logo resembles the top of an old-fashioned jukebox, reinforcing the city's claim as the "Music Crossroads of Texas".

HOW SELECTED: The logo was created in 1998 without the motto below it. In 1999, the city council passed legislation creating the motto, and authorized its inclusion below the logo. The flag was developed shortly thereafter, presumably by city hall personnel.

DESIGNER: The logo was created by the Thomas Agency (a design firm).

MORE ABOUT THE FLAG: The flag was first raised 5 April 2000 by the mayor and students participating in Local Government Week in Lubbock County.

FORMER FLAG: The previous flag of Lubbock was officially adopted on 11 February 1971, the result of a contest held in 1970 by the Women's Club of Lubbock. The design submitted by the city planning department

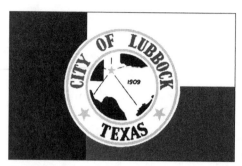

staff was the winning entry from among more than 100 received. The flag has the proportions of 2:3. Its field is the same as the state flag of Texas without the star: a vertical blue stripe at the hoist, one-third of the field's width, and the remainder of the field divided horizontally white over red. In the center of the field is the city seal, with a diameter of 1.5 units. The seal is encircled by a white band edged in gold on both sides, which in turn are edged in white on the outer and inner edges of the band. Arched over the top half of the seal, from one horizontal midpoint to the other, is **CITY OF LUBBOCK** in red block letters. Centered below, counterclockwise, is **TEXAS** in blue block letters.

On either side of the state's name is a gold five-pointed star. The inner portion of the seal has a blue field with a silhouette of the state of Texas in white that extends beyond the field's edges on all four sides. A small gold five-pointed star marks the location of Lubbock, and a thin blue ray extends from each point outward to the borders of the state. In the horizontal center, in the state's east-central portion on the map, appears **1909** in small black numerals.

Red, white, and blue echo the colors of the national and state flags. The star designating Lubbock, with rays emanating from it, symbolizes the city's nickname, "Hub City" of the south plains. The date, 1909, is the year of the city's incorporation. Since legislation adopting this flag has apparently not been repealed, and the current flag is unofficial, this flag may still be the legal version, although it has long since disappeared from city hall.

JP

MADISON, WISCONSIN ✪

Population Rank: U.S..... # 83
Wisconsin...... # 2

Proportions: 3:5 (usage)

Adopted: 12 April 1962 (official)

DESIGN: According to the resolution adopting the flag of Madison:

This flag is of light blue color and is bisected diagonally by a white band running diagonally from the lower left to the upper right of the flag, when looking at it... Superimposed on this background is a Black Cross ... and overlaid on this Black Cross is the Indian Sun symbol in gold.

SYMBOLISM: The resolution states: *The two light blue segments separated by the white diagonal band represent Lakes Mendota and Monona. The white band symbolizes the isthmus between the two lakes.* In fact, however, two additional lakes, Lake Kegonsa and Lake Waubesa, are linked to Lake Mendota and Lake Monona by the Yahara River. A Native American tribe, the Winnebago, had originally settled on the site and called it *Dejop* or "Four Lakes"; today Madison is known as the "City of Four Lakes". The four points on the black cross symbolize these four lakes. The placement of the cross in the center of the white stripe also suggests Madison's role as Wisconsin state capital, located in the center of the isthmus. The designers placed the Native American sun sign on the flag to show Madison as a "shining city" and add more color to the flag. (The same sun sign appears on the flags of the state of New Mexico and the cities of Albuquerque and Wichita).

HOW SELECTED: Adopted by a formal resolution of the common council of Madison upon the initiative of the Madison Drum and Bugle Corps. The flag was dedicated to the city by the designers and their parents.

DESIGNERS: Rick and Dennis Stone, Boy Scouts and members of the Madison Drum and Bugle Corps, with the aid of John Price, their color guard instructor.

MORE ABOUT THE FLAG: The designers' mother made the first city flags. In 1965, the city attorney, Edwin Conrad, considered using the city flag with its simple design and striking colors as the cover for a bond prospectus. Comparing the wording of the flag's resolution with the flag hanging in council chambers just a few feet from his seat, he discovered that the flag had been displayed upside down since its installation three years before.   RM

MANCHESTER, NEW HAMPSHIRE

Population Rank: U.S.... # 218
New Hampshire ...... # 1

Proportions: 2:3 (unofficial)

Adopted: Unknown

DESIGN: The flag of Manchester places the city seal in color in the center of a white field. The seal has a black ring around it, edged in gold. In the ring **CITY OF MANCHESTER** curves clockwise above, and **INCORPORATED JUNE 1846** curves counterclockwise below, all in gold. These inscriptions are separated on either side by a gold four-pointed star with a circle in its center. The shield contains three sections: it is divided horizontally, with the upper half further divided in half vertically. In the upper hoist section is a blue waterfall in front of a mountain range, with two green pine trees. In the upper fly section is a black regulator and gear on a green background. In the lower section are two factory buildings and the partial façade of a third. In front of them, a locomotive hauls a transportation-car loaded with manufactured goods below a blue sky and upon green grass. The shield's sections are separated by a narrow white line, the same width as the shield's white fimbriation. In the crest position is a workman's arm, sleeve rolled up, holding a hammer, with a heraldic ribbon behind reading **LABOR** on the hoist side and **VINCIT** on the fly side.

SYMBOLISM: The shield's first section shows Amoskeag Falls on the Merrimack River with the Uncanoonuc Mountains in the background. The falling water created the power needed to drive the many textile factories, such as the important Amoskeag Manufacturing Company, located there in the 1800s and early 1900s. The second section shows a regulator (governor) and gear wheel, symbolizing the power of steam and machinery "wisely controlled". Manchester was a center of manufacturing in New England in the 19th and 20th centuries. The third section elaborates on this theme by displaying factories or mills and a train representing transportation and commerce. The arm holding the hammer represents industry. *Labor Vincit* ("Industry Triumphant" or, literally, "Labor Conquers") is an appropriate motto for a city whose existence was based so heavily on manufacturing.

HOW SELECTED: Unknown.

DESIGNER: Unknown.

MORE ABOUT THE FLAG: As far as can be determined, the flag was first flown during the 1996 sesquicentennial celebrations of Manchester's incorporation in 1846. The seal itself was adopted by city ordinance on 22 December 1846.

FORMER FLAG: Manchester had a flag by 6 April 1965, perhaps earlier. This flag had a field of "yellowish gold" with the city seal within a dark blue ring outlined in light blue on the outside and embroidered with gold letters, but without the stars. Some of the devices on the shield also have different colors from the current version. The mountains in the upper hoist section of the former version are white, not green, and in the upper fly section the black regulator is on a white background instead of green. In the lower section, the train runs across brown land instead of green. In the current crest above the shield, the arm holding the hammer overlaps the top of the shield and is oriented toward the fly; in the older version the arm is entirely above the shield and oriented toward the hoist, which corresponds to the image shown with the official ordinance. It is likely that the differences in colors are due to the interpretation of the seal by the flags' manufacturers, since the ordinance establishing the seal sets no colors. JC

MAUI, HAWAII

[COUNTY]

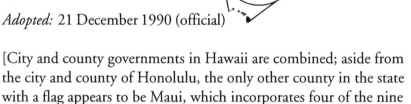

Population Rank: U.S. ..... #n/a
　　　　　　　　Hawaii .. #n/a

Proportions: 2:3 (official)

Adopted: 21 December 1990 (official)

[City and county governments in Hawaii are combined; aside from the city and county of Honolulu, the only other county in the state with a flag appears to be Maui, which incorporates four of the nine major Hawaiian islands.]

DESIGN: The flag of the County of Maui has a light blue field bearing a circular, central insignia bounded by an inverted *maile* wreath with green leaves and white highlights. The diameter of the wreath is roughly half the length of the flag. Below the wreath is a white ribbon with swallow-tailed ends and **COUNTY OF MAUI** in light blue block letters; under it is **HAWAII** in much smaller white letters. Standing within the wreath and constituting its central element is an *ahina-ahina* or silversword plant in light pink, reaching from the ribbon to the apex of the wreath. Stalks of five *ti* leaves, in a slightly lighter green and with white highlights, flank either side of the lower part of the silversword. Immediately within the wreath, arching clockwise from 9 o'clock to 3 o'clock, LĀNAʻI • MOLOKAʻI MAUI • KAHOʻOLAWE in dark blue block letters, two words on either side of the tip of the silversword. Silhouette images of the four islands appear behind the entire insignia, in proper relative scale and geographic positions, clockwise: Lanai (in orange), Molokai (in yellow-green), Maui (in bright pink), and Kahoolawe (in light pink).

SYMBOLISM: According to the county, the *maile* wreath, "probably the oldest known of leis", serves as the "tie that binds" the four islands together. The "rare and beautiful *ahina-ahina*, found on the desolate slopes of Mt. Haleakala" on the island of Maui, symbolizes "the strength, spirit, and courage of the people of the County. The *ahina-ahina*, faced against the sheer forces of worldwide extinction, and rising above the challenge for survival, clings for existence as one of the world's most exotic plants." The *ti* leaves, "the sacred symbol of the ancient gods, bestow blessings throughout the *aina*, the land of our domain." Each island has a "designated color".

HOW SELECTED: In 1987 Mayor Hannibal Tavares oversaw a contest to design a county flag for use in the Maui County Fair Parade and to fly at county facilities. An *ad hoc* committee chose the winning design from among 70 entries. Voicing concerns about the cultural interpretation of some of its symbols, however, the county council referred the design to local experts in Hawaiiana, and contracted with a local designer to assist with the details and colors. During a three-year period of consultation and revision, the culturally-sensitive *pūloʻuloʻu* (*kapu* sticks) and *ahuʻula* (cloak of Hawaiian royalty) were removed, the images of the islands were added, words were re-sequenced, and various colors were changed.

DESIGNER: Joann Hale and her daughter Janel (a student at Maui High School) designed the original winning entry and subsequent revisions, with later amendments recommended by Cheryl Logsdon, of C. J. Design.

MORE ABOUT THE FLAG: Ordinance 1965 established *Chapter 1.10, County Flag*, in the Maui County Code. Concerns about copyrighting the design dominated the council's early deliberations about the flag. The *kapu* sticks removed from the original design had been intended to indicate "protection or place of refuge to flee from danger", and the red cloak of Hawaiian royalty had signified "the charge of protectorate and guardianship entrusted to the county of Maui by the people". However, the expert from Maui Community College considered those symbols misused and perhaps offensive, and the Ali'i Nui of the Royal Order of Kamehameha I concurred, suggesting the addition of images of the islands "in relief" instead. The county council, acting as a committee of the whole, adopted the final flag design unanimously.

Ted Kaye

MEMPHIS, TENNESSEE

Population Rank: U.S..... # 18
Tennessee...... # 1

Proportions: 3:5 (official)

Adopted: July 1963 (official)

DESIGN: The flag of Memphis is divided horizontally into red over blue segments with a vertical white segment in the hoist. The white area is angled: it runs from about one-half of the length of the flag at the top to about one-third of the length at the bottom. Overlaying the intersection of the three segments is a seal in gold with black lettering, lines, and charges, forming a slightly rounded square. The seal's width is one-half of the flag's height. At the center of the seal is a full-length view of a steamboat with a paddlewheel and a very tall smokestack. To the left of the smokestack is an oak leaf. To the right of the smokestack is a cogwheel (above the paddlewheel and of about the same size). Below the paddlewheel is a cotton boll with its stem and two leaves extending to the left. Around the seal's circumference appear

MEMPHIS (top), SHELBY (left), COUNTY (right), and TENNESSEE (base), all but the last word top-outward. All of this is enclosed in a final black line parallel to the first. By ordinance the seal is double-faced on the flag so that it reads correctly on both sides.

SYMBOLISM: *The line dividing the white portion from the red and blue portions runs at an angle that is roughly equal to the angle at which the Mississippi River runs along the boundary between west Tennessee and northern Mississippi on the east, and Arkansas on the west. The colored fields of the flag, therefore, represent the geographic location of Memphis at the juncture of those three states with the red representing Tennessee, the blue Mississippi, and the white Arkansas.* (Devereaux Cannon, *Flags of Tennessee* [Gretna, LA: Pelican Publishing Co.]: 88-89). The oak leaf refers to Memphis as the hardwood capital of the world. Industry is portrayed by the cogwheel while the cotton boll reflects the importance of Memphis as a major cotton market. The steamboat represents the Mississippi River and the significant port facilities in Memphis.

HOW SELECTED: Adopted by the city commission. Whether it was part of a contest or simply on the initiative of the designer is not clear.

DESIGNER: Albert Mallory III, then a student at the Memphis Academy of Arts.

MORE ABOUT THE FLAG: The July 1963 ordinance of adoption specifies white lettering and charges on the gold seal, but because these colors contrast poorly, the city commission decided unofficially to use black instead. The ordinance was later codified as Section 1-7 of the City Code of 1967. The seal used on the flag was designed by A. L. Aydelott and adopted 21 November 1962.

FORMER FLAG: Memphis had an earlier design, consisting of the earlier seal in gold on royal blue with **Memphis, Tennessee** also in gold (with gold-colored braid). It dates from sometime between 1931, when the seal on which it was based was adopted, and 1963, when the new flag was adopted. The previous seal is described in its ordinance of adoption:

In the center of the design in bold relief shall appear a large cotton bale, upon the face of which shall be set out a modern Mississippi River steamboat, loaded with cotton bales. In the background of such design, at the top, shall be the tops of modern office buildings; on the right-hand side of the cotton bale shall appear a park scene; and at the bottom of the design and at the right-hand side shall appear cars loaded with logs; and at the left-hand side at the bottom shall appear the front of a modern locomotive engine. ... On either side of such seal, there shall be ... on the right-hand side a cotton plant, and on the left-hand side a spray of rice.   RM

MESA, ARIZONA

Population Rank: U.S. ..... # 42
Arizona ...... # 3

Proportions: 3:5 (usage)

Adopted: 1986-1997
(official status unknown)

DESIGN: The flag of Mesa places its logo on a white field. The logo consists of a square divided into orange (at the top) and turquoise segments separated by a narrow white line. The line forms a chevron, or "V" shape, starting at roughly a third from the top of the square and descending to roughly a third from the bottom of the square. The orange ranges from a dark orange at its top to an orange-yellow at its point. The motto completes the logo. It consists of segments in three rows and in different fonts. In the first line, **CITY OF** appears in thin block letters. This legend starts at the center-right edge of the square. In the second line, **MESA** appears in heavy block lettering directly below and the same length as the first line, with its lower edge aligned with the base of the square. The third line runs below the square and the second line, reading *Great People, Quality Service!*. On the existing 3 by 5 foot flag, the logo is 7 inches from the top and bottom edge, 4.5 inches from the fly end, and 4 inches from the hoist edge (with a 2-inch sleeve).

The logo was first used on 22 August 1986. The motto debuted in May 1997. Whether the flag (or as the public information office refers to it, the "banner") or any of its elements have been officially adopted is not known.

SYMBOLISM: According to the press release announcing the logo: *The new logo portrays Mesa as a strong, progressive, high growth community. Using a square, the most basic geometric shape portraying unity, balance, and strength, the logo will be an easily recognizable symbol identifying the services provided by the city ... as well as the goals of the City Council ...* The turquoise segment represents the mountains around Mesa. Its shape represents the letter "M" of Mesa. The orange symbolizes the open expanses of the desert. *The top part is depicted with colors of an Arizona sunrise, symbolic of the dawning of a bright future for Mesa. The top half also focuses attention down toward Mesa and symbolizes the City's energy and growth. The colors—turquoise, yellow, and orange—are traditional colors used in ancient times by area artists ... to represent the Southwest. The color scheme also represents the various City utility services: turquoise for water, and yellow and orange for gas and electric.*

HOW SELECTED: The public information office announced the logo in a news release. The flag itself appears to have been developed from the logo.

DESIGNER: Ellen Pence of the Public Information Office worked with a free-lance designer to design the logo. The motto was developed by a citywide team with considerable input from city employees.

MORE ABOUT THE FLAG: The flag (or "banner") is displayed only in the lobby of the municipal building and in city booths at various events and has not actually been flown out of doors.   RM 🛡

MIAMI, FLORIDA

Population Rank: U.S. ..... # 47
Florida ...... # 2

Proportions: 2:3 (usage)

Adopted: 13 November 1933 (official)

DESIGN: The flag of Miami is a horizontal tribar of equal orange, white, and green stripes. In the center is the city seal, nearly as wide as the height of the white stripe. A ring formed of two green concentric circles with an outer beveled edge on the larger circle forms the outer part of the seal. In the white ring at 9 and 3 o'clock are small orange five-pointed stars, pointing upwards. Curved clockwise above between the two stars is **THE CITY OF MIAMI**, and below, counterclockwise, **DADE CO. FLORIDA**, all in orange. In the center of the seal, occupying most of its white field, is a green palm tree with eight fronds, on a green mound. Below the leaves, and bisected by the tree's trunk is

INCORPORATED (divided between the "P" and the "O"), and below that, **1896** (divided between the "8" and the "9"), all in green.

SYMBOLISM: Orange is said to represent the orange industry for
which Florida is famous; the green is for the lush, tropical foliage of the
city.

HOW SELECTED: The city commission asked the Miami Women's
Club to submit a design for a city flag.

DESIGNER: Charles L. Gmeinder, Jr.

MORE ABOUT THE FLAG: The palm tree on the city's seal originally had seven fronds, but was changed following the adoption of a
new charter in 1921.   JP 🛡

MILWAUKEE, WISCONSIN

Population Rank: U.S. ..... # 19
Wisconsin ...... # 1

Proportions: 2:3 and 3:5 (usage)

Adopted: 21 September 1954 (official)

DESIGN: Milwaukee's flag has a field of medium blue. In the center is a large white gear, with black detail lines, its center divided into open quadrants showing the blue field. On a field of 2 by 3 units, the gear's diameter at the outside edges of its "teeth" is 1.125 units. In the upper hoist quadrant is the head of a Native American chief in profile looking toward the fly. His face is red, he wears a war bonnet of white feathers tipped in red, and his collar is white. The lower hoist quadrant shows what is intended to be a Service Flag, with three horizontal stripes of red, white, red. On the white stripe are two five-pointed stars, one blue (toward the hoist) and one gold (toward the fly). In the upper fly quadrant is an inverted black equilateral triangle bordered in white, with an ancient lamp in gold in its center. The triangle serves as a base for the bust of a male figure in white. The lower fly quadrant does not have a self-contained image, but has the top half of a factory with three smoke-stacks in use that forms a part of a horizontal depiction of important elements in the city's history. This display extends about 2 units across the field, slightly more to the fly side than the hoist side.

Adjacent to the factory on the hoist side is the tower of Milwaukee's city hall superimposed over the very center of the gear, flying a small U.S. flag. To the hoist side of city hall is the city's former sports arena, and next to that, the county stadium. These figures are all black with white detail. To the fly side of the factory is a ship out of water, seen directly in front of its stern and more to the foreground, so the bottom of the hull appears lower than the rest of the scene; its hoist side is white; its fly side, red, with a white anchor hauled up. It has a single tall red mast with a white pennant bearing a red M, reaching to the top of the gear, so that the entire figure measures about 1.25 units in height.

Beyond the ship toward the fly, the city silhouette in black and white continues, showing a home, a church, and a school. Below the city scene are three wavy horizontal lines that appear to go behind the ship; black on the hoist side, and white on the fly side. Over the home, church, and school buildings are three white seagulls in flight, one above the other. At either end of this panorama are two vertical images. On the hoist side is a stylized stalk of barley in gold edged in red, about 1.125 units tall, and one-half unit from the hoist. On the fly side is **1846**, in red numerals edged in gold, about .875 units in total height, and one-half unit from the fly's edge. Below all this, running horizontally across the bottom of the flag for a distance of 2.5 units, is MILWAUKEE, in red letters edged in gold, the "M" twice the height of the other letters.

SYMBOLISM: The city describes the flag's symbolism: *In the center the City Hall, seat of local government, is superimposed on a giant gear, representing the industrial nature of Milwaukee. The gear in turn is divided into four quadrants bearing symbols of the City's Indian origin, her culture and libraries, her military service, and her great manufacturing.*

The plumes of smoke from her factories lead the eye to a great ship seen in profile [frontal] and riding the waves of blue Lake Michigan. This stands for the city's great stature as a port, not only of the Great Lakes but now of the world.

The three buildings to the right remind us of Milwaukee's greatest treasure, her homes, her churches, and schools.

The date 1846 marks Milwaukee's incorporation as a city, and it is balanced on the left by a stylized stalk of barley, symbolic of our city's best known industry [beer]. *Next to the golden grain is our great new stadium pointing to the fame recently won by Milwaukee in the world of baseball and to her long history as a sports-loving community. Finally there is the Arena, home not only of sports and other entertainment, but of the many great conventions that are held yearly in 'the best governed big city in America.'*

HOW SELECTED: In February 1950, Alderman Fred Meyer expressed the need for an official city flag for use in Civic Progress Week to be held in April of that year. It was decided that the art commission (now the arts board) would make design recommendations to the common council for the final selection. The art commission held a citywide contest with a $75 prize for first place, $50 for second, and $25 for third. Over 150 entries were submitted; in addition to the three top prize winners, three received honorable mentions.

DESIGNER: No one design from the contest was entirely satisfactory, so Alderman Fred Steffan, a member of the art commission, incorporated elements from several of the winning designs.

MORE ABOUT THE FLAG: The small flag in the lower hoist quadrant appears at first glance to be a house flag for a shipping company, but in fact is supposed to depict a World War II service flag, which was usually oriented vertically, with a white field and wide red border. Blue stars indicated a family member in service; gold stars signified that the service person had died in the line of duty.

In late 2001, the common council conducted another contest for a new flag, believing that the current flag might be outdated. After reviewing all 104 designs, the arts board recommended in December 2001 that the common council not adopt any of them.   JP

MINNEAPOLIS, MINNESOTA

Population Rank: U.S...... # 45
Minnesota...... # 1

Proportions: 3:5, 4:6, 5:8,
and their multiples
(all official)

Adopted: 27 May 1955 (official)

DESIGN: The ordinance of adoption describes the Minneapolis flag:

A royal blue pennant on a white field or background with a white circle on the blue pennant divided into four parts; each of the four parts of the circle containing a blue symbol...

The circle is divided horizontally and vertically by a narrow cross that nearly reaches its outer edges. The circle, centered on the blue pennant at the hoist side of the flag, occupies 30% of the field, according to the official specifications. In the upper hoist quadrant of the circle is a stylized building with seven columns; in the upper fly quadrant, a draftsman's square superimposed on a cog wheel so that the square forms a right angle parallel to the angle of the cross in that quadrant; in the lower hoist quadrant, a pilot wheel with six spokes; and in the lower fly quadrant, a microscope placed so that the user would face the hoist.

SYMBOLISM: The colors were selected to harmonize with the national and state flags when flown together. The symbols on the circle have the following meanings: the building, education and the arts; the cog wheel and square, labor and industry; the pilot wheel, the city's lakes and rivers and all activities identified with them; and the microscope, research, skilled craftsmanship, and progress. The symbols combined represent the beauty, harmony, and brilliant future of the city.

HOW SELECTED: A "Committee for the establishment and procurement of an official flag for the City of Minneapolis" was established by the city council on 12 November 1954, comprising Mayor Eric C. Hoyer (*ex officio*), two aldermen, the city clerk, and three "qualified citizens of the City of Minneapolis to be designated by the aforementioned Committee members". This committee established a citywide contest to design a flag and appointed five jurors to select the winner. The top prize was a $250 U.S. Savings Bond, with four $100 Savings Bonds awarded to the runners-up in the categories of Elementary Schools, Junior High Schools, Senior High Schools, and Adult Group.

DESIGNER: Louise Sundin, a junior high school student, took the top prize.

MORE ABOUT THE FLAG: Upon adoption of the flag, a color guard comprising members of the Minneapolis Police Department Band presented the United States flag and the new city flag to the city council, placing them on either side of the rostrum.   JP 🛡

MOBILE, ALABAMA

Population Rank: U.S..... # 91
Alabama...... # 3

Proportions: 1:2 (usage)

Adopted: 4 December 1968 (unofficial)

DESIGN: The field of Mobile's flag is white. On a width of 6.5 units, a horizontal red stripe of 1 unit runs across the top of the field, about .5 units from the top edge, and a blue horizontal stripe of 1 unit runs across the bottom, about .5 units from the bottom edge. In the center of the field is the circular seal of the city, approximately 3 units in diameter and in effect, a seal within a seal. Around its outside edge is a gold ring on which SEAL OF THE CITY OF MOBILE, ALABAMA appears clockwise in black letters reminiscent of a 19th-century Barnum font. The letters begin about 7 o'clock and end at 5 o'clock. In the space remaining at the bottom of the ring, between "SEAL" and "ALABAMA" are three *fleurs-de-lis*, also in black. The field of the inner portion of the seal is also white. A smaller seal of about 1 unit in diameter, all in gold with black lettering and figures, is placed centrally in the lower half of the larger seal's field so that the smaller seal's top edge is very slightly above the field's midpoint. The smaller seal also has an outside ring on which **FROM ENCHANTING TRADITION** curves clockwise over its top and **ENDURING PROGRESS** curves counterclockwise below. In the center of this smaller seal, in its upper half, appears **MOBILE**, and slightly smaller, immediately below it, **ALABAMA**. The words fill the top half of the inner field. In the lower half are several figures: A sailing ship and seagull, upper hoist; a bale of cotton, lower hoist; a tall building, upper fly; and a mill, lower fly. Below the smaller seal is a ribbon, also gold with black letters, with **FOUNDED 1702** between the smaller seal's outer edge and the inner edge of the larger seal's ring.

Arrayed around the smaller seal in the upper portion of the larger seal's field are six partially furled flags forming a semicircle around the seal. The flags are (from the hoist): 1. France (the white *semy-de-lis* ensign, gold *fleurs-de-lis* on white, in use 1638-1790); 2. United Kingdom (national flag combining the white Cross of St. Andrew on blue with the red Cross of St. George on white, in use 1606-1801); 3. the United States of America, presumably of 1813, but generic in appearance since only four white stars of the blue canton and four red and three white stripes of the fly are visible; 4. the Confederate States of America (either the second [1863-1865] or third [after 4 March 1865] national flag, since only three white stars of the blue saltire of the red canton are shown, and a small portion of the white field at the hoist); 5. Spain, the red-yellow-red horizontal tribar (in use beginning in 1785); and 6. the Independent Republic of Alabama, after secession from the United States on January 11, 1861 (a portion of the blue field of that flag, with none of the design of it visible, in use over the capitol from January 16 to February 10, 1861). The flag of the United States is in the center and has an eagle as a finial; the other flags have spear finials.

SYMBOLISM: The flags represent the six nations that have governed Mobile: France, founding of Mobile and possession 1702-1763; Great Britain, 1763-1780; Spain, 1780-1813; the United States of America, 1813-1861 and 1865-present; the Independent Republic of Alabama, January 11 to February 10, 1861; and the Confederate States of America, 1861-1865. The figures on the smaller seal are explained by the city administration: *The sea gull and ship are significant because Mobile is* *among the nation's 10 major seaports, and the cotton bale was responsible for much of Mobile's early growth and prosperity. The tall building and mill depict the many industries which have come to Mobile in recent years.*

HOW SELECTED: Approved in a conference meeting by the board of city commissioners.

DESIGNER: Commissioner Lambert C. Mims.

MORE ABOUT THE FLAG: The Republic of Alabama flag depicted in the seal is double-faced, although all that can be seen is a portion of the blue field corresponding to the canton. The front side shows Liberty in a red sleeveless gown. In her right hand, she grasps the hilt of an unsheathed sword, pointed downward. She raises her left hand, holding a small blue flag aloft that has **ALABAMA** curved across the center of the field in gold above a single gold star. Above the female figure is a motto in gold across the top of the field: **INDEPENDENT NOW AND FOREVER.** The reverse side depicts a cotton plant ready for picking except for several red flowers. At the base of the plant, issuing from the roots on the fly side is an upright rattlesnake, facing the fly. Below, in gold, is another motto, **NOLI ME TANGERE** ("Touch Me Not"). JP

MONTGOMERY, ALABAMA

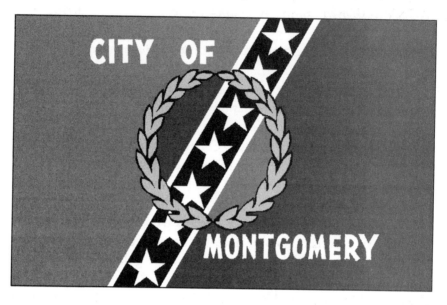

Population Rank: U.S. ..... # 85
 Alabama ...... # 3

Proportions: 5:8 (usage)

Adopted: 19 April 1952 (official)

DESIGN: The field of Montgomery's flag is divided diagonally, gray at the hoist, red at the fly. A diagonal blue stripe, fimbriated in white with seven five-pointed white stars spaced evenly on the blue, separates the gray and the red. On a field of 5 by 8 units, the blue stripe is one unit in width (including fimbriations) and slants from the top 5 units from the hoist to the bottom 2 units from the hoist. In the center of the field, superimposed on the blue stripe and adjacent fields, is an open laurel wreath in gold 2.5 units in diameter. The fields on either side of the wreath's interior are counterchanged (colors alternated) with those of the exterior, red on the hoist side and gray on the fly side. Above the wreath near the top and beginning 2 units from the hoist on the gray field is **CITY OF**, and below, on the red field beginning near the blue stripe and extending to within one unit of the fly's edge, is **MONTGOMERY**, all in white block letters.

SYMBOLISM: Gray, from the color of the uniforms of the soldiers of the Confederate States of America, represents the Confederacy. Red, the color of the saltire on the state's flag, symbolizes Alabama. Blue denotes the "blue and gray" unity of today (the uniforms of the Union soldiers during the Civil War were blue). The seven white stars symbolize the seven original states of the Confederacy, "brought together in the center wreathed in glory and honor", according to the city's chamber of commerce.

HOW SELECTED: In November 1951, the Montgomery Chamber of Commerce sponsored a contest for a new city flag. The chamber and the city's board of commissioners appointed a board of judges, consisting of Mrs. Marie Bankhead Owen, Miss Ethel Johnson, Colonel Clanton Williams, Dr. Gorden Chappell, and Rabbi Eugene Blachschleger, to select a winner from the nearly 300 entries submitted.

DESIGNER: The winner was Robert S. Ryan. The chamber, establishing the designer's credentials as a citizen of the city, gives a larger biography than usual about Ryan, who at the time was a *33-year-old native of Montgomery, son and grandson of native Montgomerians, and a great-great-grandson of a pioneer Alabamian who came to this country from Ireland in a sailboat and landed at Mobile, Alabama. He is a World War Two veteran, and both great-grandfathers were Confederate soldiers from Montgomery.* JP 🛡

MONTPELIER, VERMONT ✪

Population Rank: U.S.. Not ranked
Vermont...... # 6

Proportions: 3:5 (usage)

Adopted: 2000 (unofficial)

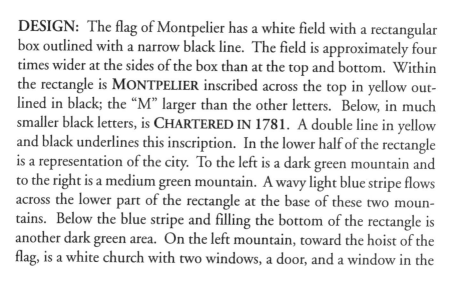

DESIGN: The flag of Montpelier has a white field with a rectangular box outlined with a narrow black line. The field is approximately four times wider at the sides of the box than at the top and bottom. Within the rectangle is MONTPELIER inscribed across the top in yellow outlined in black; the "M" larger than the other letters. Below, in much smaller black letters, is CHARTERED IN 1781. A double line in yellow and black underlines this inscription. In the lower half of the rectangle is a representation of the city. To the left is a dark green mountain and to the right is a medium green mountain. A wavy light blue stripe flows across the lower part of the rectangle at the base of these two mountains. Below the blue stripe and filling the bottom of the rectangle is another dark green area. On the left mountain, toward the hoist of the flag, is a white church with two windows, a door, and a window in the steeple, all in dark green; to its right is a representation of the statehouse in white with its yellow dome. To the right of the statehouse are three white small rectangles, one immediately to the right of the dome, the second one to its right and above, and the third, further to the right and below the first one.

The mountain toward the fly has another white church with two black windows; to its right are three more white rectangles, the first to the right of the church, the second to its right and slightly above it, and the third, which is about twice the size as the other two, is immediately below the second. To the right of these buildings is a brown barn silo and to its right a brown building with three black windows.

SYMBOLISM: The flag depicts the city of Montpelier, looking north. Montpelier is situated in a valley surrounded by mountains that feature prominently on the flag. Vermont is the Green Mountain State, and these mountains are part of the Green Mountain range. Montpelier is also the capital of Vermont, (it is the smallest capital city in the United States), indicated by the statehouse building with its yellow dome. The light blue stripe at the bottom of the flag symbolizes the confluence of the North Branch and Winooski Rivers in the valley where the city is situated. The white rectangles represent the residential and commercial buildings in the city, as well as Vermont College. White church steeples complete the scenery. The city was chartered in 1781.

HOW SELECTED: The Montpelier Travel and Tourism Committee, chaired by Jon Anderson, completed a project in 2000 to have welcome signs created and located at the major gateways to the city. Linda Mirabile, of Mirabile Designs of Montpelier, designed the signs and a city flag was created to match the signs.

DESIGNER: Linda Mirabile.

MORE ABOUT THE FLAG: In late autumn of 2000, while working on establishing welcome signs for the city of Montpelier, the city received a request for a Montpelier city flag that could be flown at the 2001 Rose Bowl Parade in Pasadena, California. Since the city had never had a flag, either official or unofficial, it was suggested the design for the new welcome signs be incorporated into a flag. This occurred as part of the initiatives by Mayor Charles "Chuck" Karparis to increase the viability and visibility of Montpelier. The design evolved out of a desire to depict key features of the city.

The flag was first presented during the general business segment of the city council meeting on 22 December 2000 by Ms. Beverlee Pembroke Hill, assistant manager to the city and liaison to the Montpelier Travel and Tourism subcommittee of the Montpelier Business Association.

To date, in addition to the 2001 Rose Bowl Parade, it has flown as part of the annual Independence Day celebrations; in December 2001 it flew along American and foreign flags during the Olympic Torch Run through the city and onto the statehouse steps.   JC ⚑

NASHVILLE, TENNESSEE ✪

Population Rank: U.S. ..... # 25
Tennessee ...... # 2

Proportions: 3:5 (usage)

Adopted: December 1963 (official)

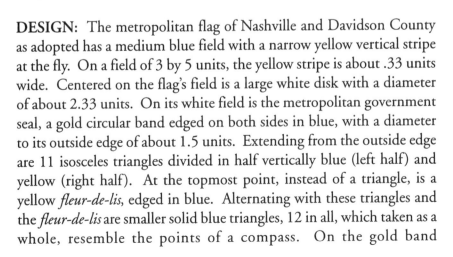

DESIGN: The metropolitan flag of Nashville and Davidson County as adopted has a medium blue field with a narrow yellow vertical stripe at the fly. On a field of 3 by 5 units, the yellow stripe is about .33 units wide. Centered on the flag's field is a large white disk with a diameter of about 2.33 units. On its white field is the metropolitan government seal, a gold circular band edged on both sides in blue, with a diameter to its outside edge of about 1.5 units. Extending from the outside edge are 11 isosceles triangles divided in half vertically blue (left half) and yellow (right half). At the topmost point, instead of a triangle, is a yellow *fleur-de-lis*, edged in blue. Alternating with these triangles and the *fleur-de-lis* are smaller solid blue triangles, 12 in all, which taken as a whole, resemble the points of a compass. On the gold band

METROPOLITAN GOVERNMENT curves clockwise over the top half and **OF NASHVILLE AND DAVIDSON COUNTY** curves counterclockwise below, separated at the midpoint on either side by a small five-pointed star, all in blue. The center of the seal has several figures in blue on a white field. Most prominent, and directly in the center, is a Native American chief, in partial profile toward the fly. His hair is braided, with two feathers extending down from the crown of his head. He wears native dress and holds a spear and bow under his right arm. His right hand holds a peace pipe, extended downwards. His left arm is slightly raised and he holds a skull in his left hand, in profile toward the hoist. On the fly side of the chief is a tobacco plant in full leaf and bloom. On his hoist side, leaning slightly away from his right leg, is the American shield with 15 stars and 15 stripes. A bunch of five arrows bristles from behind the upper hoist part of the shield. Perched on the shield's top point is an eagle, wings lifted, facing the fly.

SYMBOLISM: The ordinance of adoption explains the symbolism:

The bold heraldic blue signifies the courage and conviction of its leaders [of Nashville and Davidson County] *throughout history and the deep gold denotes the richness of its land and resources; the seal of government, encompassed by a circle of immaculate white which promises devotion to the well being of all people, lends the official designation of the strength of the government to stand behind the ideals of the flag; the seal is peaked by a fleur-de-lis, invoking the iris which brighten the springtime in the metropolitan area. The radiating compass points direct the way to opportunities unlimited; inside the compass is the historic seal of the Old City of Nashville combined with that of Davidson County; the Indian has been identified as Chief Oconostota, famous Cherokee leader who holds the skull and implements of war which he and General James Robertson buried between them as a sign of peace during the early days of the settlement of Nashville; the tobacco alludes to the wealth and cultivation of the land; the eagle, who neither flees nor fights a storm but flies above it, betokens superiority, judgment and strength in the face of danger; the stars on the shield represent the 15 states in the Union at the time Davidson County was chartered as a county by North Carolina in 1783. Tennessee became the 16th state in 1796; the seal and flag have much in common, showing the bond between all elements of our government.*

HOW SELECTED: When Nashville and Davidson County merged on 1 April 1963, the combined government adopted a new flag to replace their previous flags.

DESIGNER: Professional artists, not named.

MORE ABOUT THE FLAG: Mayor Beverly Briley officiated at ceremonies on 4 August 1964, the first public raising of the flag. He later officiated at another ceremony on 11 June 1969, when he accepted the return of a metropolitan flag that had been in combat in Vietnam with Sgt. V. R. Michaels, advisor to the South Vietnamese Air Force jet squadron. Over the years since the flag's adoption, there have been several unofficial changes in the colors and design, so that the flag currently flown in metropolitan Nashville and Davidson County differs somewhat from the original.

The current flag has a dark blue field, and between it and the yellow vertical stripe at the fly is a narrow vertical white stripe that recalls the Tennessee state flag. Moreover, the seal that was originally blue and gold on white is now shown in some additional colors on white. The lettering around the seal, originally blue, is now red. The Native American chieftain is shown in the same blue and white colors as the original, but the peace pipe has gold feathers instead of white. The tobacco plant is shown with gold leaves, not white, with dark blue shading. The American shield now has a light blue chief, but because the object is so small, the stripes below merge into a solid dark blue, as are the arrows. The eagle resting above the shield is now gold instead of white, with dark blue details on the wings. The background of the seal is divided horizontally in half with an undulating line; the lower half is green for grass, and the upper half is a light blue sky with white clouds scattered across it.

FORMER FLAG: The earlier flag of Nashville has a red field with a narrow blue border. Across the field is a broad white saltire, with arms expanding toward the corners and a blue five-pointed star in its center. Around the star is a gold laurel wreath; a large gold N appears between the upper points of the wreath, directly over the star. The flag's propor-

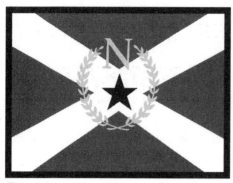

tions are 3:4. The flag's designer was Harville Duncan, a student at Hume-Fogg Technical and Vocational High School, who won a $50 prize in a contest open to all students of the city's schools. The flag was first officially used on 19 May 1961. In the ceremony presenting the flag, Mayor Ben West explained its symbolism:

The blue star in the center signifies Nashville's pre-eminence as the Capital City of Tennessee. The great white rays emanating from the star are symbolic of Nashville's reputation as a city of enlightenment, a center of education, medicine, and religion, backed by a diversified industrial economy. The City's initial, in gold, surmounts a classic Athenian wreath, symbolic of Nashville's cultural traditions which have made it widely known as 'The Athens of the South.' The design includes a field of red bordered in blue, symbolizing the City's integral position within the framework of the State and the Nation.   JP ▨

NEW ORLEANS, LOUISIANA

Population Rank: U.S..... # 31
           Louisiana...... # 1

Proportions: 2:3 (official)

Adopted: 5 February 1918 (official)

DESIGN: The ordinance of adoption describes the New Orleans flag:

The official flag of the city shall be according to the design ...which consists of a white field five-sevenths wide, with a brilliant crimson stripe one-seventh wide at the top, and a brilliant blue stripe one-seventh wide at the bottom ...There shall be three Fleurs-de-lis in the center of the white field, the height of each of which shall be one fourth of the height of the white field, and to locate their position there must be drawn an inverted equilateral triangle with an altitude of one-third the height of the white field, each angle marking the center of the Fleur-de-lis ...The three fleurs-de-lis are in gold.

SYMBOLISM: Mr. W. J. Waguespack of the Flag Committee, upon presentation of the flag to the city, explained the symbolism:

The white field is the symbol of purity of government from which alone justice and equality can flow. The crimson or red stripe ... is fraternity ... one blood or union, which is also the offspring of justice and equality ... The blue stripe ... is liberty, the offspring of purity of government ... The white field of purity is five times as large as the stripe of liberty and fraternity, because it is the mother of both. The combination of these three fundamental principles of good government constitutes 'Democracy'. The three fleurs-de-lis historically grouped in triangular form represent the birth and infancy of New Orleans under the banner of the three fleurs-de-lis, but these have since been snatched from the blue field of the banner of 'Autocracy' and now rest upon the field of purity ... and symbolize 'Democracy' triumphant over 'Autocracy' ... the red, white and blue are the colors of the United States, but are also the colors of France; and as New Orleans is the daughter of both, they are so grouped as to constitute a new and separate entity, which is now the flag of New Orleans.

HOW SELECTED: A Citizens' Flag Committee of the New Orleans Bi-Centennial Celebration, headed by W. J. Waguespack and W. O. Hart, selected a design from the 379 submitted and forwarded it to Mayor Martin Behrman and the city council.

DESIGNERS: Bernard Barry and Gus Couret, "sons and citizens of New Orleans".

MORE ABOUT THE FLAG: The New Orleans flag was first raised on Gallier Hall, at that time city hall, on 9 February 1918. Section 1-9 of the city ordinances provides that *The official flag of the city shall be displayed on the City Hall whenever the Council is in session and on all municipal buildings throughout the city on all legal holidays and whenever otherwise directed by the Mayor or the Council.*   RM

NEW YORK, NEW YORK

Population Rank: U.S. ...... # 1
New York ...... # 1

Proportions: 2:3 or 3:5 (usage)

Adopted: 27 April 1915 (official),
modified 9 January 1975

DESIGN: The *Administrative Code of the City of New York* describes the city's flag:

A flag combining the colors, orange, white and blue, arranged in perpendicular bars of equal dimensions (the blue being nearest to the flag-staff) with the standard design of the seal of the city in blue upon the middle, or white bar, omitting the legend 'Sigillum Civitatis Novi Eboraci', which colors shall be the same as those of the flag of the United Netherlands in use in the year sixteen hundred twenty-six.

The seal in the center of the flag (the same as the official city seal without the inscription, which means "Seal of the City of New York", encircling the lower half of the seal) is surrounded by a laurel wreath, open very slightly at the top. Across the center of the seal is a uniquely shaped shield with supporters. The shield's shape somewhat resembles a police badge. It bears a windmill's arms in an "X" shape, each sail showing two horizontal rows of five squares each. Where the arms meet is a four-pointed star with a small circle in the center, suggesting a flower. Between the sails on the hoist and fly sides is a flour barrel, and at the top and bottom, a beaver, facing the hoist. The supporters stand on a laurel bar. The dexter supporter is a Dutch sailor, his left arm holding the shield; his right arm slightly upraised holding a sounding line, or plummet. Angled beside him toward the hoist is a "cross-staff", a navigating instrument suggesting Henry Hudson, who reputedly determined the latitude of New York harbor with it. The sinister supporter is a Native American of the Manhattan tribe, holding a bow in his left hand, and supporting the shield with his right. Both supporters wear their native dress. Centered above the shield in the crest position is an eagle with outspread wings, perched on a hemisphere, and facing the hoist. Centered below the laurel bar is • **1625** •.

SYMBOLISM: The colors of the flag derive from the early flag of the Netherlands, the country that first settled the area in 1625 and named it New Amsterdam in 1626. The windmill sails and the Dutch sailor are further references to the first settlers. The Manhattan supporter symbolizes the tribe of Native Americans, a branch of the Algonquins, which was indigenous to the area and gave its name to the city's central island. The flour barrels and beavers suggest the flour and fur industries so important to the original settlers. The beaver also commemorates the Dutch East India Company, the first such enterprise in the area. The eagle, representing New York State, closely resembles the eagle on the state's flag and seal. John B. Pine, chairman of a special committee appointed by the arts commission associates to recommend a flag design, added a significant comment to his report to the Aldermen:

This flag is no mere decoration. It is a page of history and its colors perpetuate a great tradition. It stands for liberty and law. It represents the basic idea of civil government which the founders brought to us and which is our priceless heritage. (Seal and Flag of the City of New York, 1665-1915, John B. Pine, ed. [G. P. Putnam's Sons, New York, 1915]: 85-86.)

HOW SELECTED: In 1915, the mayor appointed a committee to design a civic coat of arms, and flag with those arms, that would be historically significant as part of the city's celebration of the 250th anniversary of municipal government in the city. The flag was officially adopted 27 April 1915 by the board of aldermen, and signed into law by the mayor 1 May 1915.

DESIGNER: The flag committee of the arts commission associates.

MORE ABOUT THE FLAG: The seal and flag first used the date **1664** to recall the year that the English first captured the city and changed its name to New York. The earlier date of **1625** was substituted by the city council in Local Law 3 of 1975, signed by the mayor on 8 January 1975. However, the seal itself was altered only by the adoption of Local Law 98 on 13 December 1977, and approved by the mayor on 30 December 1977. Since the seal change, it has not been uncommon to see the entire seal, including the inscription **SIGILLUM CIVITATIS NOVI EBORACI**, on the city flag, in

spite of the statement included in the 1977 legislation which reads: *However, the legend 'Sigillum Civitatis Novi Eboraci' may be omitted when the design is used on the city flag or for architectural or ornamental purposes.*

The change from the original legislation of "omitting the legend" to "may be omitted" appears to allow both designs to be used.

The mayor's flag is the same as the city flag, except that above the seal ("and below the crest" according to the ordinance, although this is not how the flag is made) are five blue five-pointed stars arranged in a semi-circle to symbolize the five boroughs of the city. The flag is officially 33 by 44 inches. The city council's flag, again, is the same as the city flag, but has **COUNCIL** centered above the seal below the crest. It is made like the Mayor's flag, with the word COUNCIL placed in a straight line above the seal.

The flag hangs in the Guild Hall in York, England, commemorating the historic ties of name and tradition between the two cities.

FORMER FLAG: The earlier flag of New York City dates to about  1825, likely making it the oldest U.S. civic flag to be put in use—at least, the only early civic flag for which documentation can be established. A lithographed illustration, which appeared as part of the celebration of the completion of the Erie Canal, shows a large New York City flag flying from the bow of a ship in New York Harbor.[1] The flag is white with the city's arms in the center, probably in blue (the lithograph is in black and white). A similar flag is shown in a later illustration (also in black and white) of the New York city hall during the period of national mourning after President Abraham Lincoln's assassination in 1865, with both the national and city flags at half staff. The city flag has a black border for mourning. In 1910 an advertisement by Annin & Company, at the time flag manufacturers in New York, showed the city flag as the city's arms on white in proportions of 5:8, and available either with the arms "painted and shaded" in full color, or all blue on white.

John B. Pine's 1915 book on the flag and seal (*op. cit.*, page 82), says:

Up to the present time the City of New York has never possessed an official flag in any true sense of the term. The flag which has been displayed on the City Hall, consisting of a white field bearing the seal of the City, was never formally adopted by

---

1. Lithograph entitled "Grand Canal Celebration: View of the Fleet Preparing to Form in Line," *Memoir, Prepared at the request of a Committee of the Common Council of the City of New York...at the Celebration of the Completion of the New York Canals,* Cadwallader D. Colen (New York: Corporation of New York [City], 1825): 185. (Information about this illustration, the one at Lincoln's mourning [1865], and the 1910 Annin advertisment are courtesy of the Flag Research Center.)

the City authorities...

Two points in this statement are worthy of comment. First, Pine notes that no flag before 1915 was official, although one was apparently in use for a number of years, since the aldermen from time to time provided funds for the flag's replacement. There is no definite information as to what its proportions may have been or who may have designed it. Second, Pine speaks of "a white field bearing the seal of the City," but no illustration of a flag with the seal rather than the arms is available. Dr. Whitney Smith of the Flag Research Center believes that "seal" is used here to mean "arms," an understandable allusion since the seal's primary element is the city's arms, and those illustrations that do survive of previous city flags lend support to Dr. Smith's opinion.

The pre-1915 arms, including those of the seal, are an adaptation of those adopted in 1784 after the evacuation of the city by the British. They differ from the 1915 version chiefly in artistic interpretation of the various elements. (It was, in fact, the many varied artistic interpretations of the city seal which prompted the adoption of a standardized seal in 1915, which reverts more closely to the artistic rendition of the first seal of 1686.) There is no cross-staff behind the dexter supporter, for example, and the sinister supporter holds a double bow that was not historically accurate for the Manhattan tribe, which used a single, larger bow. The eagle in the crest faces the fly rather than the hoist, and the arms rest on a wooden platform rather than a laurel bed.

OTHER FLAGS: New York City is divided administratively into five boroughs: The Bronx, Brooklyn, Manhattan, Queens, and Staten Island. Each is more populous than many U.S. cities, so it is perhaps not surprising that some of the boroughs have adopted distinctive flags. These borough flags seem to have a more formal status and usage than sub-municipal flags elsewhere in the United States, as in Cleveland, Tampa, or Portland, Oregon.

THE BRONX

The name of the borough is a contraction of "The Bronck's Land", in reference to the first settler, Jonas Bronck, a Dane who was granted a patent by the Dutch West India Company in 1639. The flag of The

Bronx echoes the 17th-century Dutch flag of three horizontal stripes of orange, white, and blue. In the center of the flag, on a large white disk surrounded by a green laurel wreath, are the Bronck family arms, a red-bordered shield bearing a gold sun with seven rays on a black field rising from a blue sea with black highlights that occupies the lower half of the shield. In the crest position is a green hemisphere on which a brown eagle is perched, facing the fly, with outstretched wings. Below the shield is a heraldic ribbon in gold with the Latin motto **Ne Cede Malis** ("Yield Not to Evils") in red letters.[2]

The laurel wreath represents honor and fame. The eagle faces eastward to suggest the hope of the New World while not forgetting the Old. The rising sun signifies the coming of peace and liberty, as well as the importance of commerce. The flag's proportions are approximately 5 by 8 units; the central disk about 3.5 units in diameter, extending well into the upper and lower stripes.

BROOKLYN

Brooklyn was an independent city before New York City annexed it in 1898. The name comes from Breukelen, the name of the original Dutch town there. The borough flag is white with a large light blue oval

2. The flag described above corresponds to a description by Gerhard Grahl, a New York resident who doubtlessly viewed the flag personally, but the colors shown on the flag at the borough's website (at <http://ww2.nypl.org/home/branch/bronx/governlment.cfm>) currently depict the shield with an orange border emblazoned by a golden sun with seven rays on a white field rising from a blue sea that occupies the lower half of the shield. In the crest position is a gray and white hemisphere on which a brown eagle is perched, facing the fly, with outstretched wings. Variations of color and detail seem to exist in other artistic renderings of the seal since there is apparently no officially prescribed version. (See Gerhard Grahl, "New York City", *The Flag Bulletin* II, No. 4 [Summer, 1963]: 43-47. Much of the information here on borough flags is based on his article.)

disk in the center. Around the edge of the oval is a darker blue ring, edged in gold. Arched over the top half in gold letters that resemble Old English font is the Dutch motto, **Een Draght Mackt Maght**, "In Unity There Is Strength". In the center of the oval stands the allegorical Justice, a woman in profile facing the hoist, dressed in a long gold gown, and holding a *fasces* and protruding axe over her left shoulder. She stands on a gray field with scattered greenery. No information is available about when the flag was designed, or by whom. The Borough of Brooklyn is coterminous with Kings County, which has a flag of its own.

MANHATTAN

The flag of Manhattan differs only slightly from the New York City flag, and is apparently used only for ceremonial purposes; otherwise the city flag is used. The difference between the two flags is entirely in the seal: on the borough's flag, the wreath around the city seal is replaced by the legend **PRESIDENT OF THE BOROUGH OF MANHATTAN**, running clockwise around most of the seal, and **N. Y. C.**, below and centered. Two five-pointed stars in outline with a space between them, replace the 1625 of the city seal.

QUEENS

At the suggestion of the chamber of commerce of the Borough of Queens in 1913, Borough President Maurice E. Connolly assigned Rodman J. Pearson, a draftsman in the Bureau of Sewers, to prepare some sketches of a flag for the chamber's approval. A special committee consisting of Commissioner of Highways G. Howland Leavitt, Louis Windemuller, and Charles G. Meyer met to confer with E. Hageman Hall, president of the New-York Historical Society and secretary of the American Scenic and Historical Preservation Society, to authenticate various elements of the design. Mr. Hall suggested some changes that were incorporated into the design, and on 3 June 1913 the chamber of commerce adopted the final design. The flag first flew officially at a celebration inaugurating the construction of the dual rapid transit system in Queens, but not until 14 October 1929 was it first raised over the borough hall.

The Queens flag is a horizontal tribar of equal light blue, white, and light blue stripes. In the upper hoist is a crown in gold over **QUEENS BOROUGH 1898**, also in gold and written in three horizontal lines, all within the top blue stripe. On the center of the flag is a large circle of gold beads with small spaces between each bead. On a field of 2 by 3 units, the beaded circle has a diameter of 1.33 units, and so overlaps the blue stripes. Within the circle are the crossed flowers, with green leaves and stems, of a yellow tulip on the hoist side over a double English rose, red surrounding a white center, on the fly side.

The flag's elements recapitulate the borough's history. The light blue and white stripes come from the shield of William Kieft, an early settler, who bought some of the present-day Queens from the Native Americans, symbolized by the circle of beads, or *wampum*, used as currency by the indigenous peoples. The beads also suggest the native name for Long Island (where Queens is situated), *Seawanhaka*, a synonym for *wampum*. The tulip represents the Dutch settlers, and the combined white and red rose (to show the unity of the Houses of York and Lancaster after years of strife) symbolizes the English colonists. The crown represents Queen Catherine of Braganza, for whom the borough is named. New York City annexed Queens in 1898.

STATEN ISLAND

The Borough of Staten Island was known as the Borough of Richmond until 1975. Its name, Staaten Eylandt in Dutch, is said to have been given by Henry Hudson. The name Richmond survives in the name of the county, which is coextensive with the borough.

The Staten Island flag was adopted in the spring of 2002, but it dates to 1971, the result of a contest that may have been held to find a replacement for the Richmond flag. The newly adopted flag has a white field on which is centered a large oval with a narrow gold border. The field of the oval is divided into three elements. A central white horizontal stripe has **STATEN ISLAND** across it in gold. Below the stripe are ten wavy lines alternating blue and white, suggesting the ocean on all sides. Above the center stripe is an elevation of the island in green with a white skyline at its base. Over the green is a blue sky, in which two white seagulls are in flight near the hoist. The green symbolizes the countryside, the white, the residential areas. The flag has a narrow gold fringe on all sides except the hoist.

As the Borough of Richmond, the island flew a flag with a blue field and the then-current seal in orange and white in the center. The seal has a beveled border around a double ring, the outer one a little more than twice as wide as the inner one. On the outer ring, centered over the top part is **RICHMOND**, in orange letters, and below, in similar fashion, **BOROUGH**. The words are preceded and followed by small stars. On the hoist side of the ring is **1683**, written vertically in white numerals, and similarly on the fly side is **1898**. The center of the seal shows two seagulls facing each other bill to bill. Between them is a letter S, and below them, just above the narrow inner ring, the abbreviation **N YORK**. The "S" stands for *Staaten* (a Dutch word for legislature). Richmond County was created in 1683, and the island was incorporated into New York City in 1898. The designers of the flag were Ferdinand Fingado and Loring McMillen, acting on the request of the borough president, Cornelius A. Hall. The flag was adopted in 1948.   JP

NEWARK, NEW JERSEY

Population Rank: U.S..... # 63
New Jersey...... # 1

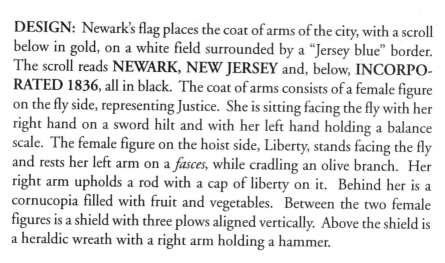

Proportions: 21:32 (official)

Adopted: 27 March 1916 (official)

DESIGN: Newark's flag places the coat of arms of the city, with a scroll below in gold, on a white field surrounded by a "Jersey blue" border. The scroll reads **NEWARK, NEW JERSEY** and, below, **INCORPO-RATED 1836,** all in black. The coat of arms consists of a female figure on the fly side, representing Justice. She is sitting facing the fly with her right hand on a sword hilt and with her left hand holding a balance scale. The female figure on the hoist side, Liberty, stands facing the fly and rests her left arm on a *fasces,* while cradling an olive branch. Her right arm upholds a rod with a cap of liberty on it. Behind her is a cornucopia filled with fruit and vegetables. Between the two female figures is a shield with three plows aligned vertically. Above the shield is a heraldic wreath with a right arm holding a hammer.

SYMBOLISM: The three plows derive from the New Jersey coat of arms and, along with the cornucopia, symbolize agriculture, for which New Jersey was once famous (the state's nickname is the "Garden State"). The two female figures each bear symbols reflecting their characters: Liberty with a wreath and *fasces*, Justice with a sword and balance scale. The image of Liberty probably comes from the state seal of New Jersey. The arm holding the hammer is a symbol of industry, as Newark, New Jersey's largest city, is an important manufacturing center.

HOW SELECTED: Unknown.

DESIGNER: Unknown.

MORE ABOUT THE FLAG: The current flag design does not comply with the city ordinance of 27 March 1916. Two dates are missing from the scroll (see "Former Flag"). Another variant design in the mayor's office and council chambers includes in large blue lettering below the scroll **NEWARK, NEW JERSEY** and on the line below in smaller letters, **INCORPORATED 1836**, repeating the information on the scroll.

FORMER FLAG: In 1916, the 250th anniversary of the founding of Newark (originally named Milford), by Puritans from Connecticut, the city adopted an official flag to coincide with the celebrations. The flag is exactly like the current flag, except with **1666**, the city's founding date, on the left loop of the scroll and **1916**, its 250th anniversary, on the right loop of the scroll.   JC 🏳️

NORFOLK, VIRGINIA

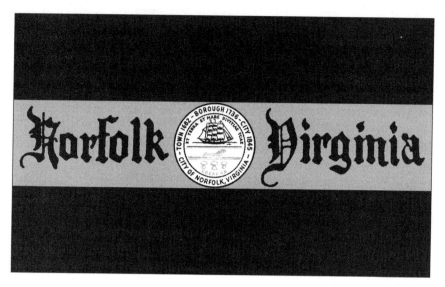

Population Rank: U.S..... # 73
Virginia...... # 2

Proportions: 3:5 (usage)

Adopted: 1946 (official status uncertain)

DESIGN: Norfolk's flag is a horizontal tribar of equal blue, gold, and blue stripes. In the center of the gold stripe is the city seal in blue and gold on a white background, separating two inscriptions, **Norfolk** on the left, and **Virginia** on the right, both in Old English script in blue. The primary element of the seal is a fully rigged sailing ship in the upper portion, sailing toward the fly. Below, past a shoreline, is a farmer's plow. At the base is a group of three wheat sheaves. The motto **ET TERRA ET MARE DIVITIAE TUAE** forms a semicircle surrounding the ship and **CRESCAS** appears below the sheaves of wheat. This Latin motto has been translated as "Your riches on both land and sea—may they increase". The images and letters in the top half are dark blue, those in the bottom half are gold, all on a white background. In a ring enclosed by inner and outer circles are inscriptions separated by dashes: TOWN 1682—BOROUGH 1736—CITY 1845 (upper), and CITY OF NORFOLK, VIRGINIA (lower).

SYMBOLISM: Navy blue emphasizes Norfolk's status as home to the world's largest naval base. Gold is for the riches of the land. The Old English inscription font reminds viewers of Norfolk's origins in England. The ship in the seal reflects Norfolk's ties to the Navy and the role of commerce in Norfolk's prosperity. Sheaves of wheat and the plow highlight agriculture's importance in the settlement and current economy of Virginia. The dates refer to Norfolk's founding as a town (1682), its charter as a borough (1736), and its recognition as a city (1845).

HOW SELECTED: Introduced by the Norfolk Advertising Board. The flag has been used since 1946. The seal, similar to the previous seal, was adopted by the board of aldermen in March 1913.

DESIGNER: A committee of the advertising board consisting of City Clerk John D. Corbell, Board Manager Francis E. Turin, W. M. Bott, and Charles A. Morrisette (an artist who painted the first draft).

FORMER FLAG: As a borough, Norfolk at one time had an earlier flag. This flag features, in the fly, an allegorical scene of a classically dressed Virginia, extending her hand in welcome to Norfolk, dressed as a daughter of the sea, rising to accept her greeting. Above, a phoenix flies toward the sun. Latin mottoes appear above, **Deo Juvante Resurgam** ("Destroyed in youth, I shall rise again with God's help"), and below, **Norfolk Reflorescens** ("Norfolk flourishes again"). On the reverse is a sailing ship with an inscription, **Norfolk, Sept. 1836.** Miscellaneous symbols are Norfolk's official flower, the crape myrtle, and its mace (the only original city mace in the United States, presented to Norfolk by Lieutenant Governor Dinwiddie in 1753). None of the available descriptions of this flag mentions its colors.   RM 🏴

OAKLAND, CALIFORNIA

Population Rank: U.S...... # 41
California...... # 7

Proportions: 2:3 (usage)

Adopted: April 1952 (official status uncertain)

DESIGN: Oakland's flag has a canary yellow field, with a green oak tree (including the trunk), wider than it is tall, centered on the middle third of the field. Above the tree, a shallow arch of green block letters proclaims **OAKLAND**. Centered below the tree and its patch of green ground is **1852** in green.

SYMBOLISM: The oak tree likely recalls the city's name. Green probably represents growth while the yellow refers to the riches of the city and region.

HOW SELECTED: Spurred by the city's approaching centennial, the flag was adopted after a design contest called for by Councilman William H. D. Clausen and approved by Mayor Clifford E. Rishell. The top prize of $200 was awarded by a jury of representatives of the art departments of the University of California, Mills College, and the California College of Arts and Crafts, chaired by Eric Stearns.

DESIGNER: George W. Lasko, Jr., a San Leandro artist and a graduate of Northeastern University in Boston.

MORE ABOUT THE FLAG: David M. Lee, eleven years old, won the grammar school prize.   RM

OKLAHOMA CITY, OKLAHOMA

Population Rank: U.S. ..... # 29
Oklahoma ...... # 1

Proportions: 13:17 (usage)

Adopted: 8 February 1994 (official)

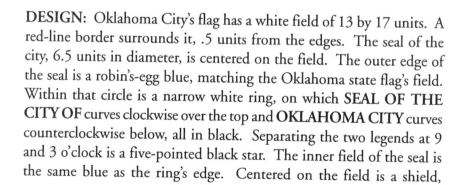

DESIGN: Oklahoma City's flag has a white field of 13 by 17 units. A red-line border surrounds it, .5 units from the edges. The seal of the city, 6.5 units in diameter, is centered on the field. The outer edge of the seal is a robin's-egg blue, matching the Oklahoma state flag's field. Within that circle is a narrow white ring, on which **SEAL OF THE CITY OF** curves clockwise over the top and **OKLAHOMA CITY** curves counterclockwise below, all in black. Separating the two legends at 9 and 3 o'clock is a five-pointed black star. The inner field of the seal is the same blue as the ring's edge. Centered on the field is a shield, divided quarterly, its first and fourth quarters in red and second and third quarters in white. A cross is superimposed over the quarters' inner edges, itself divided into four sections with their colors counterchanged (colors alternated) with the quarter they border; thus, white in the first and fourth quarters, and red in the second and third. Charged on the quarters are a plow, a hatchet hammering a stake, an atomic symbol, and a peace pipe. A green oak-leaf wreath borders the shield on either side.

SYMBOLISM: The shield represents law and protection. The plow symbolizes pioneer agriculture in the Oklahoma Territory in 1889; it is also on the seal of the original Creek Nation in whose country Oklahoma City is located. The hatchet and stake recall the "89'ers" staking land claims in the Oklahoma Territory. The atomic symbol portends an industrial and scientific future. The peace pipe echoes the pipe smoked in Native American councils, and the pendant of eagle feathers suggests the great eagle in flight, signifying high aims. The wreath of post oak leaves symbolizes Council Grove, a site in Oklahoma City founded in 1858 by Jesse Chisholm where Native Americans, military, and trade councils met. That area was set aside in 1889 by the federal government to harvest its sturdy post oak timber for Fort Reno.

HOW SELECTED: Mayor Ron Norick asked for a new design after learning that residents in the sister city of Taipei, Taiwan, could not immediately recognize Oklahoma City in its former city flag.

DESIGNER: Mark McFarland, a man with cerebral palsy, who donated his design to the city.

MORE ABOUT THE FLAG: The city council gave McFarland a standing ovation at the session where the flag was adopted. Cognizant of legal actions taken against other U.S. cities (especially, in this case, Edmond, Oklahoma) where crosses on flags have been said to represent Christianity, McFarland maintained that the cross here merely serves as an "artistic divider" to provide sufficient distance among the various symbols.

FORMER FLAG: The first flag of the city might be termed an armorial banner, since it is really the blazon of the seal's shield extended into a rectangle. Unlike the current flag, the cross on the original flag is not counterchanged, but a solid white. Mrs. Daniel C. Orcutt created the flag for the city's 75th anniversary and the city council adopted it officially on 20 July 1965. She was inspired by the design of the city's seal, adopted on 23 February 1965 (designer unnamed), and by Donald Hogland, a city resident expert in heraldry (and whose eight-page handwritten letter with carefully drawn illustrations to the council on the subject is officially appended to the ordinance of adoption). The flag's proportions are 2:3.   JP 🛡

OLYMPIA, WASHINGTON ✪

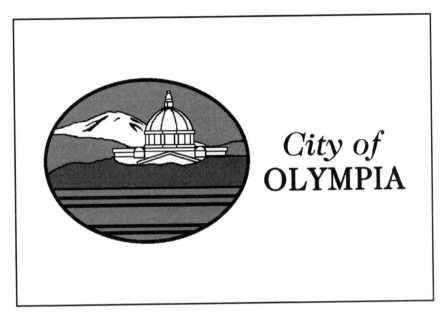

Population Rank: U.S... # 810
Nebraska.... # 18

Proportions: 2:3 (unofficial)

Adopted: 1988 (unofficial)

DESIGN: The field of Olympia's flag is white. In the hoist half is the city's ovoid logo, about 1 unit high and 1.5 units wide on a field of 2:3 units. The logo is divided more or less in half horizontally. The upper half shows Washington's state capitol toward the fly against snow-capped mountains in the background toward the hoist. A blue sky fills in the top of the logo behind the mountain peak and capitol dome. A chartreuse sward runs from the capitol to the hoist in front of the mountains. Across the center of the logo in front of the capitol is a swath of bluish green suggesting the capitol grounds. Below, in the remainder of the logo, is a section depicting water in two shades of blue—across an azure blue field, two pairs of dark blue parallel lines, one near the top and the other near the bottom, running horizontally to suggest ripples on the water. On the fly half of the field is centered *City of* over **OLYM-PIA**, in slightly larger letters, all in dark blue.

SYMBOLISM: The logo depicts a picturesque view of the statehouse amid the natural beauty surrounding Washington's state capital, situated on the southern end of Puget Sound beneath the snow-capped Olympic Mountains.

HOW SELECTED: The flag was developed by the staff at city hall after the adoption of the logo in 1988.

DESIGNER: The logo was designed by CM3 Associates of Olympia, a graphic design firm.   JP

OMAHA, NEBRASKA

Population Rank: U.S. ..... # 44
Nebraska ...... # 1

Proportions: 7:11 (usage)

Adopted: 18 March 1958 (official)

DESIGN: The field of Omaha's flag is dark blue with a Native American sun symbol in the center in gold. Its four sets of three conjoined gold rays emanate in the four cardinal directions, expanding slightly as they extend outward. The points of the rays differ: the central ray comes to a point at its center, while the outer rays come to a point at their outer edges. The diameter of the circle enclosing the sun symbol is 4 units on a field of 7 by 11 units. Overlaying the center of the sun symbol is a red disk, 1.5 units in diameter. Filling most of this disk is a covered wagon pulled by a team of oxen heading toward the fly, depicted in white with black shadings. A man leads the horses; two women are seated at the wagon's front.

SYMBOLISM: The circle enclosing the Native American sun symbol signifies continuous growth. The rays of the sun symbolize transportation on water, land, and in the air; the industries of agriculture, the livestock market, and manufacturing; city government as exemplified in the city's charter; and culture represented by education, religion, and fine arts. The covered wagon recalls the city's pioneer heritage.

HOW SELECTED: In February of 1958 the Omaha Girl Scouts thought that the city should have a flag. They contacted the mayor, John Rosenblatt, who concurred, and asked the girls to come up with a flag for an All-America City banquet just six weeks away. The troops did research and proposed two different designs. Elements from both were combined in the final flag, which was presented at the banquet.

DESIGNER: Heinz Rohde, an artist who combined the ideas into a final design.

MORE ABOUT THE FLAG: While the official flag has no lettering, words have been added at various times since, apparently unofficially. In 1963 **CITY OF** was centered horizontally above the sun symbol and **OMAHA, NEBRASKA** ran across the bottom, all in gold block letters. The current *de facto* flag uses the same lettering, but omits the name of the state.

FORMER FLAGS: Records indicate that Omaha has had two other city flags, both unofficial. A 1927 flag had the seal of the state of Nebraska on a red, green, and yellow field with **OMAHA** in large letters. A later flag apparently placed the former city seal on a plain field, no colors known. Both flags have been lost, and no images of them remain.

JP

PHILADELPHIA, PENNSYLVANIA

Population Rank: U.S. ...... # 5
Pennsylvania ...... # 1

Proportions: 3:5 (official)

Adopted: 27 March 1895 (official)

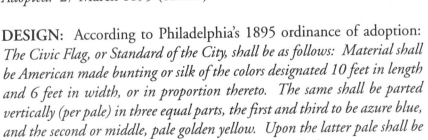

DESIGN: According to Philadelphia's 1895 ordinance of adoption: *The Civic Flag, or Standard of the City, shall be as follows: Material shall be American made bunting or silk of the colors designated 10 feet in length and 6 feet in width, or in proportion thereto. The same shall be parted vertically (per pale) in three equal parts, the first and third to be azure blue, and the second or middle, pale golden yellow. Upon the latter pale shall be emblazoned the City Arms, as borne upon the City Seal.*

In heraldic terminology the coat of arms can be described: "For a shield: Azure a fess between a plow in chief and a sailing ship in base, all Or; For a crest: A right hand and arm holding a pair of scales proper; For supporters: Dexter, the female figure of 'Peace' holding a scroll charged with an anchor, and sinister the

*female figure of 'Plenty' upholds a cornucopia. For a motto: PHILADEL-
PHIA MANETO (Let Brotherly Love Prevail).*

In lay terms, Philadelphia's flag is divided into three equal vertical stripes
of blue, yellow, and blue. In the center of the yellow stripe are the city's
arms, a blue shield divided in the center by a horizontal band, with a
plow above and a sailing ship below, all in golden yellow. Above the
shield is a right hand and arm upon a heraldic wreath, holding a pair of
scales, in natural colors. Allegorical figures flank the shield: Peace on
the left and Plenty on the right. Peace holds a scroll showing an anchor
and Plenty holds a cornucopia. On a scroll below is **PHILADELPHIA
MANETO**. The seal of Philadelphia, which contains the coat of arms,
was established by the Ordinance of Councils of 14 February 1874.

SYMBOLISM: The plow and sailing ship also appear on Pennsylvania's
arms, and together these two symbols reflect the early commercial interests of the city—agriculture and maritime commerce. Originally,
William Penn had adopted the plow as a symbol for the crest of the
coat of arms of Chester County, which was under his administration.
The ship derives from the seal of the Society of Traders, organized in
London to promote the settlement of Pennsylvania. Philadelphia is
home to the world's largest fresh-water port and has a shipbuilding
industry and government navy yard.

HOW SELECTED: Unknown

DESIGNER: Dr. Henry C. McCook.

MORE ABOUT THE FLAG: Throughout the years a variant flag
has flown without the coat of arms.

OTHER FLAGS: As in the case of Pittsburgh, which officially adopted
a civic flag four years later, Philadelphia adopted a city ensign, city pennant, and city streamer along with a civic flag. They closely resemble
their Pittsburgh counterparts.

The city ensign (merchant flag) is the same as the city flag, except in
place of the coat of arms is just its crest (the arm holding the balance

upon a heraldic wreath) surrounded by thirteen five-pointed azure blue stars, and its proportions are 2:3.

The city pennant has a triangular field of golden yellow and in the center is a blue triangle bearing the city crest surrounded by thirteen five-pointed stars, all in golden yellow; its proportions are 4:5.

The city streamer is a golden yellow field 2 feet in width and 15 in length. A blue section next to the hoist is one-fourth the length of the flag and in its center is the city crest in golden yellow. JC

PHOENIX, ARIZONA

Population Rank: U.S. .... # 6
Arizona ...... # 1

Proportions: 5:9 (usage)

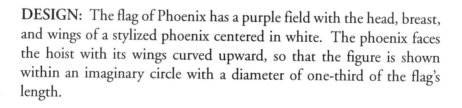

Adopted: 14 February 1990 (official)

DESIGN: The flag of Phoenix has a purple field with the head, breast, and wings of a stylized phoenix centered in white. The phoenix faces the hoist with its wings curved upward, so that the figure is shown within an imaginary circle with a diameter of one-third of the flag's length.

SYMBOLISM: The phoenix, from which the city derives it name, is the mythological bird that was consumed in flames and rose from the ashes. The flames are suggested in the central figure by the appearance of ruffled feathers. In ancient Greek, *phoenix* meant "purple," and thus also suggests the color of the flag's field.

HOW SELECTED: The city council adopted the central figure as the official logo of Phoenix in 1987 after a public vote. It was placed on a flag in 1990.

DESIGNER: The flag's logo was designed by a graphic design firm of Smit, Ghomlely, Sanft, winners of a design competition for an official city logo. The logo is protected by copyright and trademark law.

FORMER FLAG: The first flag of Phoenix is more elaborate. In 1921, the Phoenix Chamber of Commerce held a public contest for an appropriate design for a city flag. The winner of that contest is lost to posterity, as the design was considered too ornate for a flag. The second-place winner, Frederick C. Green, Sr., saw his design selected and made into a flag by a San Francisco company for $175. This flag was carried in the city's combined Industrial Week and Armistice Day Parade, 11 November 1921, and adopted by the city council at its meeting of 23 November 1921.

Second place or not, the design of this flag is also ornate. The first flag was 52 by 66 inches, made of embroidered silk. Later versions were made in proportions of 5:6. The field of the flag is blue, with a gray phoenix, head facing the fly and wings outstretched, rising from a gold sun with 48 short pointed rays (the wings, extending outward from the sun toward the top corners of the field, obscure about six of the rays on either side). Below the phoenix, in the lower quarter of the field is an elaborate white heraldic ribbon inscribed **CITY OF PHOENIX ARIZONA**, in gold.   JP 🏴

PIERRE, SOUTH DAKOTA ✪

Population Rank: U.S. #2,728
South Dakota...... # 8

Proportions: 9:16 (usage)

Adopted: 1989 (unofficial)

DESIGN: Pierre's flag has a white field with a large city seal in color in the center. On a field of 9 by 16 units, the diameter of the seal is 7.3 units. The outside edge of the seal, in gold, is beveled. Within it is a gold concentric beaded circle with a diameter of 5 units. The ring between the two circles is green. At 3 and 9 o'clock is a gold six-pointed star, with green shading to make it appear three-dimensional. Curved clockwise around the top part of the ring is **CITY OF PIERRE**, curved below, counterclockwise, in slightly smaller letters, is **INCORPO-RATED 1883**, all in gold. The central field of the seal shows a Missouri River scene from the early days of Pierre. The blue river runs across approximately the lower third of the field. Steaming from the hoist side is an old-fashioned flatbed steamboat, gray and white with black markings, its two smokestacks sending smoke toward the hoist. In small black letters on the starboard side of the boat is **MISSOURI**. The remainder of the seal shows a green plain with dark green hills in the background. A gold sun sets behind the hills, its gold rays extending into the blue sky and reflecting on the surface of the river. In the center foreground are three sheaves of wheat in gold. Approaching the center from the fly is an old gray steam locomotive and coal tender, smoke from its smokestack flowing toward the fly. A small white **83** is on the side of the locomotive, and **PIERRE** appears in miniature letters on the coal tender.

SYMBOLISM: The city describes the symbolism:

We can only assume that the sunset over the hills depicts the city of Pierre being the gateway to the west. Pierre sits directly on the east shore of the Missouri River, the hills being the rolling hills of the west river terrain. The shocks of grain and grasslands are representative of the agricultural economy of our state and community. Pierre and Ft. Pierre were a trade center and gathering place for the early trappers and settlers to meet and trade with the Native Americans. The train and riverboat are symbolic of a growing and moving mechanization of the west. The river in the foreground is the Missouri River that was and is an integral part of Pierre's quality of life.

HOW SELECTED: Mayor Grace Petersen decided the city should have a new flag, and city hall personnel concurred that it should be the newly colored seal on white. The seal, uncolored, had been adopted officially on 12 April 1883. On 22 August 1989, the city commissioners adopted colors for the seal. A local artist, John G. Moisan, was commissioned to paint the seal as specified. Upon the seal's completion, the flag was developed (apparently also in 1989).

DESIGNER: The name of the seal's original designer is not available. Mayor Petersen and staff designed the flag using John Moisan's colored seal.

MORE ABOUT THE FLAG: The seal on the flag is less striking than the colored seal Moisan created. The flag manufacturers did not reproduce all the details of the seal accurately, and so the seal on the flag is an approximation of the original. For example, Moisan's seal shows the locomotive and coal tender as black, but they appear on the flag as gray, and the lettering around the seal is smaller and in a different font from that on the flag.

FORMER FLAG: Pierre's earlier flag was officially adopted on 25 May 1937. That flag, designed by Henry M. Reed of Pierre, has a green field with a scarlet border. Its proportions are 2:3. In the center in white is a three-dimensional front view of the state capitol. Centered and arched over the capitol is **PIERRE**, and curved below, slightly smaller, is **THE CAPITAL CITY**, all in white. In the upper hoist corner is a small 48-star United States flag; in the lower hoist corner, a small French flag. The upper fly corner has a small British flag, and the lower fly corner a former Spanish merchant flag. All flags are in the correct colors. The four miniature flags were sometimes omitted when the flag was mass-produced.

The green of the field symbolizes Pierre's parks and lawns; the scarlet is for the Native American heritage surrounding the area. The capitol marks Pierre's status as the state capital. The miniature flags on the four corners represent the four nations that have claimed the area. John Cabot claimed the entire continent for Great Britain in 1497, though the claim had no real effect on the land where Pierre is situated. The French (the first whites to arrive at what is today Pierre) claimed the territory in 1743, but it was ceded to Spain in a secret treaty in 1762. Spanish control reverted to France in 1800, then in 1803 the area was sold by France to the United States as part of the Louisiana Purchase.

JP

PITTSBURGH, PENNSYLVANIA

Population Rank: U.S. ..... # 52
Pennsylvania ...... # 2

Proportions: 3:5 (official)

Adopted: 15 March 1899 (official)

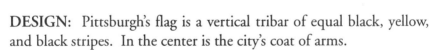

DESIGN: Pittsburgh's flag is a vertical tribar of equal black, yellow, and black stripes. In the center is the city's coat of arms.

In heraldic terminology, the coat of arms is described: *Sable, a fess chequy Argent and Azure between three bezants, 2 and 1, each bearing an eagle rising with wings displayed and inverted Sable. For a crest, a triple-towered castle Sable, masoned and windows Argent.* (On the flag the triple-towered castle is Sable, masoned Or.)

In lay terms, the coat of arms is a black shield bearing a central horizontal band with an alternating pattern of white and blue squares. Three gold disks are placed two above the band and one below. On each disk is an eagle rising with outstretched wings outlined in black. Above the shield is a black triple-towered castle with white masonry and windows (on the flag these are yellow).

SYMBOLISM: The French originally occupied this area and built Fort Duquesne. Later, in 1758, the English destroyed the fort and built another, naming it Fort Pitt after the English statesman, William Pitt, Earl of Chatham. The arms of the city are Pitt's but without the supporters (a lion and stag), the oak badge on the lion's shoulder, and the stork and anchor in the crest. The triple-towered castle denotes a chartered city.

HOW SELECTED: Unknown.

DESIGNER: Unknown.

MORE ABOUT THE FLAG: According to a letter of 18 May 1848, Judge Charles Shaler, who was on the bench of the Court of Common Pleas of Allegheny County, recounted information on the city seal: *After some discussion in which, I believe, everybody's taste was consulted, the armorial bearings of the Chatham family was made the basis of the device of our city seal (Fort Pitt having been originally named for the Earl of Chatham), and by the advice of Mr. Jones the crest on the Chatham arms was dispensed with and the castellated wall adopted in its stead, Mr. Jones conceiving that it was the proper device to designate a city, so that the device on the seal in heraldic language would read, City of Pitt.*

OTHER FLAGS: As in the case of Philadelphia, which had officially adopted a civic flag four years earlier, Pittsburgh adopted a city ensign, city pennant, and city streamer along with a civic flag. They closely resemble their Philadelphia counterparts.

The city ensign (merchant flag) is the same as the city flag, except in place of the coat of arms is the crest, or black triple-towered castle, surrounded by thirteen five-pointed black stars.

The city pennant has a triangular field of golden yellow and in the center is a black triangle bearing the city crest surrounded by thirteen five-pointed stars, all in golden yellow.

The city streamer has a golden yellow field of 2 feet in width and 15 in length. A black section next to the hoist is one-fourth the length of the flag and in its center is the city crest in golden yellow.　　　　　JC

PLANO, TEXAS

Population Rank: U.S...... # 78

Texas...... # 9

Proportions: 7:10 (usage)

Adopted: 25 August 1980 (official)

DESIGN: Plano's flag features a large **P** occupying the fly half of the flag, slanting to the right. A star shape forms the center of its loop. This star extends throughout the "P", to the top, side, and bottom edges of the loop of the "P". The stem of the "P" is red, and the loop of the "P" (the three sections segmented by the star) is blue. Centered in the hoist half is *plano* in a slanted, sans-serif font. Its baseline aligns with the bottom edge of the "P"'s loop and its height reaches the star's midpoint. The field of the flag and the star are white.

A formal resolution of the city council on 25 August 1980 enacted: *The logo approved by the City Council of the City of Plano on January 14,*

1980 is hereby further approved and adopted as the official Logo of the City of Plano. This official logo shall be used on all City of Plano equipment, materials, and flags from this day forward … (Ordinance No. 80-8-17).

SYMBOLISM: The star, as well as the red, white, and blue colors, perhaps recalls the Lone Star State of Texas. The large P seems to say "Plano" with a large capital "P", reflecting the pride of its citizens.

HOW SELECTED: Plano's flag was selected through a flag design contest sponsored by the Plano Jaycees and the Plano *Star Courier* in September 1979.

DESIGNER: Jim Wainner's design, over three others, won the contest and $50.   RM

POCATELLO, IDAHO

Copyright © Greater Pocatello Chamber of Commerce

Population Rank: U.S... # 586
                    Idaho...... # 2

Proportions: 2:3 (usage)

Adopted: 5 May 2001 (official)

DESIGN: Pocatello's flag is unusual both in design and colors. The field of the flag is white. Running boldly across the field, and occupying most of the lower half, is the motto **Proud to Be Pocatello**. "Pocatello" is in black-shadowed orange letters about twice as big as the rest of the motto in a font suggesting Academy Engraved. It takes up about two-thirds of the lower half of the field, and is in a different font from the other words. "Proud to Be" is written in black-shadowed yellow letters in a Placard-Condensed-type font that rest directly on top of the city's name. "Proud" is over the "oca" of "Pocatello", "to" rests on the "t," and "Be" is between the "t" and the first "l". Above the "P" of "Pocatello", and over the "llo", are five narrow horizontal orange lines aligned with the top of the "P" and "B". Directly above this entire element, separated only by a narrow white space, is a purple figure that occupies the upper half of the field. This figure is composed of two overlapping triangles. The larger triangle is roughly 1.5 units at its base. The smaller is roughly 1 unit at its base; its lower left point aligns with the vertical center of the larger, 0.125 units above its baseline. Extending into each triangle are four pointed cuts, sloping downward and to the left from the upper right edge, each one-third of the length of the side of the larger triangle.

A copyright notice and a trademark symbol appear on the flag.

SYMBOLISM: The purple triangles suggest the rugged mountains of the Idaho terrain, especially the Sawtooth Mountains, 190 miles northwest of Pocatello. The other colors reflect those favored in the art of Native Americans of the region.

HOW SELECTED: The city of Pocatello adopted the chamber of commerce's logo and motto for the flag.

DESIGNER: The design was created by the chamber of commerce, which has acquired a trademark and copyright for it.

MORE ABOUT THE FLAG: The city requested, and received, permission from the chamber of commerce to use the logo. The flag is now widely flown about the city.   JP

PORTLAND, MAINE

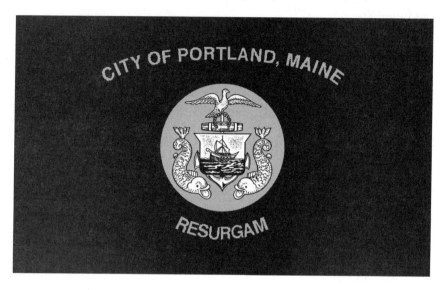

CITY OF PORTLAND, MAINE

RESURGAM

Population Rank: U.S... # 428
Maine...... # 1

Proportions: 3:5 (usage)

Adopted: Unknown (official status uncertain)

DESIGN: Portland's flag has a navy blue field bearing the center portion of the city seal in yellow, approximately half of the hoist width of the flag in diameter. This image (the city's seal excluding its outer ring with inscriptions) shows a shield overlaid on an anchor, three points of which show; one on each side of the shield and one below it. The stock of the anchor appears above the shield and on it perches a phoenix, wings outstretched, facing the fly, clutching an inverted open wreath. The device on the shield is a ship, resembling a Roman galley with oars and sails, sailing on an ocean toward the hoist. The supporters are dolphins curved downwards around the shield and facing each other. The dolphins, shield, phoenix, anchor, and ship are white with blue details, while the sea is blue with white outlines. Above the seal arches **CITY OF PORTLAND, MAINE** , and curved below it is **RESURGAM**, all in gold.

SYMBOLISM: Portland, a large coastal city, uses many maritime symbols on its flag including the anchor, the dolphins, and the ship upon the sea. The Roman galley may reflect the classical allusions popular in the mid-19th century when the seal was adopted.

What might appear to be a seagull is in fact a phoenix, holding a wreath, a mark of esteem. The phoenix, the mythical bird fabled to consume itself by fire and then rise from its own ashes, is an emblem of immortality and resurrection. Along with the motto, *RESURGAM* ("I arise"), the phoenix alludes to the rebuilding of Portland after it was twice destroyed by fire, first by the Indians in 1690 and later by the British in 1775. In 1866, the seal became an even more appropriate symbol of the city's destruction and rebuilding when one-third of Portland was consumed in a fire which left 10,000 people homeless.

HOW SELECTED: Unknown. The seal was adopted on 7 January 1835.

DESIGNER: Unknown.

MORE ABOUT THE FLAG: The phoenix as a symbol for Portland can be traced to its use on an early militia color. Recorded in *The Cumberland Gazette* of 25 October 1790: *… Amongst others, that of a Standard gave great satisfaction. The ground of it is a bright buff, and the device* [alluding to Portland's quick recovery from the two earlier disasters] *is happily designed. It represents a Phœnix rising from its ashes.*

JC

PORTLAND, OREGON

Population Rank: U.S. .... # 28
        Oregon ...... # 1

Proportions: 3:5 (official)

Adopted: 4 September 2002 (official), originally adopted 1969

DESIGN: *There is designated an official flag for the City to be known as the City Flag and described as follows: The standard size measures 5 feet in length by 3 feet in height. The background shall be green, symbolizing the forests and our green City. The design includes a four-pointed directional star, formed by the vertical and horizontal intersection of counterchanged blue stripes, symbolizing our rivers. The blue stripes are paralleled with yellow stripes, symbolizing agriculture and commerce. The yellow stripes are separated from the green background and the blue river stripes by white lines called fimbriations. The white central star is positioned slightly left of center, toward the staff end of the flag, called the hoist.* (Ordinance 176874, amending Portland's *City Code* Section 1.06.010.)

The ordinance specifies the components in one-inch units: The star is 9 units high and wide, formed by 4-unit-radius quarter-circles. The center point of the star is 26.5 units from the hoist and 17 units from the top. The canton is 18 units wide by 13.5 units high, the second quarter is 30 units wide and 8.5 units high, the third quarter is 23 units wide and 8.5 units high, the fourth quarter is 25 units wide and 13 units high. The blue stripes are 4 units wide, the white stripes are 1 unit wide, and the yellow stripes are 2 units wide. (These result in a flag 34 units high by 60 units wide.) The colors are Kelly or Irish Green, U.N. Blue, Gold, and White.

SYMBOLISM: Green symbolizes Oregon's forests, which surround Portland. The vertical and horizontal blue stripes represent the Columbia and Willamette Rivers, with the central white star (hypocycloid) signifying Portland at their confluence. The yellow stripes symbolize the harvest of golden yellow grain (Portland is a major international exporter of wheat) and the gold of commerce. The white stripes are merely decorative. The offset cross is not intended to resemble a Scandinavian cross.

HOW SELECTED: In July of 2002, the Portland Flag Association, including NAVA members Doug Lynch, Mike Hale, Harry Oswald, John Hood, Ted Kaye, and Mason Kaye, proposed an adjusted and improved version of the 1969 flag, with four major changes: removing the city seal from the canton, changing the canton to green, doubling the width of the blue stripes, and enlarging the central star to nine times its former size. Working with the mayor's chief of staff, Sam Adams, the group drafted the ordinance and testified before city council on behalf of the new flag. Mayor Vera Katz applauded the initiative and oversaw the raising on the council chambers' pole of the first new flag (manufactured and donated by Elmer's Flag & Banner).

DESIGNER: Douglas Lynch, 89, a nationally-known, award-winning graphic designer, created this revision of his previous flag. Believing his original design could be simplified, and seeking an opportunity to remove the city seal placed upon it by the former city council, he developed a new version after his presentation to the Portland Flag Association on the history of the 1969 flag.

MORE ABOUT THE FLAG: To allow for normal attrition in flag stocks, the ordinance of adoption made the previous flag equally valid until 31 December 2004.

In the 1980s, the city's Office of Neighborhood Associations sponsored the development and adoption of flags for the city's 70+ neighborhoods, modeled in proportion (3:4) on the flags of Sienna, Italy. These flags are occasionally displayed in city hall.

FORMER FLAGS: Portland has recognized four previous flags, of varying levels of acceptance.

In April 1969 the Commercial Club of Portland proposed a flag for the city, asserting that previous designs had never been officially adopted. That proposal consisted of a white field with the city seal in gold in the center, flanked by two red roses with **World Port of the Pacific** above and **City of Roses** below.

Mayor Terry Schrunk referred the design to the Portland Art Commission. Mrs. Gus (Libby) Solomon, chair of the commission, instead announced a plan to hire a qualified designer to design an official Portland flag for $500. She invited Douglas Lynch, former commission chair and prominent graphic designer to compete. He declined, describing the process of creating and adopting an acceptable flag as "a project where even angels fear to tread". Instead he offered to draft criteria "by which an appropriate flag might be created", and polled the members of the city council and art commission in writing concerning the general character of the flag, color choice, and the use of the city seal. He found that all four city council members and none of the nine art commission members favored using the seal.

At Mrs. Solomon's urging, Lynch relented and designed a flag. On a field of bright medium green, its light blue stripes represent the Columbia and Willamette rivers in an offset cross, set toward the hoist. The stripes are fimbriated in white, gold, and white, with proportions of 1:2:1:2:1:2:1. Their intersection forms a small four-pointed star (a hypocycloid) in white, representing the city at the confluence of the rivers. Overruling Lynch's preference, the city council altered his final design, changing the canton to a dark blue and adding the city seal. The canton is dark with the seal centered in yellow and white. The dimensions of the canton are 13:14; the upper fly quarter, 11:36; lower hoist quarter, 11:16, and the lower fly, 13:34. The width of the cross figure is 10 units. The city council adopted the flag by ordinance amid lively citywide discussion on 8 January 1970. Lynch called the design process "as much diplomatic as it was artistic".

In December 1957, the Lang Syne Society, composed of "senior citizens of Portland who have been engaged in its businesses, industries and professions for 30 years or more", launched a contest among the local high schools for a city flag design. The society felt that Portland, one of the only large cities without a flag, needed a municipal flag. Among 51 designs, the prize of $200 went to the winner, Philip Schaffer of Franklin High School, at the 2 April 1958 meeting when the flag was introduced to the city council by city commissioner Ormond R. Bean. Although the flag was not adopted officially, the Lang Syne Society did have a flag made and presented it to Mayor Terry Shrunk on January 1, 1959. It hung in the council chambers until 1970.

The flag has a medium blue field, with proportions of 3:5. At the hoist, about one-sixth of the field's length, is a vertical gold stripe on which **1851** (the year of the city's incorporation) runs downward vertically in large black numerals. Centered on the remaining blue portion of the field is a circular figure depicting the city's pioneer beginnings, although it is not Portland's official seal. The circle is bordered by a green ring edged on both sides by a narrow yellow line. Centered over the top portion is **Portland**, in black, clockwise. On the lower portion, beginning about at 8 o'clock and ending at about 4 o'clock, appears **Rose Festival City**, also in black (several other cities were also known as "The City of Roses"

at the time, so "Festival" was added as a distinction). On either side of the ring, centered are two roses, yellow over red, with stems and leaves. The central portion of the circle shows a snow-capped mountain scene with evergreen trees, and in the center foreground is a covered wagon and a pioneer cabin. The diameter of the circle is about one-third of the length of the entire field.

In June 1950, Mayor Dorothy McCullough Lee sought a municipal flag to fly along with the state flag. Benson High School's band director Norman Street worked with art teacher Harry Matheson to design a flag. It consists of the city seal centered on a white background. **City of Roses** appears centered above the seal, and **Portland, Oregon** appears centered below. Although Mayor Lee liked the flag very much, she failed to have it adopted, perhaps because of her rocky relationship with the city commissioners. While she had promised to use "whatever legal hocus pocus" necessary to make the flag official, one commissioner later reported "Mrs. Lee might have 'hocused', but she forgot to poke us." However, a flag was manufactured, and Benson's marching band and armed color guard carried it for several years in the annual Rose Festival Parade.

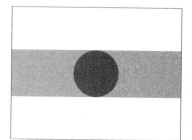

In 1917, Mayor Harry R. Albee appointed a committee to ascertain if Portland needed a flag to accompany its new slogan, "Your Portland and Mine". The committee examined the flags of 31 other prominent U.S. cities and determined Portland should have a flag, appointing Morris H. Whitehouse to lead a flag design contest. Having published extensive specifications, the committee received several proposals. Design number 8, by H. W. Frederick, won first place and $25. It is a horizontal tribar of equal white, blue, and white stripes, the blue stripe representing the Willamette River. A red circle centered on the blue stripe represents the city of Portland. However, the committee found that the best design did not measure up to the standards outlined in the contest guidelines. The flag did not appear to have "certain important requisites, such as historical association dating back to the earliest periods of the city's history", as Whitehouse made clear in the specifications. The flag did not express any apparent "robust civic ideal" or "common aim and purpose", nor did it convey "civic spirit". Joining the patriotic fervor of World War I, the committee recommended that Portland instead fly the Stars and Stripes for the time being. The Frederick design was never adopted. Mason Kaye

PROVIDENCE, RHODE ISLAND

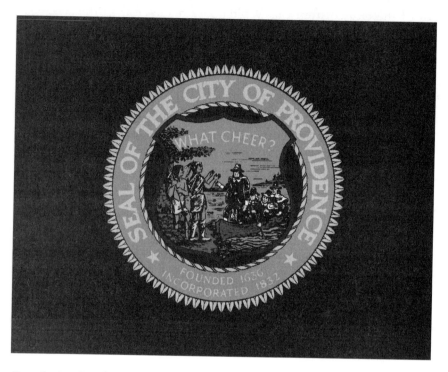

Population Rank: U.S... # 119
            Rhode Island ...... # 1

Proportions: 43:55 (official)

Adopted: 9 April 1915 (official)

DESIGN: According to the latest ordinance of adoption of the flag of Providence:

The flag of the city shall be of silk and the color shall be dark blue. In the center of the flag there shall be a white circle thirty-six inches in diameter. The seal of the city shall be embroidered on or painted in natural colors in the said white circle. In general all lettering and numbering shall be in gold.... (Ordinance 1941, ch. 1058 & 14; *Rev. Ordinances* 1946, ch. 13 & 14.)

SYMBOLISM: Another city ordinance gives the meaning of the city seal:

The blazon or description of figures on the city seal shall represent the historical story of the founding of the City of Providence in 1636. The Indians are standing on slate rock which is on a point of land covered with forest trees on the west bank of the Seekonk River. The Indians are extending friendly greetings, by raising their arms and crying out 'WHAT CHEER, NETOP?' to an approaching canoe which contains the early settlers, Roger Williams and his companions. Roger Williams, the founder of the City of Providence, and the State of Rhode Island, stands in the bow of the canoe and acknowledges the greetings of the friendly Indians by raising his right arm. (Ordinance of 1941, sec. 2-336.)

Although there is no official symbolism regarding the colors blue and white, in a 1920 newspaper article mentions the "adherence to the traditional 'blue and white' of colony and early Statehood days". *NETOP* is omitted on the seal.

HOW SELECTED: A city council committee solicited designs.

DESIGNER: Alderman E. Merle Bixby.

MORE ABOUT THE FLAG: In a photograph in the *Providence Sunday Journal* of 19 December 1920, the seal on the city flag has **PROVIDENCE** on the top section of the seal and the numerals **1636** below it. There is a ring of gold encircling the seal and the scene of the Indians greeting Roger Williams and his companions is within the inner circle, without the shield. It also has a different artistic rendition of this historical encounter.

Today the flag has the correct seal on the flag, as described in the ordinance of 1941. The scene showing Roger William's arrival at the site of Providence is on a shield in the center of the seal and a circle of rope surrounds the shield. The outer circumference of the seal is saw-toothed. The wording, **SEAL OF THE CITY OF PROVIDENCE**, is along the top of the seal and in smaller lettering is **FOUNDED 1636** above **INCORPORATED 1832** at the bottom the seal. Two stars separate the upper and lower inscriptions.

The flag came about when Alderman Bixby noticed the color company in a Providence police force parade carrying the United States flag and the Rhode Island state flag, but not a city flag. He brought the matter to the attention of the city council in 1914. A committee then solicited designs but found none acceptable. The committee then asked Alderman Bixby to create a design, which it adopted in 1915.

OTHER FLAGS: The Providence City Council has its own flag. It is white with two narrow dark blue stripes, one at the top and one at the bottom of the flag (the blue stripes represent the old Providence Plantations, which ran in narrow strips of land from the river). In the center is a dark blue disk with the seal of the Providence City Council embroidered or painted on it in gold. Encircling the seal are 15 gold stars, one for each ward of the city.   JC

PROVO, UTAH

Population Rank: U.S... # 219
Utah...... # 2

Proportions: Approximately
4:7 (usage)

Adopted: 1989 (official status uncertain)

DESIGN: Provo's flag has a white field with **Provo** running across the center in gray-shadowed black letters slanting slightly from lower hoist to upper fly. Below, and slanted parallel to the letters but beginning about two letter-spaces ahead of it, is a narrow multicolored stripe beginning with red at the hoist and shifting respectively into violet, blue, green, yellow, orange, and back to red. (The stripe is also sometimes shown as omitting the red at the hoist and beginning with violet.)

SYMBOLISM: The colored stripe "indicates diversity, technology, and the exciting upward growth of the city", according to the city's administration.

HOW SELECTED: By the municipal council.

DESIGNER: Stephen Hales Creative Design.

MORE ABOUT THE FLAG: The city's administration lends city flags to civic groups for use in special ceremonies.

FORMER FLAG: An earlier flag of Provo was in use for some years after 1989. The field of this flag is 3 by 5 units, red at the hoist and blue at the fly, separated by a large, white, square-block P, slightly slanted toward the fly, and extending from the bottom edge of the flag to the top edge. The lower stroke of the "P" curves downward to the field's center, but does not close completely. In the lower fly is **1849**, the year Provo was founded, in white block numerals. (The illustration of this flag in the official ordinances shows proportions of 6:7 and no date, which may have been added later.)

JP

RALEIGH, NORTH CAROLINA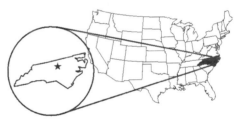

Population Rank: U.S. ..... # 62
North Carolina ...... # 2

Proportions: 14:23 (official);
2:3 (usage)

Adopted: 31 May 1899 (official); modified 25 April 1960

DESIGN: Raleigh's flag is one of the very few double-sided U.S. civic flags, no doubt because such flags are more costly to manufacture. Both sides have the same field, a vertical tribar of equal red, white, and red stripes. The front of the flag displays in its center the city seal, surrounded by a gold ring. On it **CITY OF RALEIGH** curves clockwise in the upper half and **NORTH CAROLINA** curves counterclockwise in the lower half, separated by dots, all in black. On the seal's white field is a green oak tree, with **ESTABLISHED 1792** curved counterclockwise below in small black letters. Surrounding the seal is an open wreath of green oak leaves and gold acorns, tied with a gold ribbon at its base.

The reverse of the flag displays in its center the arms of Sir Walter Raleigh with crest and motto, described in the 1960 ordinance:

A shield in red with five lozenges in silver from the dexter or left hand upper corner, touching at points, in a diagonal line to the sinister or right hand lower curve (pale-wise in bend). The crest shall be a stag upon a bandeau of six twists, straight, and having the same tinctures as shield and charges, the metal being the first twist on the dexter side. Beneath the shield shall be a red ribbon bearing the Motto of Sir Walter Raleigh, Amore et Virtute ....

SYMBOLISM: Red and white are the colors of Sir Walter Raleigh, the 16th-century English nobleman for whom the city is named. The oak tree and wreath with acorns recall the city's nickname, "City of the Oaks". The deer on the crest of the arms is a play on the name Raleigh, derived from two Anglo-Saxon words meaning "meadow of the deer".

HOW SELECTED: In 1899 the city wanted to present a city flag to the captain of the cruiser *USS Raleigh* (launched on 31 March 1892). The board of aldermen established a flag committee to develop a new flag, which was sewed by a Miss Kate Densen for $52.

DESIGNER: The flag committee.

MORE ABOUT THE FLAG: The ordinance of 1960 modified the flag slightly from the original ordinance of 1899. The later version omits the date from the seal's ring and places it with **Established** in small letters at the base of the tree. On the reverse, the full depiction of the arms was simplified in the later ordinance. The original flag of 1899, sewn by Miss Densen, is displayed in a glass case in the city's government complex.   JP

RAPID CITY, SOUTH DAKOTA

Star of the West
Rapid City, South Dakota

Population Rank: U.S. ... # 539
                South Dakota .... # 3

Proportions: 2:3 (usage)

Adopted: 1990 (official)

DESIGN: Rapid City's flag has a white field, 2 units high by 3 units wide. About a quarter-unit from the top **Star of the West** is centered in red, in a font resembling Brush Script MT, with its capital letters about an eighth-unit high. Another eighth-unit below that legend is **Rapid City, South Dakota**, centered in the same size and type of script, in dark blue. Centered in the lower half of the field is the city's seal, all in gold white. Its top is at the field's midpoint and its bottom is approximately an eighth-unit from the flag's lower edge. The seal's diameter is 1.5 units; its outer edge is surrounded with 50 small triangles, points outwards, as if it were affixed to a document. Immediately within the outer edge is a ring about an eighth-unit in width. It is divided into an upper and lower segment, each with rounded ends that do not quite meet at the seal's horizontal midpoint on either side, where a small white dot on the gold background marks the divisions. Arching clockwise in the upper segment is **RAPID CITY**, and curving counterclockwise in the lower segment is **SOUTH DAKOTA**, all in an Ariel-type font. The central disk shows Mount Rushmore National Memorial in outline. Centered above the memorial in small capital letters is **INCORPORATED**; centered below it is **1882**.

SYMBOLISM: "Star of the West" is the city's motto. Mount Rushmore stands 35 miles southwest of Rapid City in South Dakota's famed Black Hills. The memorial was carved between 1927 and 1941 under the direction of sculptor Gutzon Borglum to exemplify the first 150 years of American history. Depicting four U.S. presidents (George Washington, Thomas Jefferson, Theodore Roosevelt, and Abraham Lincoln), the memorial symbolizes the birth, growth, development, and preservation of the nation. The seal also commemorates the city's incorporation in 1882. The indented edge of the city seal recalls the shape of the South Dakota seal on the state flag; its golden color recalls the outer rim of that seal. The other colors in the Rapid City flag—red, white, and blue—reflect those of the national flag.

HOW SELECTED: Developed by the mayor's office staff.

DESIGNER: Kay Rippentrop and the staff in the mayor's office.

MORE ABOUT THE FLAG: Information from available sources about the flag's proportions is uncertain. The ratio of 2:3 seems to be the most accurate.   JP

RICHMOND, VIRGINIA ⊙

Population Rank: U.S. ..... # 94
Virginia ...... # 4

Proportions: 3:5 (official)

Adopted: 24 May 1993 (official)

DESIGN: Richmond's flag has a field of dark blue on its upper two-thirds. The lower third is divided into four horizontal stripes of white, red, white, and red, in proportions of 1:3:1:3. In the center of the blue field is a three-quarter silhouette of a bareheaded boatman in white, standing with his right leg slightly raised as if it rests on a seat, and poling his boat toward the hoist. The white boat melds with the top white stripe, which has four slight bumps resembling waves and thus gives the appearance of water. In a three-quarters circle around the boatman are 9 five-pointed white stars (were the circle closed, there would be 12 stars). The boatman and stars occupy just slightly less than half the total field.

SYMBOLISM: The city describes the symbolism in "Richmond and Its Flag":

The faceless boatman, as he poles to the honor side of the flag, symbolizes the tens of thousands of anonymous individuals, composed of a multiplicity of nationalities and races, who through the ages determined Richmond's homogeneous character and contributed to the City's success, growth and progress. Surrounding this symbol of our river's power is an arc of nine stars. Each represents a present state that was once part of the Commonwealth of Virginia over which Richmond was their capital in the nation's infancy— Virginia, West Virginia, Kentucky, Ohio, Indiana, Illinois, Michigan, Wisconsin, and Minnesota.

The city's colors, red and blue, date to 1784 when the mayor, Robert Mitchell, added strips of red and blue ribbon when he affixed the city seal to documents. When asked why, he responded, "The blue signifies the river from which all life flows, and the red is for the infernal red clay that is always under our feet." Richmond is situated on the James River.

HOW SELECTED: On 22 July 1991, an anonymous donor gave $12,000 "to be used for the design of a devisal of arms, including shield, crest, supporters and badge, in connection with the creation of a new City flag". The city council authorized establishing a flag committee to design the flag.

DESIGNER: The flag committee.

MORE ABOUT THE FLAG: Use of the city flag "except for the usual and customary official purposes, including decoration and display" is prohibited by ordinance (28 February 2000) unless specifically authorized by the city manager.

FORMER FLAG: The earlier flag of Richmond is double-sided with a dark blue field. On the front side occupying about the center third of the field is a "Norman" shield in white, featuring the central figure from the city's seal. In the center of the field is the allegorical Justice, also called *Vindicatrix*, or "the Spirit of the South", robed in a pink *chiton* (Greek gown) and a *himation* (drape) in white with blue shadings. Her hair is brown and she is blindfolded. In her right hand she holds a sword upright; in her left, the scales of justice. A green tobacco plant behind her symbolizes one of Richmond's early important products. Above her head, running across the center third of the shield, is the Latin motto **SIC ITUR AD ASTRA** ("Such is the way to the stars") in black. Arched over all this, beginning and ending at the shield's vertical midpoint, in similar letters, is **RICHMOND VA, FOUNDED BY WILLIAM BYRD MDCCXXXVII.**

On the reverse side in the center is a red shield. The top half of the shield bears the Confederate Battle Flag: on a red field, a blue saltire edged in white with 13 white five-pointed stars. Below it is a white horizontal bar, with **DEO VINDICE** ("Vindicated by God"), centered in two lines in blue.

This flag was designed by Carlton McCarthy, an early 20th-century mayor of Richmond, and adopted officially in 1914. Its proportions are 3:5. The designers intended its symbolism to recall Richmond's role as "the capital of the great southern Confederacy [1861-1865] and the leading city of the south", and strongly defended the "historic connection with the Confederate cause … [as] part of the history of the world from which we cannot be separated."   JP

RIVERSIDE, CALIFORNIA

Population Rank: U.S. .... # 67
                California .... # 10

Proportions: 5:8 (usage)

Adopted: 17 January 1967 (official)

DESIGN: The field of Riverside's flag is divided horizontally, gold over blue. In the center of the flag is the city's logo, 7.5 units in diameter on a field of 10 by 16 units. The outer ring of the logo is edged in blue. The field within the ring is white and has a width of one unit. Curved clockwise above is **RIVERSIDE**, below, counterclockwise, is **CALIFOR-NIA**, all in blue. In the logo's center, blue on a white field, is a symbol described as a Native American "rain cross", a trapezoidal figure surmounted by a double cross. The sides of the rain cross, which cross each other at their junctions, are 3 units, as is the top; the bottom side is 4 units. Within the rain cross is a bell, 1.5 units from its top to the bottom of the clapper, suspended from the top side.

SYMBOLISM: The bell and rain cross are taken from "the world-famous collection of the Mission Inn", according to the city's publications. The bell recalls the many missions of the Spanish missionaries along *El Camino Real* in early California; the rain cross recalls the Native Americans who were the first to live in what is today Riverside.

HOW SELECTED: By recommendation of the chamber of commerce.

DESIGNER: Charles L. Bridges, Chairman of the Mayor's Conference on Civic Beauty.

MORE ABOUT THE FLAG: After the flag's design was adopted, the city ordered 16 flags to fly at various sites around the city, and two flags of rayon taffeta with a white fringe for indoor use.

FORMER FLAG: On 22 November 1966, barely two months before adopting the current city flag, the city council had approved a similar flag in the same colors with a modified version of the city seal, but apparently it was never used. The city seal is shaped somewhat like a shield, so that, ironically, the logo looks more like the traditional seal than the seal itself. The top of the seal curves upward. Following the same curve, immediately below it is **INCORPORATED 1883** in blue on white. Below that legend, and forming the top of an "inner shield", is what appears to be the Native Americans rain bird, in gold. On a blue field below the rain bird are three figures: On the hoist side is a branch of three oranges; in the center, what appears to be a bundle of rods (the Roman *fasces*, or symbol of authority); and on the fly side a cornucopia curved over two small figures, all in gold. At the bottom of the "outer" shield is **CITY OF**, in blue on white. Across the lower stripe is **RIVERSIDE, CALIFORNIA**, in gold on blue. (Seal colors reconstructed.)   JP

ROCHESTER, NEW YORK

ROCHESTER

Population Rank: U.S. ..... # 79
New York ...... # 3

Proportions: 10:19 (official)
2:3 and 3:5 (usage)

Adopted: 25 June 1934 (official)

DESIGN: According to the ordinance of adoption:

*The flag presented to the City of Rochester by The Rochester Historical Society, June 21st, 1934, is hereby designated as the official flag of the City of Rochester, having the following description: Said flag to be of three colors, arranged in perpendicular bars of equal width, federal blue nearest the pole, white in the center, and golden yellow on the extreme of the flag, from the pole. Upon the white center shall be inscribed the Coat of Arms of the Rochester Family, as allowed by the Herald's Visitation to the County of Essex, England, in the year 1558. Beneath the said Coat of Arms shall appear the word **Rochester** in a downward curved line. The hoist and fly* *of said flag shall correspond with those of the Flag of the United States of America, particularly so when used in conjunction with our National flag.* (Ordinance 4079.)

SYMBOLISM: According to Mayor Hiram H. Edgerton, who designed the flag in 1910: *The blue represents our exceptional water and electric power; the white, the cleanliness of our city; the gold, our financial strength and industrial prosperity....* The city is located at the mouth of the Genesee River on Lake Ontario. It is also on the New York State Barge Canal system (the Erie Canal created an industrial boom for Rochester in the 1820s).

Originally Ebenezer "Indian" Allen had settled here in 1789, but by 1791 he had abandoned his sawmill and gristmill. Then in 1803, Colonel Nathaniel Rochester, traveled with two companions by horse from Maryland to Genesee country. Colonel Rochester purchased 100 acres of land when he saw the abundance of water resources in the area and the potential for factories. By 1817 Rochester had become a village. The Rochester family coat of arms commemorates Colonel Rochester and recognizes his contributions to its history.

In 1933 Edward R. Foreman, the city historian, wrote a brief history on *The Official Flag of Rochester,* in which he described the symbols on the Rochester family coat of arms. The shield is gold with a horizontal black bar midway across it and occupying one-third of the width of the field. Three black waxing crescent moons (horns up) are placed two above and one below the bar. The shield has a narrow red border. According to Foreman, the crane (in the crest) represents vigilance; the three crescents symbolize fertility and prosperity; and the black bar represents a waistband, one of the symbols of high command in knighthood. The red border on the shield symbolizes military affiliation. (Although these emblems are given traditional heraldic meanings, there is no documentary proof that they relate to the symbols on the Rochester family arms).

HOW SELECTED: Upon learning that the flag had never been formally adopted by the city council, the historical society brought the matter to the council at the urging of the city historian, Edward R. Foreman.

DESIGNER: Mayor Hiram H. Edgerton.

MORE ABOUT THE FLAG: On 15 September 1910, Mayor Edgerton had formally designated this flag as official but the common council never voted on it. The Rochester Chamber of Commerce, by resolution, approved the design on 19 September, but because the common council never made a decision, the flag remained unofficial until 1934.

A variant of the official flag contains a narrow blue line surrounding the entire coat of arms in the center of the flag. 10:19 are the same proportions as the United States flag.

OTHER FLAGS: In 1979, the city adopted a "city banner" but this did not replace the official Rochester flag. The flag has a royal blue field with a stylized five-petal lilac flower divided by five lines representing a water wheel, all in white. • **Flour City** • **Flower City** • **City of Rochester, N.Y.** surrounds the petal in gold. The city was at one time a major flour-milling center, and later known for its tree nurseries and seed houses, hence the play on the words "Flour — Flower". The gold is PMS 124, the blue is PMS 287.

FORMER FLAG: Mayor James G. Culer created and used a "mayor's flag" during his 1904-08 term of office. It was white with the city seal in gold in the center.   JC 📛

SACRAMENTO, CALIFORNIA ✪

CITY OF SACRAMENTO

Population Rank: U.S. ..... # 40
California ...... # 6

Proportions: 1:2 (usage)

Adopted: 15 August 1989 (official)

DESIGN: Sacramento's flag has a modernistic design with five colors on its field. The central figure is a stylized white S curving lazily from the upper fly to the lower hoist. On a field of 16 by 32 units, the figure is 3 units wide at the fly and 1 unit below the upper fly corner, and 2 units wide at the hoist and 4 units above the lower hoist corner. The figure is 6 units wide at its widest point in the center of the flag. The field above the "S" is a medium blue. At the upper hoist corner is a green half-disk, 3 units at its widest point, and extending 6 units from the top edge. The field below the "S" is a dark blue. At the center fly is a half-disk in gold, smaller than the disk at the hoist, 4 units from the bottom edge and 6 units from the top edge. At its widest point it is about 3 units. Across the bottom of the dark blue field is **CITY OF SACRAMENTO** in white letters one unit high in an Arial-type font.

SYMBOLISM: White represents the city's virtue, strength, and bright future. The two blue sections represent the city's rivers (the Sacramento and the American), green stands for the agricultural heritage, and the gold color represents the gold miners so important in the history of California and of Sacramento, the center of the Gold Country and the 1849 Gold Rush.

HOW SELECTED: On 21 February 1989 the city council approved a resolution setting aside $5,000 for the design and manufacture of a new city flag by the Art Directors and Artists Club of Sacramento in preparation for celebration of the city's Sesquicentennial on August 13 of that year. A team of five designers from the club was chosen to develop a flag. The team proposed four designs from which the city council chose the finalist, after public display and comment.

DESIGNER: The design team comprised Lisa Bacchini, of Lisa Bacchini Graphic Design and Illustrations; Frank Burris, Kramer Carton Co.; Kyp Griffin, Tackett-Barbaria Design; Laurie Lewis, University of California at Davis, Publications Department; and Mark Price, Trimline/ 3M and Graphic Design by Price.

MORE ABOUT THE FLAG: The design team undertook the flag design as a community service project without compensation.

FORMER FLAG: The design of the previous Sacramento flag resulted from of the efforts of E. A. Combatalade, the founder of the Camellia Festival Association that held an annual celebration in the city. Combatalade felt that the city should have a flag to celebrate its 125th anniversary, especially since it was one of the last major California cities without a flag. He suggested key design elements to Goodwin & Cole, flag manufacturers, who prepared a sketch of a possible flag. Combatalade took the sketch to Max Depew, assistant editor of the *Sacramento Bee*, who thought that the elements could be rearranged more attractively. He and Combatalade made a new sketch of what ultimately became the city's first flag. The city council officially adopted the design on 23 January 1964.

The flag's proportions are 7:11. The white field has four major elements. Centered at the hoist is the C. P. Huntington locomotive, in profile toward the fly, commemorating Sacramento as the terminus of the nation's first transcontinental railroad. The locomotive is black with a red side, a red "cow-catcher" in front, and a red coal tender following. Centered at the fly is a Pony Express rider on horseback, headed at full gallop toward the hoist, marking Sacramento's role as the western terminus of the Pony Express. The rider, bent over the horse, wears a coonskin cap, a red kerchief and red shirt, and dark blue pants.

In the lower center, extending from slightly above the field's midpoint down about one-third of the flag's width is the state capitol dome, denoting Sacramento as the state's capital. The dome is gold, supported by two stories of white columns detailed in black. At the base of this figure is a red camellia flower, a green leaf on either side. In the upper center, above the dome, is a bearded miner, kneeling by a stream, panning for gold, and symbolizing the discovery of gold in California. The figure is in partial profile toward the hoist. He wears a brown wide-brimmed hat, a red shirt, and black pants. A miner's pick-ax lies on the ground at his right. Arched over the miner's head in the center of the field is **SACRAMENTO**; running horizontally and centered below the camellia is **CALIFORNIA**, all in blue block letters.   JP 🛡

St. Louis, Missouri

Population Rank: U.S. ..... # 49
            Missouri ...... # 2

Proportions: 5:8 (official)

Adopted: 3 February 1964 (official)

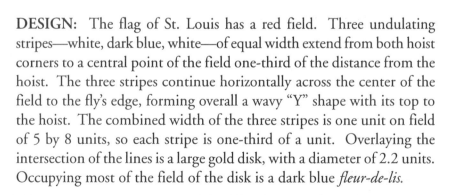

DESIGN: The flag of St. Louis has a red field. Three undulating stripes—white, dark blue, white—of equal width extend from both hoist corners to a central point of the field one-third of the distance from the hoist. The three stripes continue horizontally across the center of the field to the fly's edge, forming overall a wavy "Y" shape with its top to the hoist. The combined width of the three stripes is one unit on field of 5 by 8 units, so each stripe is one-third of a unit. Overlaying the intersection of the lines is a large gold disk, with a diameter of 2.2 units. Occupying most of the field of the disk is a dark blue *fleur-de-lis*.

SYMBOLISM: The wavy lines emanating from the hoist corners symbolize the Missouri and Mississippi Rivers, which meet at St. Louis. The horizontal wavy line across the field symbolizes the Mississippi River continuing alone. The gold disk (*bezant*) represents the city of St. Louis itself, located at the confluence of the two rivers. It also symbolizes the Louisiana Purchase, in which the city was included. (The ordinance of adoption explains that heraldically, the bezant, or Byzantine coin, signifies money, or simply, purchase.) The *fleur-de-lis* recalls the early French history of the city and the French saint for whom the city is named. The flag's colors reflect those of Spain (red and yellow), Bourbon France (white and yellow), Napoleonic and Republican France (blue, white, and red), and the United States (red, white, and blue).

HOW SELECTED: On 28 November 1962, Mayor Raymond R. Tucker appointed a five-member committee to design a new flag for the city's bicentennial celebration in 1964. The committee consisted of Charles Nagel, director of the City Art Museum (chairman); Dr. Arthur W. Proetz, a retired physician versed in St. Louis history; George R. Brooks, director of the Missouri Historical Society; Charles van Ravenswaay, a former director of the Missouri Historical Society and president of Old Sturbridge Village in Massachusetts; and Professor Theodore Sizer of Bethany, Connecticut, director emeritus of the Yale Gallery of Fine Arts. An anonymous gift of $1,000 through the City Art Museum funded the design project.

DESIGNER: Professor Theodore Sizer, of the committee.

MORE ABOUT THE FLAG: The ordinance of adoption does not specify the proportions, but does make Sizer's design official, and the proportions of that flag are 5:8. Sizer's original design had the field between the two rivers at the hoist in blue, but at the suggestion of the Rev. Maurice McNamee, S.J., chairman of the fine arts committee of St. Louis University, the board of aldermen changed the field to one of all red.

FORMER FLAG: The previous flag of St. Louis was designed by Edward A. Krondl in 1916; although it was apparently in use from that time, it was not made official until much later (either 1946 or 1950,

according to conflicting reports). The flag is a horizontal tribar of equal red, white, and dark blue stripes. In each of the four corners of the field is a white five-pointed star. On the center of the field is a large blue shield, almost as broad at the base as it is at the top, outlined in white. On a field of 2 by 3 units, it measures 1 unit in width by 1.25 units in height. On the shield is a crowned St. Louis in profile toward the hoist, his right arm holding a cross aloft, astride a horse (right foreleg raised). The ground on which they stand is marked with a line, and below, centered, is a *fleur-de-lis*. The entire charge is white, detailed in dark blue.

The four stars represent St. Louis's rank as the fourth largest city in the United States in 1916. By 1964 the eponymous figure on the shield seemed to many in the city inappropriate for the city's flag, a sentiment that helped spur the adoption of a new flag.   JP 🛡

ST. PAUL, MINNESOTA

Population Rank: U.S. ..... # 59
         Minnesota ...... # 2

Proportions: 4:5 (usage)

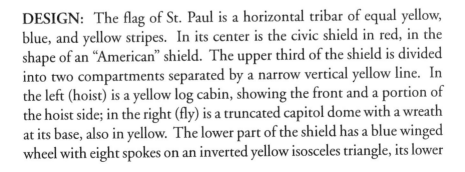

Adopted: 22 November 1932 (official)

DESIGN: The flag of St. Paul is a horizontal tribar of equal yellow, blue, and yellow stripes. In its center is the civic shield in red, in the shape of an "American" shield. The upper third of the shield is divided into two compartments separated by a narrow vertical yellow line. In the left (hoist) is a yellow log cabin, showing the front and a portion of the hoist side; in the right (fly) is a truncated capitol dome with a wreath at its base, also in yellow. The lower part of the shield has a blue winged wheel with eight spokes on an inverted yellow isosceles triangle, its lower point truncated in a concave arch. Above the shield, on the upper stripe, is a small blue five-pointed star. Below the shield, on the lower stripe, is a red ribbon with **SAINT PAUL** in yellow.

SYMBOLISM: According to the St. Paul Junior Chamber of Commerce:

A blue mid stripe represents the Mississippi River; a small cabin stands for Father Gaultier's original St. Paul chapel; a dome represents Minnesota's Capitol and capital; and a winged wheel indicates St. Paul's position as a transportation hub. The flag also contains a star of the north, symbolic of Minnesota, and a red shield, representing the progress and spirit of the city, while gold stripes are symbolic of the future.

HOW SELECTED: A citywide contest was sponsored by the St. Paul Association of Commerce.

DESIGNER: Gladys Mittle, an art student at the College of St. Catherine.

MORE ABOUT THE FLAG: Gaultier's log mission chapel was erected in 1841; called "St. Paul's", it gave the name to the village that grew up around it. The first major display of the city flag was on 30 March 1935, when thousands of the flags decorated the city for St. Paul Day.

JP

ST. PETERSBURG, FLORIDA

Population Rank: U.S. ..... # 68
Florida ...... # 4

Proportions: 11:18 (official)

Adopted: 17 February 1983 (official)

DESIGN: St. Petersburg's flag has five equal horizontal stripes of orange, red, green, dark blue, and medium blue, separated by white fimbriations. In the center, stretching from the top to the bottom edge, is a large white pelican in partially transparent silhouette, perched on a rock and facing the hoist.

SYMBOLISM: Red and orange are for St. Petersburg's abundant sunshine, green for the land, and the blues for the waters of Tampa Bay and the Gulf of Mexico that surround the city. The pelican, indigenous to the area, represents the environmental concerns of the citizens.

HOW SELECTED: In 1983, city officials determined that the old city logo (the city seal) was not easily reproduced or recognized by the public. They commissioned the city illustrator to design a new logo, a rectangle, which was also adopted as the city's flag.

DESIGNER: Ronald F. Whitney, Jr.

MORE ABOUT THE FLAG: Research by the city concerning the effectiveness of the flag/logo as seen by the public shows widely popular acceptance. The pelican has become something of a city mascot, which has translated into a "Feed the Pelican Fund" to provide food for the endangered brown pelican during the winter months.

FORMER FLAGS: St. Petersburg's first flag was adopted on 14 July 1927 after a contest supervised by a committee named by Mayor C. J. Maurer. The committee consisted of Ernest Kitche (the public works director who had initiated the idea of a municipal flag), Commissioner R. C. Purvis, and Lillian Moore. No monetary prize was offered, the city deeming that it would be sufficient honor to have one's design chosen as the city's flag. Not surprisingly, there were few entrants in the contest, which was won by Betsy Ross Flag Co. of Newburgh, New York.

The design finally chosen was a vertical tribar of equal blue, gold, and blue stripes, with the city's seal (adopted 11 July 1921) in the center. The seal has a beveled edge resembling a rope. A smaller concentric circle within the seal's edge forms a ring around the seal. On the ring's white field **CITY OF ST. PETERSBURG, FLORIDA** arches clockwise over the top half, and **RE-INCORPORATED A.D. 1903.** curves counterclockwise below. The color of the letters is not specified, but is likely dark blue. In the seal's center, on the hoist side, is a white pelican perched on a post, facing the hoist. On the fly side is a green palm tree, growing from the base of the seal. The foreground shows a sandy beach, probably golden yellow, with a white seven-petaled poinsettia lying at the base of the palm tree. From the beach to the horizon line, the horizontal midpoint of the seal, is the blue ocean. Above, between the pelican and the palm tree, is a gold sun, reflected in the water below. The sky is probably a light blue. An official mayor's flag, with the colors of the stripes reversed, was also adopted.

By 1951, Mayor S. C. Minshall and city council were unhappy that the city's name was not featured prominently on the flag. On January 16 of that year, the city council passed a resolution amending the 1927 ordinance *to provide that the flags have the words St. Petersburg, Florida in a crescent over the seal and the words The Sunshine City in a reverse crescent under the seal, the letters to be 2 to 3 inches in height, and to be in navy blue on the City Flag and in yellow on the Mayor's flag.*

The new flag design was never made. A flag manufacturer notified the city that he could not make an attractive flag according to the new specifications, and presented a different design in miniature form that converted the vertical tribar to a horizontal one, with nearly the same colors: dark blue, yellow, and dark blue. The seal remains on the center stripe. On the top stripe, in large gold letters is **ST. PETERSBURG, FLORIDA**, taking up most of the space on the stripe. On the blue stripe below, in a large gold script, is *"Sunshine City"*. The proportions are 4:7. A provision was initially made for the mayor's flag to be in reverse colors, but this idea was later abandoned, with the declaration that one city flag would serve all the city's needs. The horizontal design was adopted on 17 April 1951.

JP

SALEM, OREGON

Population Rank: U.S... # 158
Oregon...... # 3

Proportions: 2:3 (usage)

Adopted: 14 August 1972 (official)

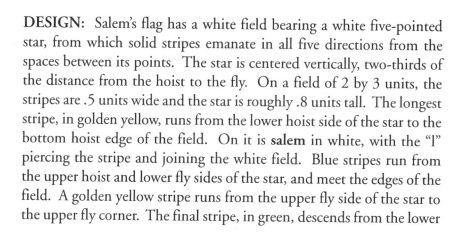

DESIGN: Salem's flag has a white field bearing a white five-pointed star, from which solid stripes emanate in all five directions from the spaces between its points. The star is centered vertically, two-thirds of the distance from the hoist to the fly. On a field of 2 by 3 units, the stripes are .5 units wide and the star is roughly .8 units tall. The longest stripe, in golden yellow, runs from the lower hoist side of the star to the bottom hoist edge of the field. On it is **salem** in white, with the "l" piercing the stripe and joining the white field. Blue stripes run from the upper hoist and lower fly sides of the star, and meet the edges of the field. A golden yellow stripe runs from the upper fly side of the star to the upper fly corner. The final stripe, in green, descends from the lower side of the star to the bottom edge of the flag. On it in white is a stylized image of the top portion of Oregon's state capitol, surmounted by its statue.

SYMBOLISM: The city describes the symbolism:

The flag's design symbolizes the essence of the City of Salem. It is the capital of Oregon. Into Salem flows the input of the State and from Salem comes the decision and directions for Oregon. The star—the symbol used on maps to indicate a State capital ... The decorative element is the landmark sculpture of the Oregon Pioneer on the top of the Capitol Building. The colors were chosen to symbolize the ideals of the City of Salem ...the dominant background of white shows peace and honor. The design utilizes summer blue, autumn golden yellow, and spring green; the blue being sky and water, the green showing freshness and eternal hope, the golden yellow of harvest indicating fulfillment and the enjoyment of nature's bounty. Together these colors also indicate the four seasons and are reminiscent of Salem's setting, between mountains, rivers, and fields.

HOW SELECTED: Chosen from designs submitted in a flag contest beginning 1 February and closing 1 March 1972. An outside consultant examined and combined the designs. A final version was presented to a joint meeting of the mayor's flag committee and the city council on 4 May and at a ceremonial meeting on 8 May, where the winners were announced. Ordinance 104-72 made the flag official.

DESIGNER: Arvid Orbeck, a local designer, from a composite of ideas from the flag contest.

MORE ABOUT THE FLAG: The Salem Federal Savings & Loan Association paid for the costs of the flag contest, including radio and television advertising and Mr. Orbeck's fee.   RM

SALT LAKE CITY, UTAH

Population Rank: U.S... # 111
Utah...... # 1

Proportions: 3:5 (usage)

Adopted: 23 September 1969 (official)

DESIGN: Salt Lake City's flag places the arms of the city in the center of a white field. They measure approximately 2.5 by 2.25 units on a field of 3 by 5 units. An outline of a beehive in dark brown takes the place of the traditional shield. The field within shows a green plain in the lower half, the bottom of which is partially obscured by a heraldic ribbon. At the fly side of the scene is a covered wagon, white with orange wheels, pulled by a team of four dark brown oxen headed toward the hoist. The lead oxen are approximately three-fourths of the distance from the fly. Immediately below them is "**THIS IS THE PLACE**" in black.

The midpoint of the scene forms a horizon with low dark blue mountains across the plain. Between the mountains and the plain is a narrow white line shaded in blue. An orange setting sun with 32 rays of varying lengths fills the white sky. The hoist supporter is a pioneer woman, dressed in a long-sleeved dress; a boy stands in front of her. The fly supporter is a pioneer man, holding a long handled shovel. The figures are in natural colors. The heraldic ribbon below is dark blue, backed in white, with **SALT LAKE CITY** curved across the central part in an Arial-type font in white. Above the beehive alight two seagulls, in natural coloring. Both have wings outstretched, and while the gull toward the fly (which faces front) has landed and its feet are not visible, the gull toward the hoist and facing the fly has yet to touch down.

SYMBOLISM: The beehive refers to Utah's nickname, "The Beehive State". The scene suggests the arrival of the Mormon pioneers at the Great Salt Lake in 1847, when their leader, Brigham Young, said, "This is the place", indicating where they would settle and found the city. The seagulls, the state bird, recall the seemingly miraculous arrival of a flock of seagulls early in the state's history to devour a plague of crickets (Mormon grasshoppers) that had threatened the new settlers' crops.

HOW SELECTED: In 1963, *The Deseret News*, a Salt Lake City newspaper, and the junior chamber of commerce sponsored a contest for a new city flag, with a prize to the winner of $100.

DESIGNER: J. Rulon Hales was the winner.

MORE ABOUT THE FLAG: The flag was not made until 1969, owing to the cost of manufacturing a flag with such a detailed design and with so many colors. Sue Larson and Cherie Horricks of the Highland High School Art Class, under the direction of Jack Vigos of the Art Department, created the first flag.   JP

SAN ANTONIO, TEXAS

Population Rank: U.S........ # 9
                      Texas....... # 2

Proportions: 5:9 (official)

Adopted: 27 August 1992 (official)

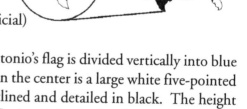

DESIGN: The field of San Antonio's flag is divided vertically into blue at the hoist and red at the fly. In the center is a large white five-pointed star on which is the Alamo outlined and detailed in black. The height of the star is nine-tenths the flag's width; the height of the Alamo is one-fourth the flag's width.

SYMBOLISM: The colors are those of the flags of Texas and the United States. The star also suggests the nickname of Texas, "The Lone Star State". The Alamo, a fort in San Antonio and the site of an important battle fought on 6 March 1836 by Texans in their war to gain independence from Mexico, symbolizes the city's role in that struggle.

HOW SELECTED: The flag is an updated version of an earlier flag which bore the name of the city and state. Pete Van de Putte, president of Dixie Flag Company, suggested to Mayor Nelson Wolff that more people might fly the flag if it were less expensive, perhaps by eliminating the costly lettering.

DESIGNER: The original flag was designed by William W. Herring, a Spanish-American War veteran. The sketch he made of the flag is dated 28 May 1933.

MORE ABOUT THE FLAG: The earlier version of the flag had large white block letters curved over the star, with **SAN AN** on the blue half and **TONIO** on the red. In the same letters, **TEXAS** was centered horizontally between the star's two lower points, with the "X" half on the blue and half on the red field. The flag was presented to city council on 18 April 1935 by the United Spanish-American War Veterans, but not adopted officially until 1976. The depiction of the Alamo is described variously as having been rendered as gray and as silver and gold. The official colors are PMS 286 (blue) and PMS 200 (red).

FORMER FLAG: San Antonio's first official flag was adopted on 25 January 1917. The flag has a white field with a large blue silhouette map of Texas in its center and **SAN AN-TONIO** in large white block letters across the center portion of the state. Below the city's name is the Alamo, in a buff color and marking the geographical location of San Antonio. The flag is 48 by 65 inches and its designer was Arthur Storms, a Shriner from the Alzafar Temple. The Shriners (a social and philanthropic men's organization) used the flag regularly at their national conventions in various cities for many years, but as time went by it was all but forgotten at city hall, even though it apparently was the official city flag until 1976.   JP

SAN DIEGO, CALIFORNIA

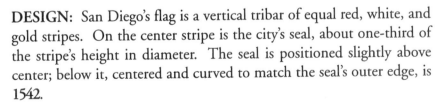

Population Rank: U.S. ...... # 7
California ...... # 2

Proportions: 2:3 (usage)

Adopted: 16 October 1934 (official)

DESIGN: San Diego's flag is a vertical tribar of equal red, white, and gold stripes. On the center stripe is the city's seal, about one-third of the stripe's height in diameter. The seal is positioned slightly above center; below it, centered and curved to match the seal's outer edge, is 1542.

The seal is elaborate. A white band, edged on both sides in gold, surrounds the seal. Beginning at 8 o'clock and extending to 4 o'clock, • THE CITY OF SAN DIEGO • STATE OF CALIFORNIA • runs clockwise in gold. In the remaining space on the band below, on a white heraldic ribbon edged in gold, is the city's motto, **SEMPER**

VIGILANS ("Always Vigilant") also in gold. The shield is slightly curved on both sides on the top edge, and indented slightly on either side near the top. Its field is gold, with a wavy blue bar across its center. At the top is a black Spanish caravel with red sails, flag, and pennon facing the hoist. In the base is an orange tree, in natural colors with fruit, with a black winged wheel on either side. The supporters are the Pillars of Hercules, entwined with gold ribbons, each pillar resting on a green dolphin with red eyes and fins, facing the shield's edges, their red tails linked below the shield. In the crest is a blue Carmelite belfry, from which hangs a gold bell.

SYMBOLISM: The explorer Juan Rodríguez Cabrillo discovered San Diego, the first California port entered by a Spanish ship, in 1542. Red and gold recall the Spanish flag, and red and white are also found in the United States flag. The gold is a reminder of the precious metal that transformed California from a wilderness to a prosperous state.

HOW SELECTED: The Native Sons of the Golden West, the hereditary organization also responsible for the adoption of the California state flag in 1911, developed the city flag and presented it to the city council.

DESIGNER: Uncertain. The designer is not specifically named, but the ordinance of adoption mentions Albert V. Mayrhofer as presenting the flag to the council. Whether he is the designer or just the representative of his organization is not certain.

MORE ABOUT THE FLAG: The detail on the seal does not permit any lettering to be seen on the ribbons entwined about the Pillars of Hercules and, in fact, there is no official reference to such lettering. However, the pillars as depicted on the flags of Spain typically have **PLUS** on the dexter ribbon and **ULTRA** on the sinister, together meaning "More Beyond". Since the ribbons are gold, one supposes that the lettering would be in red (the reverse of the pillars on the Spanish arms). None of the available examples of the seal, all small, show any lettering on the ribbons. JP

San Francisco, California

Population Rank: U.S..... # 13
          California...... # 4

Proportions: 3:5 (usage)

Adopted: 14 April 1900 (official); revised 30 December 1940

DESIGN: According to the 1940 ordinance:

The City and County of San Francisco shall have an official flag to be known as 'The Flag of San Francisco'. The flag shall be as hereinafter described, to-wit: 'A Phoenix rising from the flames, below which shall appear the motto **Oro en Paz—Fierro en Guerra'***, both in a golden yellow hue on a field of white, with the Flag itself bordered with gold.*

The words **San Francisco** *shall appear horizontally along the lower portion of the Flag, below the Phoenix and the Motto, in letters of appropriate size, rich blue in coloring.*

The wings of the phoenix are outspread and pictured above a ring of red flames, resembling an open crown, with eight points outlined in golden yellow. The scroll is segmented into three sections and is bordered in black to separate it from the white field. The Spanish motto means "Gold in Peace, Iron in War". The width of the gold border is one-eighth the height of the flag.

SYMBOLISM: In the words of Mayor Phelan in 1900, *It is singularly appropriate by reason of the fact that California is the Golden State and San Francisco has become the point of debarkation for our troops* [in the Spanish-American War] ... *Gold is emblematic of the abundance of nature, and iron of the fortitude and courage of men; but when the war ceases let us hope that the productive industries ... may permit us to read the inscription, 'Gold and Iron in Peace.'*

This motto, however, predates the Spanish-American War, appearing on a seal dating from 1859 (perhaps anticipating the Civil War). Others attribute the origin to Don Quixote and his instructions to Sancho Panza. The phoenix first appeared on a seal in 1852 as a crest to symbolize the city's resurgence from an earlier fire (Kenneth M. Johnson, *California Governmental Seals*, Castle Press, 1963: No. 8). The phoenix is a symbol of human aspiration and achievement, a mythological bird that lives for 500 years, then is consumed by flames and rises again from its ashes. In an alternate interpretation, the phoenix represents the city's emergence under the 1856 Municipal Consolidation Act as a city and county separate from San Mateo County. In any case, the symbol was unintentionally prophetic, as the flag was adopted six years before the great earthquake and fire of 1906.

HOW SELECTED: Chosen in a competition initiated by the mayor, James D. Phelan. He appointed as judges the commissioner of public works, the parks commissioner, and three members of the board of supervisors. The winning design was selected from among over 100 entries.

DESIGNER: Policeman John M. Gamble won the prize of $50 for his design.

MORE ABOUT THE FLAG: The words **SAN FRANCISCO** were not on the original flag. They were added by a resolution, first passed on 29 August 1938, that later resulted in the 1940 ordinance. The language of the resolution explains the addition with these words:

Whereas, many have marveled at the beauty of the Official Flag of the City and County of San Francisco and have inquired 'What flag is it?' because there is no wording to show; now, therefore, be it

Resolved, That there be added to the Official Flag ... of San Francisco the words San Francisco so that it will be identifiable to all who view it; and be it

*Further Resolved, That the words **San Francisco** be placed horizontally along the lower portion of the Flag, below the Phoenix and the Motto, in letters of appropriate size ... so that the Flag will be blue and gold on a field of white, symbolic of the blue skies of San Francisco, the gold of her commerce and industry and the white of her pure purpose to be a city of happy homes and contented, prosperous people.*

The original city flag had a plain white field, and was entrusted to the chief of police in May 1900 for use in parades and ceremonies. According to tradition, it was rescued in a paddy wagon from the flame-engulfed city hall in April 1906. That flag was replaced by a duplicate in 1926. In 1940, when pre-war patriotic fervor led the board of supervisors to authorize making more than one flag, the drafter of the specifications described the gold fringe of the 1926 ceremonial flag with the phrase *bordered with golden yellow.* This misinterpretation added the golden border to the flag's otherwise white field.   RM

SAN JOSE, CALIFORNIA

Population Rank: U.S..... # 11
            California...... # 3

Proportions: 3:5 (usage)

Adopted: 5 June 1984 (official)

DESIGN: The flag of San José is a horizontal tribar of gold, white, and blue stripes in proportions of 1:4:1. Centered on the white stripe is the city seal, one unit in diameter on a field of 3 by 5 units. The seal is encircled by a black-edged gold band, the outer edge of which is bordered by a narrow gold stripe, which in turn is bordered by a slightly wider black stripe. On the top half of the gold band in black block letters, clockwise, runs **CITY OF SAN JOSE**. Centered on the lower portion of the band is **CALIFORNIA**, in the same letters. Separating the two legends on either side is a small black six-pointed star. The field of the seal is white. In its center is a shock of wheat, with a bunch of purple grapes on either side curved along the seal's inner edge, their stems joined in a gold bow below the wheat. Centered below the seal, and attached to it, is a small gold cartouche-shaped oval bearing the legend **FOUNDED 1777**. The seal was adopted officially on 9 September 1850.

SYMBOLISM: The grapes and wheat sheaf indicate the area's main agricultural products in the mid-19th century.

HOW SELECTED: The flag was developed by the rules committee and the Historic Landmarks Commission of San José, beginning in August 1968, at the request of the city council.

DESIGNER: Unknown.

MORE ABOUT THE FLAG: The city's name is written with an accent on the letter "e" of "José", a convention that is frequently ignored. In any case, capital letters in Spanish are normally not accented unless the accent is needed for clarity.

FORMER FLAG: The first flag of San José was designed by Clyde Arbuckle, the city historian, who worked with the historic landmarks commission. The flag has a white field bordered with three stripes, one inside the other. From the outside edge, they are white, gold, and blue, the last two colors being those of California. The city seal, without the lettering around the seal or the cartouche below it, is in the center of the field. Above the seal, **SAN JOSÉ, CALIFORNIA** runs horizontally; below the seal is **FOUNDED 1777**, all in large black letters. The flag's proportions are 3 by 4.5. It was officially adopted 2 June 1969.   JP

SANTA ANA, CALIFORNIA

Population Rank: U.S..... # 51
California...... # 8

Proportions: 7:10 (official)

Adopted: 2 July 1984 (official)

DESIGN: Santa Ana's flag is divided diagonally from upper hoist to lower fly. The hoist triangle is medium blue; the fly triangle is yellow. On the center of the field is the city seal, approximately 4 units in diameter on a field of 7 by 10 units. The seal is surrounded by a dark blue ring which is fimbriated in gold where it overlaps the blue hoist triangle. On that ring CITY OF SANTA ANA arches clockwise over the top half and CALFORNIA is centered on the lower half, counterclockwise, all in gold. At 8:30 and 3:30 o'clock is a small five-pointed star. The center of the seal has a white field. In the upper fly portion, between about 1:00 and 2:30 o'clock, half of a gold sun is visible with 8 gold equally-spaced rays emanating in straight lines to the inner edge of the blue ring. In a similar position on the hoist side is a line drawing in blue of the Orange County government building, in partial profile toward the hoist. Below it, and close to the hoist side, is **ORANGE COUNTY SEAT OF GOVERNMENT**, in blue centered in three lines, two words over two words over one. In the center lower half of the seal is a blue line image of city hall, in partial profile toward the fly, with trees and shrubs. Centered below this building, in the same lettering, is **THE GOLDEN CITY**, directly above **FOUNDED 1869**. The seal was adopted officially in 1972.

SYMBOLISM: Blue and yellow (or gold) are the official colors of the city. The sun no doubt alludes to the abundant sunshine of the city. Santa Ana is the county seat of Orange County, hence the county building on the seal. The city's nickname is "The Golden City".

HOW SELECTED: Little is known about the flag's history. The ordinance of adoption is a scant four lines, and mentions nothing about how the flag was developed. City hall personnel have no other information available about the flag.

DESIGNER: Not available.

FORMER FLAGS: In 1976, the city council sponsored a contest among city residents for a design of the first official flag, with a deadline of May 31 of that year. Mayor John Garthe and Frank Blaszcak, the public information officer, were to choose the three top designs for council to select the winner. Evidently no design pleased the council sufficiently, for no flag was adopted as a result of the contest.   JP 🏴

SANTA FE, NEW MEXICO

Population Rank: U.S... # 447
New Mexico ...... # 2

Proportions: 2:3 (assumed)

Adopted: 20 September 1915 (official)

DESIGN: The field of Santa Fe's flag is yellow with the city's seal in its center. The seal consists of a narrow blue circle around a white field. Immediately within this circle, running clockwise around the seal from its base is the complete name of the city in Spanish, in a Flat Brush-type font: **La Villa Real de la Santa Fé de San Francisco de Asís** . Within the circle of lettering is a heraldic "American" shield divided so that the top portion bears on its fly half the principal charge of the arms of Mexico (in a 19th-century version): an eagle with a serpent in its beak perched on a *nopal* cactus, all in a blue silhouette on white. The hoist half shows a portion of the arms of Spain, a yellow turreted castle in silhouette on a red field on the hoist side, and a silhouetted upright red lion, on the fly side. The lower part of the shield is the modified American blazon, 13 white five-pointed stars (staggered 7 above and 6 below) on dark blue, over 13 vertical stripes (7 red, 6 white). Below the shield is a white heraldic ribbon, edged in blue and folded in thirds. On the three sections appear, in blue: **1610** at the hoist, **1846** in the center, and **1821** at the fly. Emanating from behind the shield in a circle are 85 short gold rays, appearing to be scalloped, since every fifth ray is longer. Several rays are hidden by the shield's upper corners and the center portion of the heraldic ribbon.

SYMBOLISM: The complete name of the city in English is "The Royal Town of the Holy Faith of Saint Francis of Assisi". The emblems on the shield represent the nations that have had sovereignty over Santa Fe, with their initial date of control on the heraldic ribbon: Spain, 1610; Mexico, 1821; and United States, 1846. Spanish settlers named the town for St. Francis and chose him as its patron saint. Over time the name shortened to simply "Santa Fe".

HOW SELECTED: Ralph Emerson Twitchell, at the time a former mayor of the city, proposed the design to the city council on the date of its adoption. On 19 March 1915 his design had been adopted as the first official state flag of New Mexico.

DESIGNER: Not specified; presumably former Mayor Twitchell.

MORE ABOUT THE FLAG: The current version of the flag in use differs from that specified in the ordinance of adoption: it now uses a field of white instead of gold. The city's seal according to that ordinance consists only of the shield and heraldic ribbon and is termed a "heraldic seal". The ordinance further specifies that on the front side of the flag *shall be delineated in painting, printing, or embroidery an ideal representation or portrait of St. Francis of Assisi with the legend, in crimson:* **SAN FRANCISCO DE ASSISI** ... It is not known if such a flag was ever manufactured, but the current version has only the city's seal on both sides, a much less expensive rendering than would be the case with a double-sided flag. Moreover, the ordinance stipulates 1606 as the date of the city's founding by Don Juan de Oñate, the first Spanish governor-general of New Mexico. Historians now generally accept that the city was founded in 1610 when his successor, Don Pedro de Peralta, moved his capital to the site of today's city. The illustration accompanying the ordinance shows the date on the fly third of the ribbon as 1822, but it is correctly 1821 in the text of the ordinance. Also, the Mexican emblem is shown in its original colors of brown (for the eagle) and green (for the serpent and *nopal*).

FORMER FLAG: At some time in the past several decades (the date is uncertain) the city used a flag that departed more radically from the official ordinance. That flag is double-sided, with a red field on the front and a blue field on the back. The "heraldic seal" of the ordinance is prominently displayed centered in the lower half of the field, but the Spanish arms are rendered in two colors only (white castle on red, red lion on white) and the Mexican arms show a white eagle on light blue. Centered in two lines across the top of the flag is **City of** over **Santa Fe** in red letters outlined in white on the front side and, in blue on the back. The city's name is in letters slightly larger than "City of". No further information about the flag is available.   JP 🏴

SCOTTSDALE, ARIZONA

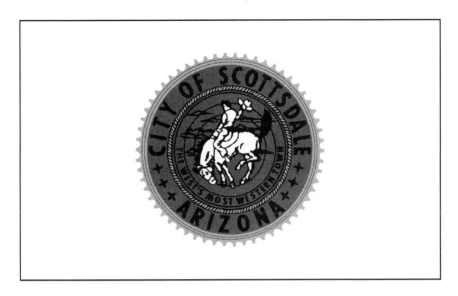

Population Rank: U.S. ..... # 86
 Arizona ...... # 4

Proportions: 6:11 (usage)

Adopted: After 1951 (apparently unofficial)

DESIGN: Scottsdale's flag has a white field with a large city seal in the center. On a field of 6 by 11 units, the seal is 4 units in diameter. The seal's field is a dark blue. The outer edge of the seal is a narrow gold band from which emanate 72 evenly-spaced tiny triangles, in imitation of the cut edge of an embossed seal. Two parallel narrow blue lines encircle the gold band. Within the gold band is another band, in dark blue, the inner edge of which is a beveled gold ring. On the blue band is **CITY OF SCOTTSDALE** arched clockwise over the top half, and **ARIZONA** centered counterclockwise on the lower half, all in black block letters. Both before and after "ARIZONA" are three black four-pointed stars. Another blue ring is inside the beveled gold circle, bordered in a narrow black line on both sides. The outer black edge is flush with the inner side of the beveled gold ring. On this ring, in small black letters centered counterclockwise on the lower half, is **THE WEST'S MOST WESTERN TOWN**. Yet another blue ring, slightly narrower, also with black edges (the outer edge of this ring is the inner edge of the preceding ring) is next. The inner portion of the seal, in blue, has a bucking bronco and rider in white detailed in black, facing the hoist. In traditional rodeo fashion, the rider is holding on with his left hand and raising his hat into the air with his right. The horse's mane and tail are black.

SYMBOLISM: The seal bears the city's motto, "The West's Most Western Town", and depicts a well-known symbol of the west, the bucking bronco. The rider was inspired by a long-time wrangler Gerbacio "Harvey" Noriega, who was the "head honcho" at what was then Brown's Ranch in Scottsdale.

HOW SELECTED: The flag evidently resulted from a sense in city hall that there should be a city flag, and the city's seal was simply placed on a white background. The seal was adopted about 1951, the same year as the city's incorporation (on June 25). The flag was developed some time after that (records are unavailable), and is apparently unofficial.

DESIGNER: The seal's designer is Gene Brown Pennington, the granddaughter of one of the city's early settlers, E. O. Brown.   JP 🛡

SEATTLE, WASHINGTON

Population Rank: U.S. ..... # 23
Washington ...... # 1

Proportions: 11:15 (usage)

Adopted: 16 July 1990 (official)

DESIGN: Seattle's flag has an elaborate design in two colors. The field is a teal blue/green—a dark aquamarine, "the color of Puget Sound at dusk", according to the ordinance of adoption. From the top half of the hoist on a white background run four equally-spaced teal stripes, generally horizontal, but slanted slightly upward and ending in a curved shape resembling a hook. The top stripe is 3.5 units in length on a field of 11 by 15 units. Each of the stripes below decreases in length one-half unit. The width of the stripes is .5 units; the bottom edge of the top stripe is 2 units from the top edge of the field, and the stripes are approximately 1 unit apart.

Emanating from below the "hook" of each of the top three stripes is a teal ribbon that undulates toward the center of the flag and intertwines with the others to form a sort of wreath around the center of the flag, averaging about 8 units in diameter, all on white. Within this wreath, which appears to be cast from the foam of surf, is a stylized rendition of the city's seal, in its center a profile of Chief Seattle, facing the hoist. Around the chief's head are two teal curved bands that appear to be cut ribbons, about the same width as the hoist stripes, one from his chin to the top of his head, and the other beginning lower at the back of his head, and extending beyond his neck. Together these form a stylized "S". Around this figure, in teal letters beginning about 9 o'clock and ending at 3 o'clock, is **CITY OF GOODWILL**. Dots at 8 and 4 o'clock separate the remainder of the legend, **SEATTLE**, which curves from 7 to 5 o'clock.

SYMBOLISM: Chief Seattle, leader of the local Suquamish tribe, is known best for giving his name to the city and for his 1854 speech defending the preservation of nature. His profile also represents other Native Americans of the region. "City of Goodwill" was chosen as the city's nickname at the same time as the flag was adopted. The design suggests Seattle's location as a port city.

HOW SELECTED: The council adopted a city flag and nickname in preparation for the Goodwill Games (an international athletic event) and Goodwill Arts Festival to be held in Seattle in 1990.

DESIGNER: Councilmember Paul Kraabel.

MORE ABOUT THE FLAG: The central seal design is much like one proposed for a new city flag in 1976 designed by the David Strong Design Group, but never adopted.

FORMER FLAGS: Few cities have made so many unsuccessful attempts to adopt a city flag as Seattle before 1990.

In 1962 and 1964 various council members called for a city flag. A Seattle designer, William Werrbach, created two designs, but neither was adopted. In 1968, local flag enthusiast Dr. Willard Goff designed a flag, but council rejected it as too contemporary (it showed the Space Needle and a supersonic transport). In 1976 Mayor Wes Uhlman recommended the flag designed by the David Strong Design Group for commemoration of the United States bicentennial, but the council declared its agenda too busy to consider it. The following year council member Phyllis Lamphere promoted the idea of adopting a city flag once again, but she finally gave up, saying that her efforts "didn't excite anyone". There the matter rested until 1990 when the current city flag was finally adopted.

In 1943, Councilman Frank McCaffrey designed and had manufactured a city flag that he presented to the council, although it was apparently unofficial. Very similar to Washington's state flag, it has a green field of 3 by 5 units with the city's seal in gold in the center. The seal shows a profile of Chief Seattle toward the hoist, • CITY • OF • SEATTLE • curved over his head, and **1869** centered below it. Surrounding this portion is ring that declares over the top half, **CORPORATE • SEAL • OF • THE** as a preface to the city's name below.

In the lower half of the ring are two dolphins, one on either side facing the lower center point, where two fir cones are shown. The dolphins, according to the seal's designer, James A. Wehn, symbolize Seattle as a center of deep-water commerce; the fir cones represent the Evergreen State (Washington's nickname). (The seal was adopted 13 January 1937.) McCaffrey's flag was known as "Council's Flag", and hung in council chambers for at least two decades.

About 1934 Mayor Charles L. Smith presented an unofficial city flag to the Nile Temple of the Shrine Legion of Honor (a Masonic marching body) and the Shriners used it for years to represent the city at their national meetings. This flag, apparently one of a kind, is 5:7 in proportions. The white field has a narrow blue border. In the center of the field is a frontal portrait of Chief Seattle, presumably in natural colors, surrounded by a white ring edged in gold on which **CHIEF** curves above and **SEATTLE** curves below, all in gold. Emanating from the top of the band is a gold flourish extending to either side. Across the top of the flag is a broad heraldic ribbon, white and edged in gold, with **CITY OF SEATTLE** in gold, "OF" smaller than the other words. Centered below the ribbon and immediately above the gold flourishes is the legend, in smaller gold letters, **INCORPORATED 1869**. Centered at the bottom in larger gold letters is **WASHINGTON**. Whether city officials may ever have used the flag is unknown.   JP

SHREVEPORT, LOUISIANA

Population Rank: U.S. ..... # 88
                   Louisiana ...... # 3

Proportions: 2:3 (official);
               3:5 (usage)

Adopted: 1935 (official)

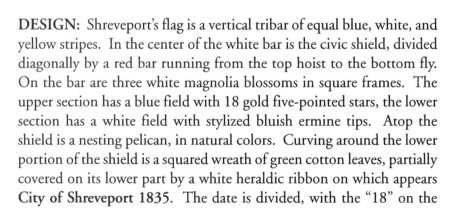

DESIGN: Shreveport's flag is a vertical tribar of equal blue, white, and yellow stripes. In the center of the white bar is the civic shield, divided diagonally by a red bar running from the top hoist to the bottom fly. On the bar are three white magnolia blossoms in square frames. The upper section has a blue field with 18 gold five-pointed stars, the lower section has a white field with stylized bluish ermine tips. Atop the shield is a nesting pelican, in natural colors. Curving around the lower portion of the shield is a squared wreath of green cotton leaves, partially covered on its lower part by a white heraldic ribbon on which appears **City of Shreveport 1835**. The date is divided, with the "18" on the hoist side and the "35" on the fly side. The city's name is in the center.

SYMBOLISM: The colors of the tribar are said to represent the three nations that had owned Louisiana: France (blue), United States (white), and Spain (yellow). The 18 stars in the shield's topmost third symbolize Louisiana as the eighteenth state to join the Union. The three magnolia blossoms, the state flower of Louisiana, represent Shreveport as the center of the tri-state area known as Ark-La-Tex (Arkansas, Louisiana, and Texas). The ermine in the lower portion of the shield comes from the arms of the Shreve family, in honor of Captain Henry Miller Shreve, the city's founder. The cotton leaves show Shreveport's importance in the cotton industry, and the pelican is Louisiana's state bird.

HOW SELECTED: A contest was held in 1934 with a top prize of $50. A seven-member contest committee chose a winner, then submitted the design to the eleven-member design committee, which approved it and submitted it to the flag committee, made up of 31 members, where it received final approval. A seven-member publicity committee was charged with the responsibility of having an actual flag manufactured.

DESIGNER: Stewart G. Davis, a local artist.

MORE ABOUT THE FLAG: As the local chamber of commerce was planning a large celebration in honor of the city's centennial in 1935, it felt that a suitable flag for the city should be adopted to generate interest in the city's citizenry.   JP 🏴

SPOKANE, WASHINGTON

Population Rank: U.S. ..... # 98
Washington ...... # 2

Proportions: 3:5 (usage)

Adopted: 6 October 1975 (official)

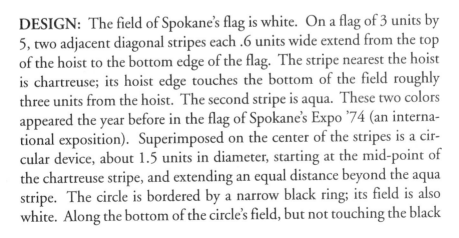

DESIGN: The field of Spokane's flag is white. On a flag of 3 units by 5, two adjacent diagonal stripes each .6 units wide extend from the top of the hoist to the bottom edge of the flag. The stripe nearest the hoist is chartreuse; its hoist edge touches the bottom of the field roughly three units from the hoist. The second stripe is aqua. These two colors appeared the year before in the flag of Spokane's Expo '74 (an international exposition). Superimposed on the center of the stripes is a circular device, about 1.5 units in diameter, starting at the mid-point of the chartreuse stripe, and extending an equal distance beyond the aqua stripe. The circle is bordered by a narrow black ring; its field is also white. Along the bottom of the circle's field, but not touching the black ring, are silhouettes of four children in black, standing in a row with their hands clasped. The children on either end have their free hands raised. Above them and to the left is **CHILDREN OF** with **THE SUN** centered immediately below, all in small black letters. Overlapping the upper right side of the circle is a gold sun .7 units in diameter with some 30 short, pointed rays. Centered in the lower third of the fly portion beyond the stripes is **CITY OF SPOKANE** in black.

SYMBOLISM: *Spokane* means "Children of the Sun", or the "Sun People", in the language of the Spokane tribe, from which the city derives its name.

HOW SELECTED: By the city council.

DESIGNER: Lloyd L. Carson, art director for the DeVine, Miller, Carlson, and Donaldson Advertising Company.

MORE ABOUT THE FLAG: Chartreuse is extremely rare in flags, especially in combination with another uncommon color, aqua, making this flag very unusual.

FORMER FLAG: The earlier flag of Spokane is also remarkable for its unusual colors. The field of this flag is lilac on which is centered a solid skyline behind a bridge with an arch below it, all in white. White ripples shaded in blue suggesting the water run below the bridge. Curved along the hoist skyline and extending about one-fourth of the way across the bridge is a spray of lilacs, highlighted in white and blue. Above and behind the skyline is the suggestion, in white, of a mountain peak.

From each of the field's four corners, a white line extends about halfway toward the central figure. Each of the divisions thus formed has a figure centered on it. On the hoist side is an evergreen tree in blue and shaded in white. Above is a gold sun, depicted as the Native Americans might, with three lines extending from each of the sun's four sides, each center ray slightly larger than the other two. On the fly side is a white five-pointed star. Below, in stylized white script pierced by a white arrow in the direction of the hoist, is **Spokane**. Centered below, in smaller white letters, is **THE LILAC CITY**. The flag's proportions varied in use between 3:4 and 5:7. The flag was officially adopted 25 July 1958. It was designed by S. Luther Essick, who had become convinced of the value of a city flag when working in displaced persons camps in Vienna after World War II. He was impressed by how much it meant to the Viennese to once again fly their city flag. The chamber of commerce and representatives of the city's Lilac Festival helped persuade the city council to adopt the flag.

The flag is replete with symbolism. According to a city brochure, *The lilac color and the flower represent Spokane as the "Lilac City" and her position as the "Queen City of the Inland Empire". The buildings represent planned progress. The bridge symbolizes Monroe Street Bridge and Falls, important local landmarks. The white star stands for loyalty to the state of Washington. The mountain peak is Mount Spokane, part of the city's scenic beauty and historic legend. Both the gold sun of Native American design and the name of the city pierced by an arrow reflect the origin of the city's name, "Children of the Sun". The evergreen (Douglas fir), Washington's state tree, indicates the city's connection with the state. The white lines represent the city's basic freedoms, focused on Spokane. White represents purity of purpose; blue, trueness and loyalty; and lilac, the city's royal heritage.*   JP 🛡

SPRINGFIELD, ILLINOIS ✪

Population Rank: U.S... # 201
　　　　　　　Illinois...... # 4

Proportions: 2:3 and
　　　　　　3:5 (both official)

Adopted: 22 October 1917 (official)

DESIGN: Springfield's flag has a dark blue field. On a flag of 3 by 5 units, 20 white five-pointed stars (all oriented upward) form a circle 2 units in diameter in the upper hoist half of the flag, about one-quarter unit from the top and one-half unit from the hoist. In the center of the circle is a large red five-pointed star bordered in white, one point oriented to the top. Centered across the bottom of the flag in gold block letters in an Arial-type font one-third unit in height is **SPRINGFIELD ILLINOIS** (without punctuation).

SYMBOLISM: The 20 white stars represent the number of states in the Union before Illinois was admitted in 1818. The large red star represents Springfield as the capital of Illinois, the 21st state.

HOW SELECTED: A contest was conceived by the poet, Vachel Lindsay (1879-1931), a native of Springfield, and sponsored by the Springfield Art Association.

DESIGNER: S. T. Wallace, a citizen of Springfield.

MORE ABOUT THE FLAG: The early version of the flag does not have the city's name across the bottom, and the circle of stars is centered vertically. Moreover, the red star points downward rather than upward. It is not known when the original design was altered, or by whom, but the original design was still in use in 1953. The flag was first exhibited on 8 November 1917.   JP

STOCKTON, CALIFORNIA

Population Rank: U.S..... # 70
　　　　　　California.... # 12

Proportions: 2:3 (usage)

Adopted: 27 August 1999 (unofficial)

DESIGN: The field of the flag of Stockton is divided in half, red at the hoist and blue at the fly. In its center an oversized seal spans the height of the field. The flag is 26 by 39 units. A white outer ring of the seal, 2 units wide, encloses three concentric rings; the first and third are gold edged in black, and one-half of a unit wide, and form the outer and inner edges of the second ring, which is white, and 3 units wide. **STOCKTON FOUNDED JUNE 1849** curves clockwise around the top portion of the white ring, **INCORPORATED JULY 1850** curves counterclockwise below, all blue. Red five-pointed stars separate these legends. In the center of the seal is a large, light brown, antlered tule elk facing the fly. In the background, a dark brown mountain range rises from the horizontal center of the seal. The range has four peaks, the highest in the center, and above them is a light blue sky. The lower half of the scene depicts a blue river below the mountains, about one-third the width of the scene's lower half. On the fly side is a small red sailboat with two white sails and a red pennant, billowing toward the fly. The lowest portion of the seal shows green grass below the elk.

SYMBOLISM: The tule elk is native to the region. The central peak has traditionally represented Mount Diablo, a prominent peak in the area, but others consider the mountains depicted on the seal to be the Sierra Nevada, a mountain range to the east of the city. The water behind the elk reflects Stockton's dependence on water as a main transportation artery for supplies during the California Gold Rush. A modern interpretation of the water would be the importance of Stockton as a seaport, as well as the 1,000 miles of Sacramento River Delta waterways used for fishing, boating, and other recreational activities.

HOW SELECTED: Developed by the city clerk in 1999, but never officially adopted. The seal on the flag was adopted 25 July 1994.

DESIGNER: Katherine Gong Meissner, city clerk. The redesigned seal of 1994 was the project of the previous city clerk, Frances Hong, who felt that the original majesty of the elk as it appeared on the first seal had been lost over the years due to poor renditions as it was copied.

MORE ABOUT THE FLAG: When Stockton was a finalist for the All-America City award in 1999, Meissner developed the flag so that the city would have a flag with its new seal for the delegates to take along to the competition in Philadelphia.

FORMER FLAG: The original seal was designed by Stockton's first

mayor, Samuel Purdy, in 1850. It is identical to the current seal, except that the elk walks toward the hoist, looking over its left shoulder. This version of the seal in gold on a green field was used unofficially as the city's flag until 1999. JP

TACOMA, WASHINGTON

Population Rank: U.S..... # 99
Washington ...... # 3

Proportions: 2:3 (usage)

Adopted: 18 June 1991 (official)

DESIGN: The field of Tacoma's flag is a bright medium (royal) blue, with the city seal in blue and gold in the center. On a field of 2 by 3 units, the diameter of the seal is 1.25 units. A gold ring edged in blue encircles the seal. Arched over the top half in blue is **SEAL OF THE CITY OF TACOMA**, preceded and followed by a small blue-outlined star at the midpoints of the ring. Centered below is **1884**, also in blue. Immediately preceding and following the two legends are small three-lobed objects, edged in blue. The center of the seal shows Mount Tacoma (now Mount Rainier) in blue, rising from a horizontal line about one-third of the way from the top of the seal. A gold sun with rays appears over its hoist shoulder. Centered below the mountain is a bridge with four arches over a waterway that widens to fill the bottom of the seal. An old-fashioned train with coal tender and two boxcars is crossing the bridge in the direction of the fly. On the promontories on either side of the bridge are factories with smokestacks in operation. Wharves run along the edge of the banks where the factories meet the water. Two small steamships are moored, one on either side of the waterway. The water and the sky behind the mountain are a lighter shade of blue; the rest is gold with blue shadings.

SYMBOLISM: The seal captures a scene from the area at the city's founding. Mount Rainier is a prominent landmark overlooking the city, drawn on the seal in 1884, the year of the city's incorporation.

HOW SELECTED: The flag was developed as part of the city's Corporate Identity Program, which calls for the use of the city seal on all materials related to official, policy-making activities of the mayor and city council. It was felt that the seal, because of its historic significance, would reinforce the official status of the flag.

DESIGNER: Not available.

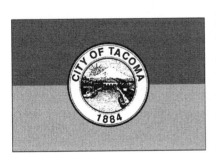

FORMER FLAGS: Tacoma has had two previous flags. The first flag was designed by C. A. Darmer, a member of the Military and Naval Affairs Committee of the Tacoma Chamber of Commerce, which proposed the adoption of the flag to city council. The flag is a horizontal bicolor, crimson over gold, with the city seal in the center in black and white, with proportions of 2:3. It was officially adopted on 30 November 1931.

The second flag was adopted officially on 11 April 1972. This flag has a white field with proportions of 3:5 units. In the center is a circular emblem with an overall diameter of about 2.25 units consisting of a semicircular rainbow composed of 3 stripes, from the top red, orange, and yellow, curved over a circular blue emblem. Complementing the rainbow below is **CITY OF TACOMA** in blue in an Arial-type font,

curved counterclockwise from one end of the rainbow to the other. There is a white space between the rainbow/city-name circle and the central symbol, enclosed in a narrow blue circle of about 1.25 units in diameter.

The symbol has a white field and is divided approximately in half. The upper portion shows a stylized Mount Rainier in blue; the lower portion, open water, representing Commencement Bay, detailed with four curved blue lines and a blue seagull, centered, flying toward the hoist. The flag was designed by John Wallerich and Larry Lawson of the city, and recommended to the city council by the Tacoma-Pierce County Civil Arts Commission. The rainbow symbolizes the bridge of communication; the seagull, the union of sky and abundant waters; and the circle, the timeless union of these qualities leading to a bright future.

JP

TALLAHASSEE, FLORIDA ✪

Population Rank: U.S... # 135
Florida...... # 8

Proportions: 4:7 (usage)

Adopted: 1957 (official)

DESIGN: Tallahassee's flag is a white saltire on a dark blue field, with the city seal in blue on a gold background overlaying the center. On a field of 4 by 7 units, the seal is about 2 units in diameter. Immediately within the seal's outer edge is a narrow white ring, into which emanate some 80 tiny black triangles, suggesting the cut edge of a seal. Within the white ring is a gold ring, the inner edge of which is formed by a narrow black ring. Curved over the top of the gold ring is **CITY** *of* **TALLAHASSEE**, and counterclockwise below is **FLORIDA**, all in black and an Arial-type font. The dome of the capitol appears in the center of the seal, its lower portion white detailed in black and its upper portion black detailed in white. A small United States flag flies atop the dome, blowing toward the hoist. Clouds on either side of the dome are gold edged in black.

SYMBOLISM: The capitol dome on the seal represents Tallahassee's status as the capital of Florida. No particular symbolism is given for the colors or saltire, although the flag has the same basic design as the Florida state flag, with different colors. In the choice of colors for the Tallahassee flag, the designer, whose name is of Scottish origin, may have been influenced by the flag of Scotland, a white saltire on blue.

HOW SELECTED: At the urging of Mrs. Florence R. S. Phillips, one-time secretary of the Tallahassee Booster Club (a forerunner of the chamber of commerce), and City Engineer Miller Walston, the city commission held a contest for a new city flag sometime in 1916.

DESIGNER: Miss Abernathy, an art teacher at Florida State College for Women.

MORE ABOUT THE FLAG: From its creation, the flag was apparently considered the city flag, even though not officially adopted, since an ordinance existed prohibiting its use for advertising or commercial purposes without the approval of the city commission. The original flag had the seal in blue on white. It was evidently changed to gold about the time of its official adoption in 1957. According to a number of references, the flag appeared for years on city postcards with an account of its history.   JP 🏴

TAMPA, FLORIDA

Population Rank: U.S..... # 58
Florida...... # 3

Proportions: 3:5 (unofficial)

Adopted: 8 July 1930 (official)

DESIGN: Tampa's flag has a shape unlike any other U.S. city flag. It is a modified burgee with a shallow indentation between the two traditional end points, and a third point (suggesting the tongue found on some swallow-tailed war ensigns), about half as long, between the other two. At the hoist are three narrow equal vertical stripes—red, white, and blue—each .2 units wide on a white field of 3 by 5 units. Spaced evenly on the blue stripe are 7 white five-pointed stars. 1.6 units from the hoist are five approximately equal vertical stripes (three yellow and two red) that form a central bar .75 units wide. Centered on this red and yellow bar is the city's seal, 1.1 units in diameter. From the seal's fly midpoint, three stripes—red, white, red—each .2 units wide, bend in a chevron oriented to the fly. At the end of the fly is a dark green stripe about the same width as the red stripes of the chevron and oriented in the same fashion. The top and bottom of the stripe have diamond-shaped red tips at the top and bottom points of the fly. The tongue between these two points forms a diamond, and is itself divided into four smaller equal diamonds; the top and bottom of these are dark green and meld into the green chevron, while the fly diamond at the tip of the tongue is red like its counterparts above and below. The hoist diamond is dark blue and displays a single white five-pointed star.

Extending across the center of the field horizontally from the blue stripe at the hoist, is another blue stripe .2 units wide that runs behind the seal and over the chevron stripes, stopping at the border of the green chevron at the fly's edge. Two white stars are on the hoist portion of this stripe, in line with the center star of the vertical stripe, and four more are on the fly side, evenly spaced. The blue diamond of the tongue with its lone star gives the impression that the blue stripe is overlaid by the green chevron. All of the stars on the flag are oriented point-upwards.

The seal is blue on white. The outer ring around the seal is edged in blue. The white field of the ring is divided into two semicircular bands with rounded ends, one above and one below, that do not quite meet at the center, where a small white star on blue separates them on both sides. Arched on the top band is **CITY OF TAMPA FLORIDA** and on the lower band, counterclockwise, is **ORGANIZED JULY 15, 1887**, all in blue. In the center of the seal is the steamer *Mascotte* on a blue sea headed toward the fly. Midway across the lower portion of the sea is a white horizontal stripe with **MASCOTTE** on it in blue. The seal was adopted in 1887.

SYMBOLISM: The designer suggested rather creative symbolism for his design. The colors are inspired by the national flags of the immigrants who settled the area: France, Great Britain, and the United States (red, white and blue); Italy (green, white, and red); and Spain (red and yellow). British contributions to the area (1763-1821) are also suggested by portions of the crosses of St. Andrew and St. George. Florida is acknowledged by the red and white colors of its state flag and by a stylized "F". A stylized "H" suggests Hillsborough County, of which Tampa is the seat of government. The seal superimposed on a stylized "T" commemorates the official birth of Tampa in 1855. (Some imagination is required to trace out the letters intended by the designer.) The Mascotte on the seal recalls the ship built for railroad magnate Henry B. Plant, which ran passengers and freight from Tampa to Key West, Florida, and Havana, Cuba, in the late 19th century, allowing Cuban cigar workers to travel inexpensively between factories in Florida and Cuba.

HOW SELECTED: Presented to Mayor D. B. McKay by the designer. The mayor recommended it to the board of representatives, who adopted the flag.

DESIGNER: F. Grant Whitney, a local industrial engineer.

MORE ABOUT THE FLAG: A photo in the *Tampa Tribune* of 24 February 1944 shows the flag with a white vertical stripe centered over the red vertical stripe behind the seal. Neither the original version nor the official version on file in the city shows that stripe, which was apparently added in error by the manufacturer.

OTHER FLAGS: Tampa is one of the few cities, including Cleveland and New York, with a sub-municipal flag, in this case the flag of Ybor City, which comprises Tampa's Latin Quarter. Ybor City was founded as a village devoted to cigar manufacturing in 1885 and was annexed to Tampa in 1887. There is no information available about the flag's history or designer, but it is at least forty years old.

The flag is divided into four triangular quarters (per saltire), yellow at the hoist, green at the top, red at the fly, and blue on the bottom. Overlaying the center is a white disk resembling a seal, the outer edge of which has a white band bordered in gold. In the lower half of the disk is a gold cigar slanting up from the hoist toward the fly, with a blue tip at the hoist end. Over the cigar in script is **Ybor**, in white outlined in blue. Below the cigar, in small blue letters, is **CITY**. A narrow white vertical stripe runs from the center edges of the disk to the top and bottom edges of the flag. The colors come from the flags of the original countries of the city's many ethnic groups. A rather comical "Pledge of Affection" for the flag reads, in "Spanglish":

> *I pledge affection to the flag of Ybor Ciudad*
> *The symbol of fame and fine calidad*
> *It should always wave proudly arriba*
> *With friendship and good will ever viva!*
> *Yesterday, today and mañana,*
> *My it always inspire our hazañas*
> *We are españoles, italianos, and cubanos*
> *But together we make americanos.*
> *Salute our flag and alcalde*
> *Trust them to always be salve.*
> *Respect this ensign we demanda*
> *Let's be gay when see it, caramba!*

JP

TOLEDO, OHIO

Population Rank: U.S. ..... # 56
Ohio ...... # 4

Proportions: 3:5 (usage)

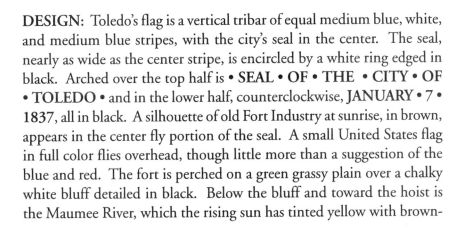

Adopted: 18 January 1994 (official)

DESIGN: Toledo's flag is a vertical tribar of equal medium blue, white, and medium blue stripes, with the city's seal in the center. The seal, nearly as wide as the center stripe, is encircled by a white ring edged in black. Arched over the top half is • **SEAL** • **OF** • **THE** • **CITY** • **OF** • **TOLEDO** • and in the lower half, counterclockwise, **JANUARY** • 7 • **1837**, all in black. A silhouette of old Fort Industry at sunrise, in brown, appears in the center fly portion of the seal. A small United States flag in full color flies overhead, though little more than a suggestion of the blue and red. The fort is perched on a green grassy plain over a chalky white bluff detailed in black. Below the bluff and toward the hoist is the Maumee River, which the rising sun has tinted yellow with brownish waves. The orange sun, its top half visible, is aligned with the fort horizontally. Orange rays in varying sizes form a hemisphere over the sun, and the sky is also yellow with brownish tints. Arched immediately below the inner circle of the outer ring, and in black letters about two-thirds the size of those on the ring, is the city's Latin motto, • **LABORARE** • **EST** • **ORARE** • ("To work is to pray").

SYMBOLISM: Fort Industry was the first building, constructed around 1800, in what would later become the city of Toledo, at the junction of Swan Creek and the Maumee River. The rising sun, prominent on the state seal, symbolizes Ohio.

HOW SELECTED: Mayor Carleton S. Finkbeiner and city council adopted a "modification" of the city's official flag in 1994 in preparation for a celebration of the city's 160th anniversary in 1997 by placing the city's first engraved seal on the flag. (This seal was adopted in 1873; before that a kind of generic seal with a scroll on which "L. S."—for the Latin *Locus Sigilli*, or "Place of the Seal"—was used.) In effect, however, it is a new flag.

DESIGNER: Presumably Mayor Finkbeiner, who thought that a return to the old seal was appropriate. The designer of the 1873 seal was an engraver, O. J. Hopkins.

MORE ABOUT THE FLAG: Because of the seal's many colors, Toledo's current flag is considerably more costly to manufacture than the previous flag, so it is not flown as widely about the city as was its predecessor.

FORMER FLAG: The former flag of Toledo was adopted by city council on 11 January 1909. The ordinance of adoption describes the design and proportions of the flag:

A field divided into three vertical bars of equal width, each bar to be one-third of the whole; the width of the flag to be five parts of its whole length; the two outer bars to be of navy blue, the center bar of pure white; in the middle of the center bar a conventionalized figure of the blockhouse of old Fort Industry, in red, surrounded by a circle of blue; the diameter of the outer edge of the circle to be 2.4 of a part.

Robert M. Corl designed the flag based on suggestions by the mayor, Brad Whitlock. Corl also designed a new city seal (also repealed in 1994 in favor of the 1873 version), which incorporated the blockhouse design, and was adopted along with the flag. The symbolism of the flag is explained in the 1 February 1947, issue of *The Toledo City Journal* (p. 74): *On our city flag the blockhouse stands for security, industry, and the pioneer spirit of advancement. The circle denotes unity, completeness, and eternity and also represents the state of Ohio. The colors of the flag, red, white, and blue stand for the nation; blue for constancy, white for purity, and red for labor, courage, and brotherhood.* JP 🛡

TOPEKA, KANSAS ✪

Population Rank: U.S.... # 176
            Kansas.... # 14

Proportions: 2:3 (usage)

Adopted: 1977 (official)

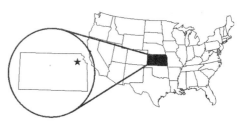

DESIGN: The field of the flag of Topeka is divided vertically, with a shield and ribbon on a white field on the hoist half, and gold stripe over a dark green stripe on the fly half. The shield has a gold field; its images, lettering, and its dividing lines and chevron are all in dark green. In a compartment across its top is **GOLDEN CITY** in outlined letters, centered in two lines. The rest of the field is divided into three portions by a chevron (upside-down "V"), the top point of which is in the center of the shield, and a line extending upwards to the top compartment. In the hoist third are a beehive and a locomotive drive wheel. In the fly third is a grass hut of the Kaw Tribe, with an arrow and stalk of corn on either side of the hut. In the lower third is the dome of the Kansas state capitol. The chevron has a zigzag band design in gold, forming ten unequal divisions separating nine five-pointed gold stars. Below the shield is a heraldic ribbon in gold, on which **TOPEKA 1854 KANSAS** appears in green outlined letters.

SYMBOLISM: The gold on the flag reflects the city's nickname, "The Golden City", given by the early settlers because of the beauty of the city's sunlit rolling hills and autumn elms. The dark green represents the fertility of the Kaw Valley and corn, an important agricultural product of the region. The beehive and locomotive drive wheel symbolize industry and the major part the railroads contributed to the region's development. The Kaw hut recalls the original settlers of the land, and the arrow and corn stalk suggest that the Kaw were both hunters and farmers. The capitol dome shows that Topeka is the capital of Kansas. The zigzag design on the chevron symbolizes the first bridge over the Kansas River, a structure that contributed to the city's growth. The nine stars stand for the nine founders of the city.

HOW SELECTED: The flag was a United States bicentennial project of Boy Scout Troop 43.

DESIGNER: Dana Villeme, a 13-year old Eagle Scout, with the advice of some local architects. The city coat of arms that appears on the flag was designed in 1960 by Ed Bruske, an artist for the city-county planning agency.

MORE ABOUT THE FLAG: Beginning in 1975, it took Boy Scout Troop 43 two years of hard work to embroider the first flag on poplin. This flag was 4:7 in proportion; later versions are 2:3. In 1996, after Villeme died in an automobile accident, the city dedicated a memorial plaque in his honor on the flagpole at city hall where the city flag is flown.   JP

TRENTON, NEW JERSEY

Population Rank: U.S... # 297
New Jersey...... # 5

Proportions: 3:5 (usage)

Adopted: 18 April 1985 (official)

DESIGN: Trenton's flag is divided in half, blue at the hoist and gold at the fly. In the center is the city seal in gold. The seal, nearly the height of the flag, has a white field bordered by a fancy blue ring. In its center is a blue shield with three wheat sheaves, 2 over 1, in buff. From the upper corners of the shield hang tassels or chains. Above the shield on a heraldic wreath is a nag's head, in profile facing the hoist, and encircling the coat of arms is **SEAL OF THE CITY OF TRENTON**, with 1792 below.

SYMBOLISM: The nag's (horse's) head, which also appears on the state seal, and wheat sheaves represent agriculture, an important economic resource when the area was first settled by English Quakers in

1679. They are also appropriate symbols for the capital city of New Jersey, "The Garden State". The state legislature granted the city's charter in 1792. Since 1909, blue and gold have been the city's official colors; buff has been a traditional color of New Jersey since the 1700s.

HOW SELECTED: Attorney George Dougherty researched the Trenton flag in 1985 and discovered that an earlier version was unofficial. He suggested a flag, based on a former design, be officially adopted by the city council.

DESIGNER: Unknown.

MORE ABOUT THE FLAG: Although not directly related to the flag, the first city seal bore just one wheat sheaf and **CITY OF TRENTON** with the city motto **E PARVIS GRANDES** ("Out of the Small [come] the Great") around the circumference. The seal was later changed, adding two more wheat sheaves, the nag's head, and the year 1792, eliminating the motto.

FORMER FLAG: Before the adoption of this official flag, the city had used a similar unofficial flag for a number of years, except the city seal was centered on the blue stripe at the hoist.

JC

TUCSON, ARIZONA

Population Rank: U.S..... # 30
            Arizona...... # 2

Proportions: 3:5 (usage)

Adopted: 5 January 1953 (official)

DESIGN: Tucson's flag has a white field with the city seal in the center. No size is specified for the seal, but it usually occupies a significant portion of the field. The seal's outer edge is blue, surrounding a white interior ring. Curved on that ring from about 10 o'clock to 2 o'clock is CITY OF TUCSON, and centered below, counterclockwise, is ARIZONA, all in blue in an Arial-type font. The seal is circular, but its field is divided in half between the upper hoist side and the lower fly side, resembling a tilted yin-yang symbol.

The upper part of the seal is yellow with its curved edge suggesting the sun, with 33 short rays emanating outward, every fourth ray slightly longer. The rays are shadowed in red on the hoist side. Horizontally across the center of the upper portion is Tucson's 1949 skyline, with buildings in beige, blue, brown, and gray, and a green saguaro cactus in the hoist foreground.

The lower part of the seal shows the historic San Xavier mission, in white with black shadowing, as if guarding the city at night, on a blue background. Very narrow red rays in sets of four in alternating sizes extend from the edge of the blue portion to balance the sun's rays above, perhaps suggesting moonlight. Loosely surrounding the seal's lower half is a brown lariat, portions of which extend into the white ring of the seal.

SYMBOLISM: The designer wished to contrast the modern Tucson with the historic city. The lariat symbolically binds the two eras together.

HOW SELECTED: The Tucson Press Club sponsored a contest for a new city seal in 1949 after Mayor E. T. "Happy" Houston mentioned to the club's president that a new seal was needed. The winning design was adopted 1 March 1950 as the city's registered trademark, but was not officially made the city seal until 1953, when the flag was also adopted.

DESIGNER: Mrs. Norman (Mary) Crowfoot, an artist who had just recently arrived in Tucson, learned of the contest and entered it.

MORE ABOUT THE FLAG: The original seal's colors were much brighter than the current version, with a lighter yellow and blue, and red on the buildings of the skyline and mission. The current shades of color seem to be a "cooler" variation. Also, earlier flags had been made in proportions of 4:5 units, as well as 8:13.   JP

Tulsa, Oklahoma

Population Rank: U.S..... # 42
Oklahoma...... # 2

Proportions: 12:19 (official)

Adopted: 17 August 1973 (official)

DESIGN: Tulsa's flag is described in the ordinance of adoption:

The flag design shall be the corporate seal of the City of Tulsa as described herein, positioned on both sides of a white material measuring six (6) feet, four (4) inches by four (4) feet, with the seal measuring two (2) feet, six (6) inches from top to bottom located in the center of the white material.

The corporate seal is also described in its own ordinance of adoption (27 December 1967):

The Corporate Seal of the City of Tulsa shall be in the shape of a modified vertical ellipse. The upper one-third of this ellipse shall be a gold field. Superimposed on this field, in the optical center and pointing upward shall be an Indian [Native American] *projectile point (arrowhead) of the Snyder variety in black and white facets. To the left [hoist] and adjacent to the base of this arrowhead there shall be the numerals "1" and "8". To the right [fly] and adjacent to the base of this arrowhead there shall be the numerals "9" and "8", together representing the year 1898. Superimposed upon and circumscribing the curved edge of the gold field there shall appear two rows of five-pointed blue stars, forty-six (46) in number.*

The lower left [hoist] quadrant of the seal shall be a black field with a stylized white oil derrick superimposed upon and centered in the field.

The lower right [fly] quadrant of the seal shall be a blue field with parallel horizontal white lines. Each line shall be composed of a series of arcs to suggest a wave form.

The upper gold field, the lower left black quadrant and the lower right blue quadrant shall be separated from each other to form the letter "T" in white. Circumscribing the lower half of the seal in Lincoln Gothic type style shall be the words "CITY OF TULSA OKLAHOMA" in gold capital letters.

SYMBOLISM: The "T", of course, is the initial letter of the city's name. The arrowhead recalls the importance of the early Native Americans in the region and their continuing influence today. The 46 stars symbolize Oklahoma as the 46th state to join the Union (16 November 1907). Tulsa was incorporated in 1898. The oil derrick suggests the importance of the petroleum industry in the rapid development of the city from its founding in 1879. The blue waters suggest the important waterways of the region, the Arkansas and Caney Rivers and Keystone Lake.

HOW SELECTED: The flag was adopted as part of celebrations of the city's 75th anniversary.

DESIGNER: Unknown.

FORMER FLAGS: Tulsa's first flag is non-rectangular, the fly ending in an isosceles triangle. The proportions are:

hoist, 25 units; length, 43 units; triangle sides, 13 units, for a total of 26 units at the fly. The field is white, with a large red circle in the center, about 13 units in diameter, with **TULSA** in large narrow white letters curving to conform to the circle. From the red circle emanate eight blue rays that widen as they reach the flag's edges. Four rays meet the flag's corners, four more meet its upper and lower edges. Another set of narrow white pointed rays, varying in length and suggesting sun's rays, overlay the broader blue rays, and in the six broad white rays formed in the spaces between the blue rays at the top and bottom are corresponding thin blue rays, for a total of 14 narrow rays.

In both broader white sections in the center portions of the hoist and fly is a broad red arrow, fimbriated in white with red edges, pointing to the center. On the hoist arrow is **UNLIMITED**, and on the fly arrow, **OPPORTUNITY**, both in white. The design suggests the brashness of early Tulsa as it grew rapidly with the petroleum industry, attracting visitors, settlers, and businesses, loudly proclaiming a bright future for all. The flag was designed by Alfred Perry, and adopted by the city commission on 5 June 1924. Mrs. W. A. (Rose) Cease made the first flag.   JP

VIRGINIA BEACH, VIRGINIA

Population Rank: U.S..... # 38
Virginia ...... # 1

Proportions: Indoor flags, 3:5;
outdoor flags, 2:3
or 5:8 (usage)

Adopted: 11 January 1965 (official)

DESIGN: The flag of Virginia Beach centers the city seal on a light blue field. The edge of the seal, in gray, appears to be scalloped, but is in fact made up of 39 tiny marlins linked nose-to-tail counterclockwise, enclosing a white ring around the seal. The inner edge of the ring is composed of a wreath of 54 gray strawberry leaves, half counterclockwise and half clockwise. On the white field between the ring's two edges, beginning at 9 o'clock and ending at 3 o'clock, is • CITY • OF • VIRGINIA • BEACH • VIRGINIA • in gray. Between the same two points, running counterclockwise, is LANDMARKS OF OUR

NATION'S BEGINNING, in gray letters about half the size of the first legend. The central portion of the seal depicts the Cape Henry lighthouse, in a dusty rose with gray shadings. It stands on a rocky shore, a dark gray fading into white beach at either side. An aquamarine sea is behind the lighthouse, its horizon line at the midpoint of the seal. On the upper hoist side is an orange sun with rays emanating from it. The sky is a light blue, and white clouds float overhead and on the horizon on the fly side. The diameter of the seal is about half the width of the hoist. The seal was officially adopted 21 January 1963.

SYMBOLISM: The city describes the seal's symbolism:

The Virginia Beach City Seal reflects our nation's beginnings and highlights, Virginia Beach landmarks and features ... Leaping marlins form its outer edge and represent sport fishing, boating, and other water activities. Strawberry leaves are linked together to create an inner circle, representing the importance of agriculture to the City. Bright sunshine and blue water join the sandy beach to show the importance of tourism and the pleasures of nature available to Virginia Beach residents and visitors. In the seal's center is the Cape Henry Lighthouse and a white cross. The cross marks the first landing of settlers on this nation's soil "Cape Henry" at Virginia Beach in 1607. The lighthouse is the first ever approved by the Continental Congress ... The lighthouse and cross symbolize the beginnings of Virginia Beach and the United States. As the Cape Henry Light signals a safe haven, so its replica erected in 1881 beams a warm welcome to Virginia Beach, a vibrant year-round city.

HOW SELECTED: On 24 June 1963, city council established a committee of three to develop a city flag.

DESIGNER: The committee, consisting of Richard B. Kellam, Laura Lambe, and A. R. Mailhes.

MORE ABOUT THE FLAG: The original version of the seal clearly shows a white cross on the horizon on the fly side of the lighthouse (and is still part of the city code), but today that seems to have been replaced by clouds.   JP

WARWICK, RHODE ISLAND

Population Rank: U.S... # 291
Rhode Island ...... # 2

Proportions: 2:3 (usage)

Adopted: Unknown

DESIGN: Warwick's flag has a white field with the city seal centered in full color. The seal consists of a white disk bearing the shield of the city's coat of arms. In heraldic terminology, the shield is described as: *Gules, a chevron between three crosses botonny Or, on a chief Azure, an eagle displayed Or.* In lay terms, the shield is a red field with a chevron (inverted "V") between three crosses, each tip shaped like a trefoil (cloverleaf), all in gold. The upper third of the shield is blue with a gold eagle facing the hoist with wings extended. Around the white disk is a dark blue ring with the inner lining resembling a chain and the outer lining resembling a rope. On the blue ring **THE CITY OF WARWICK, R.I.** curves over the top clockwise, **1642** and **1931** are paired at the bottom counterclockwise, and two five-pointed stars separate the inscriptions, all in gold.

SYMBOLISM: Warwick was founded on 12 January 1642. It was originally called Shawomet, after a local Indian tribe, a branch of the Nanhiganset (Narragansett) Nation. The land, on the west shore of Narragansett Bay, was purchased from this tribe by Samuel Gorton and his friends. Gorton, like Roger Williams, the founder of the Colony of Rhode Island and Providence Plantations, was a fugitive from Massachusetts for championing religious freedom.

In 1644 Gorton left for England to defend the title to this land, as the Massachusetts-Bay Colony was challenging its ownership. In 1647, a charter was granted by Robert Rich, the Earl of Warwick and Governor-in-Chief of Foreign Plantations. The grateful townspeople then renamed the settlement after their benefactor and adopted his family coat of arms as the town's arms, changing some colors on the shield. For the next thirty years Massachusetts would dispute the title to this land near Narragansett Bay. At the age of 84, Gorton had to return to England again to secure this land against a Massachusetts challenge.

HOW SELECTED: Unknown.

DESIGNER: Unknown.

MORE ABOUT THE FLAG: Nathaniel Tiffany designed the seal. Although the shield has an "azure" or blue chief (upper section) with a spread-winged golden eagle, on the shield of the family of Warwick the chief is "Or" or gold and the eagle is "Gules" or red. Heraldic tradition requires a city or other entity adopting a coat of arms from a family to change ("difference") it in some manner, by adding another symbol or changing the colors. Although the bird is clearly an eagle, there has been controversy over this creature. A Warwick Heritage Committee publication entitled: *Origin of the Seal of the City of Warwick, Rhode Island* (n.d.), argues that the eagle is really a *wyvern*, a heraldic beast.

JC 🛡

WASHINGTON,
DISTRICT OF COLUMBIA ✪

Population Rank: U.S...... # 21
    District of Columbia...... # 1

Proportions: 7:12 (official)

Adopted: 15 October 1938 (official)

DESIGN: The flag of Washington, DC, the nation's capital, has a white field with two horizontal red stripes below three red five-pointed stars spaced evenly across the top of the field. The placement of these elements was carefully detailed upon adoption:

The upper white portion is 3/10 of the hoist; the two horizontal bars are each 2/10 of the hoist; the white space between bars is 1/10 of the hoist; and the base, or lowest white space, is 2/10 of the hoist. The three red five-pointed stars have a diameter of 2/10 of the hoist and are spaced equidistant in the fly or horizontal dimension of the flag. So long as the proportions herein prescribed are observed, the dimensions of the flag both in hoist and fly may vary in accordance with the size of flag desired.

SYMBOLISM: The symbolism is described in a publication of the District of Columbia (*The Government of the District of Columbia*, 1963, p. 32):

The flag for the District of Columbia is based on the shield of the Washington family coat of arms, which is described as follows: "Arms—Argent, two bars, gules; in chief, three mullets of the second. Crest—Out of a ducal coronet or, a raven, wings endorsed, proper." This coat of arms was confirmed to Laurence Washington of Sulgrave, in the County of Northampton, and his descendants, by Cook Clarenceux, King of Arms, in 1592.

In lay terms, "Argent" is silver or white, "Gules" is red, "chief" is the upper part, and "mullets" are five-pointed stars deriving from the rowels of spurs.

HOW SELECTED: On 16 June 1938, the Congress of the United States (which oversees the District of Columbia) passed an act creating a commission to procure a design for a flag. Commission members included Melvin C. Hazen, president of the Board of Commissioners for the District of Columbia, chairman; Harry H. Woodring, secretary of war, represented by Captain A. D. Hopping, Office of the Quartermaster General; Claude A. Swanson, secretary of the navy, represented by Lieutenant J. W. Murphy, Jr., Office of Naval Communications; A. E. DuBois, Heraldic Section, Quartermaster Corps; and G. M. Thornett, secretary to the board of commissioners. The commission also received advice from the Commission on Fine Arts.

DESIGNER: Not stated. During the previous five years, designs had been submitted from various unidentified sources, anticipating the work of the yet-to-be-named commission, but no designer was ultimately identified.

MORE ABOUT THE FLAG: There are 14 paragraphs detailing how the flag of the District should be displayed, accompanied by 20 illustrations. There are also 18 "cautions" detailing how the flag should not be displayed or handled. These regulations are among the most detailed of any civic flag in the United States

FORMER FLAGS: The District of Columbia apparently had at least two former flags, both unofficial, and both designed to fulfill a ceremonial need in the military. The more recent is depicted in *The National Geographic Magazine*, LXVI, No. 3 (September 1934): 367. The text accompanying it is brief:

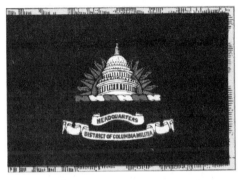

In the absence of any official flag for the District of Columbia, the District Militia devised the one reproduced here, and until such time as it shall be replaced by law, it will be the flag of the District of Columbia, just as formerly the one with the hatchet had that status. (p. 361).

The flag has a dark blue field. Horizontally across the center third of the flag is a heraldic wreath of six alternating stripes, red and white. Above the wreath is the white dome of the U.S. Capitol, superimposed on a sunburst in gold emanating from either side. Below the wreath is a short white heraldic ribbon, arched, with **HEADQUARTERS** across it in blue. Below that ribbon is another, curved in opposition to the arched one, and folded into three sections. On the center, and longest, section is **DISTRICT OF COLUMBIA MILITIA**, also in blue. The flag has proportions of 3 by 4.5, and is fringed in gold.

The earlier flag appears in *The National Geographic Magazine*, XXXII, No. 4 (October 1917): 335, with a short description on p. 340:

The flag of the National Guard of the District of Columbia has a rectangular field, the fly end of which is swallow-tailed. Centered thereon is a small hatchet, whose alleged manipulation in connection with an apocryphal cherry tree is reputed to have put the Father of His Country to a very trying test in the matter of veracity. The designation of the forces appear on scrolls above and below the hatchet.

The field of the flag is dark blue, with a gold fringe. The hatchet, in brown, has the blade facing down and toward the hoist, the handle slanting from upper hoist to lower fly. The heraldic ribbons are similar to those on the later flag, but in red with gold lettering and with the hatchet between them. The wry reference to the cherry tree relates to the oft-told legend that when Washington was a boy, he chopped down his father's cherry tree with a small hatchet. When confronted by his father, the tale goes that he said he could not tell a lie, and confessed to the deed, thus becoming a role model for generations of American school-children.   JP

WICHITA, KANSAS

Population Rank: U.S. .... # 50
Kansas ...... # 3

Proportions: 2:3 (usage)

Adopted: 14 June 1937 (official)

DESIGN: The field of Wichita's flag would be described in heraldry as "Gyronny of six, Gules and Argent", that is, alternating red and white rays that expand from the center to the field's borders. On a field of 2 by 3 units, the rays emanate from a point .875 units from the hoist. The hoist segment is white, the remaining rays alternate in color. The hoist and fly rays are 2 units at their widest; the upper and lower hoist rays, 1.33 units; and the upper and lower fly rays, 1.67 units. A blue disk of 1 unit in diameter, fimbriated in white, overlays the center. A Native American sun sign in white fills the disk. The sun sign differs slightly from those on the New Mexico state flag and the Albuquerque and Madison city flags: the arms comprise three rays rather than four (the central ray is slightly longer than the others) and it contains a small white disk in its center.

SYMBOLISM: The symbolism is explained by the designer:

The white circle around the field of blue in the center and containing the Indian design for the sun, symbolizes a 'hogan', or permanent home. Superimposed on the field of blue is the white sun. The blue indicates happiness and faithfulness in a town of happy people and permanent homes. Radiating from the circular field of blue are red and white stripes. The red means virtue and honor, the white stands for courageous virtues. The stripes lining the red and white background are symbols of rays of light and ways to come and go, open and free to all—hence, the red, white, and blue.

HOW SELECTED: Bert Wells, the city manager, asked the American Legion to develop a contest for a new city flag. A committee was appointed by the Legion, consisting of Paul Henrion, head of the Civic Flag Committee of the Legion, chairman; H. M. Van Auken, secretary of the chamber of commerce; Glen Thomas, a local architect; John Rydjord, Wichita University professor; and W. H. Allen, publisher of the *Wichita Beacon*. Six prizes totaling $85 were supplied by the Wichita Rotary Club, ranging from $40 for the first place to $2 for sixth place. Judging was done by R. T. Aitchison, Charles M. Capps, and William Dickinson, who had been appointed by the American Legion and the Wichita Art Association.

DESIGNER: Cecil McAlister, a resident of the city, took first place in the American Legion contest.

MORE ABOUT THE FLAG: An interesting footnote to the flag's adoption followed. McAlister's original design shows **WICHITA** in white on the fly's red segment, appearing to emerge from the center as the letters grow steadily larger toward the fly's edge. The first flags sewn, however (by Mrs. Mary J. Harper), did not have the city's name on them. On 25 March 1940, at the suggestion of Mrs. W. E. Haines of Haines Tile and Mantel Co., the city commission adopted a resolution to add the city's name to the flag, perhaps unaware that it had been part of the original design. The resolution, however, went into the

"pending" file, and was never acted upon, even though there were peri-
odic calls for the name to be added in later years. The reluctance of the
city government—in opposition to an overwhelming trend among U.S.
cities to place the name of the city on its flag—leads the vexillologist to
wonder if there is a wise flag designer in the Wichita city hall who has
never been persuaded to tamper with success!   JP

WILMINGTON, DELAWARE

Population Rank: U.S... # 387
　　　　　Delaware...... # 1

Proportions: 5:8 (assumed)

Adopted: 28 March 1963 (official)

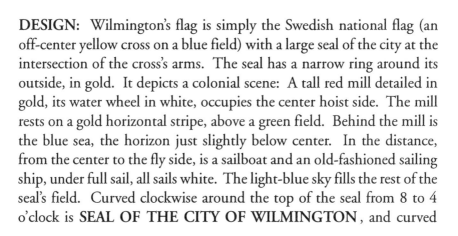

DESIGN: Wilmington's flag is simply the Swedish national flag (an off-center yellow cross on a blue field) with a large seal of the city at the intersection of the cross's arms. The seal has a narrow ring around its outside, in gold. It depicts a colonial scene: A tall red mill detailed in gold, its water wheel in white, occupies the center hoist side. The mill rests on a gold horizontal stripe, above a green field. Behind the mill is the blue sea, the horizon just slightly below center. In the distance, from the center to the fly side, is a sailboat and an old-fashioned sailing ship, under full sail, all sails white. The light-blue sky fills the rest of the seal's field. Curved clockwise around the top of the seal from 8 to 4 o'clock is **SEAL OF THE CITY OF WILMINGTON**, and curved counterclockwise below is **DELAWARE**, all in black letters superimposed over the edges of the scene.

SYMBOLISM: The city was founded by Swedes on March 28, 1638; the flag was adopted for the city's 325th anniversary commemoration. The seal shows Wilmington soon after its founding and suggests the milling and shipping industries that would become important in the city's development.

HOW SELECTED: The flag's design dates to 18 February 1927, as a result of a request by Robert J. Forman, superintendent of the public buildings, for a city flag for an official dinner in honor of Superintendent of Police George Black. The seal dates from 1832, but its official adoption date is uncertain.

DESIGNER: Stanley M. Arthurs, a local artist.

MORE ABOUT THE FLAG: The flag was apparently first used unofficially in 1927 and occasionally thereafter. Wilmington formally adopted the design before presenting a city flag to its Swedish sister city, Kalmar, whose officials were attending the 1963 anniversary celebration. The designer based his design on information, obtained from various Swedish officials, about the flag most likely used by the Swedes who first landed at the Wilmington site. That flag was "nearly square", so the first flag made followed that pattern, but by the time of the official adoption it had assumed a longer rectangular shape. Its proportions are not specified, but presumably the same as Sweden's flag.

The seal shown on the flag differs somewhat from a more traditional version also used by the city. In the alternate version the seal has a blue ring around the outside, edged in gold. The lettering appears on the ring, and a five-pointed star is shown before and after **DELAWARE**, all in gold.

FORMER FLAGS: Another unofficial city flag existed around 1960, a blue field with the city seal in the center (presumably in gold), but it was apparently rarely used, and little is known about it.   JP

WORCESTER, MASSACHUSETTS

Population Rank: U.S... # 121
Massachusetts...... # 2

Proportions: 10:19 (official)

Adopted: 11 December 1967 (official)

DESIGN: The flag of Worcester centers the city seal on a green field. The seal contains a white disk with a red heart encircled by a green wreath. On an outer white ring runs **WORCESTER** at the top, clockwise, and **A TOWN JUNE 14, 1722, A CITY FEB. 29, 1848** below, counterclockwise, all in gold.

As stated in a city ordinance: *The flag of the city shall bear on both sides a representation of the seal of the city upon a green field in the proportion of hoist to fly of one to one point nine. The diameter of the seal shall be one-half the hoist.*

SYMBOLISM: Worcester is the geographic center of the Commonwealth of Massachusetts, and often referred to as "The Heart of the Commonwealth". This motto was first noted on 4 October 1831, on the 100th anniversary of the incorporation of Worcester County, of which Worcester is the county seat. During the celebrations, Levi Lincoln, Worcester's first mayor and a former governor of Massachusetts, paid tribute to Chief Justice Isaac Parker of the Supreme Court, who had just died. Mr. Lincoln stated: *It was the wish of his heart that the county of Worcester should remain one and indivisible. Whatever changes may in evil times await it, in honoring his virtues there will be no division in the 'Heart of the Commonwealth'.*

HOW SELECTED: Committee.

DESIGNER: Unknown.

MORE ABOUT THE FLAG: According to a photograph and article in the *Worcester Telegram* of 11 December 1968, the city flag "was exhibited for the first time yesterday in the City Council Chambers", apparently just one day short of a year after adoption. 10:19 are the same proportions as the United States flag.

Alderman Stephen Salisbury headed a committee to adopt a city seal on 18 December in 1848, Worcester's first year as a city. On 23 January 1849, the city council unanimously adopted the seal.

FORMER FLAG: Although not official, during the Tippecanoe convention in Worcester on 17 June 1840 a flag flew during a parade displaying a heart clasped by joined hands and below it on a scroll: **With Heart and Hand** and the dates **1674**, the first attempt to settle Worcester, and **1684**, when Worcester adopted its name. JC 🏴

YONKERS, NEW YORK

Population Rank: U.S. .... # 95
New York ...... # 4

Proportions: 3:5 (official)

Adopted: Unknown

DESIGN: The flag of Yonkers centers the city seal on a white field. The city seal portrays a bust of George Washington facing toward the fly with a furled United States flag below. On an outer ring, **CORPORATION** runs over the top of the seal clockwise and **OF THE CITY OF YONKERS** runs counterclockwise below, separated by five-pointed stars. The outlines of the seal, the lettering, and the bust are dark blue on white; the stripes of the flag are red.

According to *An Ordinance Adopting the Code of the Ordinances of the City of Yonkers*, Article I, Section 1. Corporate Seal (*Code of Ordinances of the City of Yonkers*), adopted 26 December 1911:

The corporate seal of the city shall consist of the device of the bust of Washington with the American flag folded underneath, surrounded by the words Corporation of the City of Yonkers.

However, an even earlier description appears in the *Bylaws and General Ordinances of the Village of Yonkers* amended and adopted as amended on 28 June 1860:

The seal of this corporation shall be of some suitable metal, with the words Corporation of Yonkers engraved around the same, and the head of Washington with the American flag folded under the figure.

The seal's design used by Yonkers as a village was apparently carried over when it was incorporated as a city on 1 June 1872.

SYMBOLISM: There is no official symbolism assigned to the flag. George Washington's image may have been chosen for the seal because during the American Revolution he led the Continental Army, which was often in the area of today's Yonkers.

HOW SELECTED: Unknown.

DESIGNER: Unknown.

MORE ABOUT THE FLAG: Indoors, the flag has dark blue fringe. The flag dates at least from 3 February 1956 when it appeared in the *Yonkers Herald Statesman.* JC

Contributors to This Issue

James Croft, *NAVA News* editor in 1996-1997, has been a NAVA member since 1969. Founder of the Institute of Civic Heraldry in 1980 and its director since then, his vexillological interests focus on city flags and coats of arms throughout the world. He has written extensively on municipal flags, including *The Civic Coats of Arms of Mozambique* and many articles on Canadian and U.S. civic flags. In 1975-1976 he lived in Johannesburg, studying South Africa's civic flags and coats of arms; his paper "South African Civic Flags" won NAVA's Driver Award in 1981. He organized NAVA's 37th annual meeting in Montreal in 2003.

Richard P. Monahan, currently serving as NAVA's Secretary, has been a member of NAVA since 1995. He has an associate degree from the University of Akron with aspirations to a higher degree. He is the Vice President of the Great Waters Association of Vexillology and contributes to its journal, *Flagwaver*. He also belongs to the Canadian Flag Association, the Flag Institute, and the New England Vexillological Association. His interests lie primarily in how flags relate to the broad political and historical movements they represent. He is a sergeant in the Ohio Army National Guard, having served four years on active duty in Europe and at Ft. Stewart, Georgia.

John M. Purcell, Ph.D., a NAVA member since 1969, sits on Raven's Editorial Board, and has also served as NAVA's corresponding secretary, recording secretary, and president. His vexillological writings appear in such publications as *The Flag Bulletin*, *Raven*, *NAVA News*, *Banderas*, and *Banderín*. He has been co-editor of *Flagwaver*, the journal of Great Waters Association of Vexillology, since its inception in 1996. In 1999 he received both the Whitney Award from NAVA and the New Directions in Vexillology Award from the Canadian Flag Association. He is Professor Emeritus in Spanish and Foreign Language Education at Cleveland State University (Ohio), and the author of several professional publications.

Edward B. (Ted) Kaye, managing editor of *Raven* since 1996, is also advisory editor to *The Flag Bulletin*. A member of NAVA since 1985 and an organizer of the 12th International Congress of Vexillology in San Francisco in 1987, he serves as the chief financial officer of a small technology company and as NAVA's treasurer. His articles have appeared in *Raven*, *The Flag Bulletin*, *NAVA News*, and *Flagmaster*. He recently compiled and published NAVA's guide to flag design, *Good Flag, Bad Flag*, and has consulted on several state, city, and organizational flag design initiatives.

David B. Martucci, art editor, has performed layout for the past three volumes of *Raven*. A member of NAVA since 1967, he has served as NAVA's president since 1998, works part-time for a small Maine town as assessor's agent, and is a free-lance graphic designer/desktop publisher/computer consultant. He also appraises antique flags. His articles have appeared in *The Flag Bulletin*, *NAVA News*, *Flagmaster*, and *The New England Journal of Vexillology*. He was featured on the History Channel's *This Week in History* and the Boeing Corporation presented his original essay on *Why Americans Love Their Flag* in a radio ad campaign.

Colophon

This issue of *Raven: A Journal of Vexillology* was typeset in Adobe Garamond using Aldus PageMaker, on a Macintosh Titanium PowerBook G4. Typesetting and image processing was performed by David B. Martucci, of Vexman Consulting, Washington, Maine.

The journal is printed on 60 pound Offset White paper. All printing and binding was done by Whitehall Printing Company, Naples, Florida.